Youth Voices, Public Spaces, and Civic Engagement

"In prioritizing youths' voices, *Youth Voices, Public Spaces, and Civic Engagement* offers important lessons for educators and community partners in supporting the next generation of civic leaders."

Kathryn Obenchain, Purdue University, U.S.

"In a standardized, educational climate that stifles youth voice and lived experience, *Youth Voices, Public Spaces, and Civic Engagement* provides hope and demonstrates how the arts can promote democratic practice."

Sarah Montgomery, University of Northern Iowa, U.S.

This collection of original research explores ways that educators can create participatory spaces that foster civic engagement, critical thinking, and authentic literacy practices for adolescent youth in urban contexts. Casting youth as vital social actors, contributors shed light on the ways in which urban youth develop a clearer sense of agency within the structural forces of racial segregation and economic development that would otherwise marginalize and silence their voices and begin to see familiar spaces with reimagined possibilities for socially just educational practices.

Stuart Greene is associate professor of English, University of Notre Dame, U.S.

Kevin J. Burke is assistant professor of English education, University of Georgia, U.S.

Maria K. McKenna is assistant professor of the practice, University of Notre Dame, U.S.

Routledge Research in Education

For a full list of titles in this series, please visit www.routledge.com

134 **Education, Nature, and Society**
Stephen Gough

135 **Learning Technologies and the Body**
Integration and Implementation In Formal and Informal Learning Environments
Edited by Victor Lee

136 **Landscapes of Specific Literacies in Contemporary Society**
Exploring a social model of literacy
Edited by Vicky Duckworth and Gordon Ade-Ojo

137 **The Education of Radical Democracy**
Sarah S. Amsler

138 **Aristotelian Character Education**
Kristján Kristjánsson

139 **Performing Kamishibai**
Tara McGowan

140 **Educating Adolescent Girls Around the Globe**
Edited by Sandra L. Stacki and Supriya Baily

141 **Quality Teaching and the Capability Approach**
Evaluating the work and governance of women teachers in rural Sub-Saharan Africa
Alison Buckler

142 **Using Narrative Inquiry for Educational Research in the Asia Pacific**
Edited by Sheila Trahar and Wai Ming Yu

143 **The Hidden Role of Software in Educational Research**
Policy to Practice
By Tom Liam Lynch

144 **Education, Leadership and Islam**
Theories, discourses and practices from an Islamic perspective
Saeeda Shah

145 **English Language Teacher Education in Chile**
A cultural historical activity theory perspective
Malba Barahona

146 **Navigating Model Minority Stereotypes**
Asian Indian Youth in South Asian Diaspora
Rupam Saran

147 **Evidence-based Practice in Education**
Functions of evidence and causal presuppositions
Tone Kvernbekk

148 **A New Vision of Liberal Education**
The good of the unexamined life
Alistair Miller

149 **Transatlantic Reflections on the Practice-Based PhD in Fine Art**
Jessica B. Schwarzenbach and Paul M. W. Hackett

150 **Drama and Social Justice**
Theory, research and practice in international contexts
Edited by Kelly Freebody and Michael Finneran

151 **Education, Identity and Women Religious, 1800–1950**
Convents, classrooms and colleges
Edited by Deirdre Raftery and Elizabeth Smyth

152 **School Health Education in Changing Times**
Curriculum, pedagogies and partnerships
Deana Leahy, Lisette Burrows, Louise McCuaig, Jan Wright and Dawn Penney

153 **Progressive Sexuality Education**
The Conceits of Secularism
Mary Lou Rasmussen

154 **Collaboration and the Future of Education**
Preserving the Right to Think and Teach Historically
Gordon Andrews, Warren J. Wilson, and James Cousins

155 **Theorizing Pedagogical Interaction**
Insights from Conversation Analysis
Hansun Zhang Waring

156 **Interdisciplinary Approaches to Distance Teaching**
Connected Classrooms in Theory and Practice
Alan Blackstock and Nathan Straight

156 **How Arts Education Makes a Difference**
Research examining successful classroom practice and pedagogy
Edited by Josephine Fleming, Robyn Gibson and Michael Anderson

157 **Populism, Media and Education**
Challenging discrimination in contemporary digital societies
Edited by Maria Ranieri

158 **Imagination for Inclusion: Diverse contexts of educational practice**
Edited by Derek Bland

159 **Youth Voices, Public Spaces, and Civic Engagement**
Edited by Stuart Greene, Kevin J. Burke, and Maria K. McKenna

160 **Spirituality In Education in a Global, Pluralised World**
Marian de Souza

161 **Reconceptualising Agency and Childhood**
New Perspectives in Childhood Studies
Edited by Florian Esser, Meike Baader, Tanja Betz, and Beatrice Hungerland

162 **Technology-Enhanced Language Learning for Specialized Domains**
Practical applications and mobility
Edited by Elena Martín Monje, Izaskun Elorza and Blanca García Riaza

Youth Voices, Public Spaces, and Civic Engagement

Edited by
Stuart Greene, Kevin J. Burke, and
Maria K. McKenna

NEW YORK AND LONDON

First published 2016
by Routledge
711 Third Avenue, New York, NY 10017

and by Routledge
2 Park Square, Milton Park, Abingdon, Oxon, OX14 4RN

Routledge is an imprint of the Taylor & Francis Group, an informa business

© 2016 Taylor & Francis

The right of Stuart Greene, Kevin J. Burke, and Maria K. McKenna to be identified as editor of this work has been asserted by him/her in accordance with sections 77 and 78 of the Copyright, Designs and Patents Act 1988.

All rights reserved. No part of this book may be reprinted or reproduced or utilised in any form or by any electronic, mechanical, or other means, now known or hereafter invented, including photocopying and recording, or in any information storage or retrieval system, without permission in writing from the publishers.

Trademark notice: Product or corporate names may be trademarks or registered trademarks, and are used only for identification and explanation without intent to infringe.

Library of Congress Cataloguing in Publication Data
Names: Greene, Stuart, editor.
Title: Youth voices, public spaces, and civic
  engagement / edited by Stuart Greene, Kevin J. Burke, and Maria K. McKenna.
Description: New York : Routledge, 2016. | Series: Routledge research in
  education ; 159
Identifiers: LCCN 2015039258 | ISBN 9781138951099 (hardback) |
  ISBN 9781315668376 (ebk)
Subjects: LCSH: Urban youth—Education—United States. | Community
  education—United States. | Civics—Study and teaching—United States. |
  Education, Urban—Social aspects—United States.
Classification: LCC LC5141 .Y68 2016 | DDC 370.9173/2—dc23
LC record available at http://lccn.loc.gov/2015039258

ISBN: 978-1-138-95109-9 (hbk)
ISBN: 978-1-315-66837-6 (ebk)

Typeset in Sabon
by Apex CoVantage, LLC

Printed and bound in the United States of America by Publishers Graphics, LLC on sustainably sourced paper.

Contents

List of Figures ix
Acknowledgments xi

Introduction: Literacies and the Practice of Democracy 1

PART I
Understanding Youth Perceptions of Civic Engagement and Resistance

1 Picturing New Notions of Civic Engagement in the U.S.: Youth-Facilitated, Visually-Based Explorations of the Perspectives of Our Least Franchised and Most Diverse Citizens 25
ANTHONY M. PELLEGRINO, KRISTIEN ZENKOV, MELISSA A. GALLAGHER, AND LIZ LONG

2 Speaking Through Digital Storytelling: A Case Study of Agency and the Politics of Identity Formation in School 50
REBECCA L. BEUCHER

3 "Truth, in the End, Is Different From What We Have Been Taught": Re-Centering Indigenous Knowledges in Public Schooling Spaces 68
TIMOTHY SAN PEDRO

4 Publicly Engaged Scholarship in Urban Communities: Possibilities for Literacy Teaching and Learning 88
VALERIE KINLOCH

PART II
Creating Safe, Creative Spaces for Youth Through Community Partnerships

5 "We Want This to Be Owned by You:" The Promise and Perils of Youth Participatory Action Research 111
LAWRENCE TORRY WINN AND MAISHA T. WINN

6 Writing Our Lives: The Power of Youth Literacies and Community Engagement 131
MARCELLE M. HADDIX AND ALVINA MARDHANI-BAYNE

7 "It Help[ed] Me Think Outside the Box": Connecting Critical Pedagogy and Traditional Literacy in a Youth Mentoring Program 148
HORACE R. HALL AND BEVERLY J. TREZEK

8 Where Are They Now? An Intergenerational Conversation on the Work of the Llano Grande Center for Research and Development 169
FRANCISCO J. GUAJARDO, MIGUEL A. GUAJARDO, AND MARK CANTÚ

PART III
Literacies as a Civil and Human Right

9 Black "Youth Speak Truth" to Power: Literacy for Freedom, Community Radio, and Civic Engagement 189
KEISHA L. GREEN

10 Bilingual Youth Voices in Middle School: Performance, Storytelling, and Photography 210
RUTH HARMAN, LINDY L. JOHNSON, AND EDGAR ESCUTIA CHAGOYA

11 When Words Fail, Art Speaks: Learning to Listen to Youth Stories in a Community Photovoice Project 235
STUART GREENE, KEVIN J. BURKE, AND MARIA K. McKENNA

List of Contributors 259
Index 265

Figures

1.1	The American Dream	34
1.2	"The American Dream."	35
1.3	Dreams of Equality	39
3.1	Seal and Symbol on the Outside Wall of DVHS Depicting a Stereotypical Native American	69
3.2	Hallway Intersection at DVHS	70
3.3	A Poster Titled "Explorers in American!" Taped Along the Outside Wall of an "American" History Course	71
3.4	Front View of the Stuffed Animal Used in History as Perspective Lesson Plan	74
3.5	Behind View of "Digger" the Dog, the Stuffed Animal Ms. Bee Used in a Perspective Lesson Plan	75
3.6	Timeline Poster Constructed for the History as Perspective Lesson Plan	78
3.7.1		
3.7.2		
3.7.3	Timeline Posters Constructed for the History as Perspective Lesson Plan	80
4.1	The Good Seed Community Garden	98
4.2	All It Takes Is One Hand	101
4.3	Working in the Garden	103
4.4	Community Garden	104
6.1	Student Definition of Community Engagement	137
6.2	Student Word Collage of Community Engagement	138
6.3	A Student Self-Definition Collage	141
6.4	A Student Self-Definition Collage	142
9.1	An Illustration of Youth Voices' Weekly Activities and Programmatic Goals	192
10.1	Rabbit Box Poster for Coile Storytelling in Athens	215
10.2	Edgar on Stage at Melting Point	217
10.3	One Way Sign	220
10.4	Arrival to New Home	221

x *Figures*

10.5	The Yellow Bus	221
10.6	Athens Banner Photo	224
10.7	Author at Work	229
11.1	Affective, Social, Cognitive, Civic Processes	236
11.2	A Community-Based Partnership	239

Acknowledgments

We would like to thank Diana Hess, executive director of the Neighborhood Resource Connection (NRC) in South Bend, and Naomi Penney, former board president of the NRC. Both community leaders have provided a great deal of support and inspiration for our work with youth in the Engaging Youths, Engaging Neighborhoods Project. We are especially grateful to have worked with so many bright, talented, and capable young people. They continue to open our eyes to the value of forging relationships in creating vibrant communities, to the assets that young people possess, and to the vision they have for a flourishing life. We also would like to thank the Center for Social Concerns, which awarded us with a Ganey Grant, and to the Institute for the Study of the Liberal Arts (ISLA) in the College of Arts and Letters at Notre Dame for their generous funding to support our research. The Robinson Community Learning Center, the Indiana University South Bend Civil Rights Heritage Center, and the Notre Dame Center for Arts and Culture have all generously provided extraordinary spaces where the youth we have worked with could thrive. Finally, we appreciate the support and guidance that our editor, Christina Chronister, has given us from the very beginning. The editorial staff at Routledge has been wonderful.

Introduction
Literacies and the Practice of Democracy

> *Literacy . . . [is] . . . the fundamental practice of voice and a tool for self-authoring one's place in the world. . . . When young people change the nature of conversation itself, we witness the fundamental practice of voice that is literacy.*
>
> Ruth H. Kim (2013, p. 394)

> *For democracy to survive and flourish, those who have been silenced need to find their voices. Those who have been marginalized need to seek, create, and find a myriad of possible places for themselves in society. They must be able to find their dreams in the American landscape if our nation is to enact the democratic dream.*
>
> Linda Darling-Hammond (1998, p. 91)

> *Educators need to know what happens in the world of the children with whom they work. . . . the universe of their dreams, the language [with] which they skillfully defend themselves from the aggressiveness of their world, what they know, what they know independently of schools, and how they know it.*
>
> Paulo Freire (1998, pp. 72–73)

The purpose of *Youth Voices, Public Spaces, and Civic Engagement* is to bring together researchers who share a commitment to engaging youth in ways that give them opportunities to develop their voices, to "change the nature of the conversation" in schools and communities, to reframe who youth are and what they want for themselves, and to participate in the decisions that affect youth so that they can begin to "find a myriad of possible places for themselves in [a democratic] society." The aim of this edited collection of newly commissioned research is also to advocate for socially just practices of teaching that are mindful of who youth are, "their universe of dreams . . . what they know, what they know independently of schools, and how they know it." These are practices drawn from thoughtful educators who attend to youth in respectful, caring ways, who by giving youth opportunities to use multiple literacies in places that matter to them foster community based on trust, relationships, and empathy.

The authors in this volume document ways children participate in spaces that cultivate democratic practices that are inclusive and foster civic engagement. Thus the "reframing" in our title is as much about the purpose of education in a multiethnic and multilingual context (Paris, 2011) as it is about the value of seeing youth as significant social actors. Education can serve as a site of possibility and cultivate in students an ethic of action, democracy, dialogue, and interdependency. Such a view challenges efforts that have narrowed the curriculum to ensure college readiness in schools through increased standardization, testing, and accountability.

We have invited researchers to contribute to this edited collection who have sought to make visible the stories of youth who continually demonstrate the depths of their thinking but whose voices are often muted in public discourses about schooling and a changing urban landscape. Youth as a term is itself politically charged. We are reminded of Bishop's (2015) point in her own work on youth activism and organizing. As she explains, youth "recognizes the power of young people not as 'kids' to be controlled and 'children' to be quieted but as growing adults who possess the capacity to be leaders in the present" (p. 2). We also sought researchers who share the assumption that art serves as a site of engagement—an affordance for creative expression, imagination, play, and civic engagement. As a number of scholars have pointed out, youth already occupy rich, fertile spaces that are generative and that serve as affordances for building relationships and community. We can listen to what youth can teach us about what a flourishing community or neighborhood looks and feels like and support their efforts to create safe spaces where they can create positive changes in their day-to-day lives. Understanding youth's perspectives on what it means to flourish is especially important at a time when neighborhood schools are disappearing and policies have eroded public spaces (Greene, 2013) where youth have opportunities to build relationships and a sustaining sense of community. Without schools as anchors in neighborhoods, it is more essential than ever to understand how to create and maintain vibrant communities that support youth's sense of identity, agency, and development.

In our research (Greene, Burke, & McKenna, 2013), youth have used multiple sign systems to develop a sense of agency as authors of their space within the structural forces of racial segregation and economic development that would otherwise naturally marginalize and silence their voices. Youth began to see familiar spaces in new ways (Hull & James, 2006) by reimagining possibilities in what can be conceived of as youth's performance of literacy (e.g., through reading, writing, speaking, taking photographs, public presentations, coding, painting murals, collage, digital media and communication). It seems appropriate for us to characterize children's enactments of self through image and text as performance because the ways in which children construct meaning are always in concert with others, and often they are expressed more readily through means other than those privileged by schools (Hull & Katz, 2006). In our work, they used cultural tools of language, image, and text in new contexts and reappropriated these tools in ways that enabled them to develop a sense of agency within social structures that can also limit who they are and can be (Greene, Burke, & McKenna, 2013). This agency can be a catalyst for deeper engagement in their own education and issues that matter in their community, such as redesigning and refurbishing a park (Greene, Burke, & McKenna, 2014) or advocating to keep a library from closing in a low-income neighborhood (Burke & Greene, 2015).

With others, we challenge deficit perspectives about "urban" and "inner city" youth that limit policy makers' and educators' understanding and appreciation of youth's capacities for contributing to meaningful change in the places they inhabit. Studies of low-income minority students' underachievement emphasize pathology in a "culture of poverty," the lack of parental support and stability, high rates of students dropping out, and the extent to which schools support a school-to-prison pipeline (e.g., Wright Edelman, 2012). The statistics can indeed be alarming, and reform-minded policy makers blame children (and their teachers) rather than examine social and economic conditions that limit their ability to flourish. Indeed, reports can mask larger inequalities in school and in economic development that create spaces of inequality and distort educators' perceptions of youth who grow up in unsafe neighborhoods amid abandoned houses and a dearth of material resources (Greene, 2008). Thus this edited collection is an attempt to reframe youth voices and encourage more spaces for socially just educational practices. Equally important, we challenge assumptions about the impacts of poverty on communities, families, and children and what education can look and feel like in a democratic society.

When we fail to recognize schools as arenas to cultivate community and civic identity, we are left with much less powerful means to do such work. Without community relationships, beginning with schools, community engagement and civic identities become much more difficult to engender. As a consequence, the very fabric of our democracy becomes threatened. Perhaps, then, our greatest challenge in our efforts to empower children is to find ways to integrate and cultivate schools and communities as mutually supportive spheres in youth's lives. If schools and communities are to play such roles, then it follows that understanding the specific nuances of building and maintaining relationships within these different spheres should be a central focus.

This edited collection of original research foregrounds stories of "community . . . resilience, and identity formation" that can make visible the challenges that youth and their families face in their day-to-day lives (Schein, 2006, p. 14). Material spaces can limit or enable youth and their families when they seek opportunities for growth, development, and economic wellbeing. Just as important are the ways youth, in particular, reimagine those spaces to take ownership of their lives and envision possible futures that transcend the material and racialized contexts of abandonment and conflict that leave low-income families of color, in particular, behind.

Rodriguez (2006) suggests the extent to which "stories build consensus, a common culture of shared understandings" (p. 1070). If this is true, then the stories of spaces that often are silenced by policies that tend to disempower youth, and particularly youth of color, have agential and long-lasting possibilities:

> Agency is the empowerment enabled at particular sites and along particular vectors. Thus when we speak of the agent of articulation, we need to distinguish between the fact that people do things that have effects, often while they are struggling to change their circumstances or even history, and the existence of agents—places and vectors—that make history. Agency points to the existence of particular formations of practices as places on social maps, where such places are at least potentially involved in the making of history. Agency, as a site is, of course, only realized if specific investments are enabled and articulated.
> (Grossberg as cited in McLaren, 1999, p. xxxvi)

In other words, the stories that students tell, particularly in spaces neglected by cities working to reinvent themselves in the image of a neoliberal economic model, can serve as a counter-narrative with possibilities for creating sites of agential change. Their stories constitute a call for action and provide a road map for ways that social reform work can begin. This counter-narrative is especially important given the changing demographics of youth spaces in and out of school that reflect a changing American economic and geographic landscape.

As editors, we echo Kinloch's (2013) understanding that research should continue to examine how children, youth, and adults

> make sense of our own spaces, how we come to, or are taught to, question the meanings of the spaces we occupy, and how spaces help to foster our sense of agency, of power, and of belonging to something or someone or to somewhere in order to become "authentic chroniclers" of their own experiences. (p. 111)

Doing so, Kinloch has argued, can enable us to discover youth's potential for analyzing, interpreting, and interrogating those spaces that otherwise limit opportunity. We would argue further that engaging youth in the multiple affordances of literacy can help complicate both the visible and invisible signs of inequity within schools and communities that mask seemingly democratic principles of equal opportunity and access. Youth need both the educational and rhetorical spaces that value their experiences (see also Roberts, Bell, & Murphy, 2008), give them the ability to participate in critical, creative analyses of their lived experiences, and engage them as full partners in their own learning (Greene, Burke, & McKenna, 2013, 2014). Similarly, policy makers and educators need to be reminded of (or in some cases introduced to) the value of treating the voices of youth in respectful and robust ways. Through attending to youth stories, we can, as educators, begin to see familiar spaces in new ways as well. Moreover, understanding multilingual and multiethnic youth spaces provides an "opportunity to re-vision" approaches to teaching language and literacy and challenge traditional conceptions of difference that often fail to acknowledge youth's "sociocultural practices" from which they can gain "sustenance" (Paris, 2011, pp. 163, 165).

Like others, we see the importance of creating safe spaces for youth to take risks and experience success; the importance of identifying problems that are meaningful to youth; the significant role that adults can play in supporting youth by providing structure but then fading as an effort to give youth more autonomy in organizing, developing, and implementing a plan for action; and the need to ensure that youth have time for critical reflection to help them identify structural problems that reproduce inequality and to develop a sense of agency. And our goals include "challeng[ing] young people to hear and get in touch with what they think, see, and hear in their communities and social worlds" (Soep & Chavez, 2010, p. 6). Doing so can help reframe what it means to learn, the places where learning occurs, and the roles that youth play in connecting their lived experience to larger social, economic, and political issues. Thus, we also challenge *where* this teaching and learning can (and should) happen.

With the contributors to this volume, we question assumptions about teaching and learning, that is, "what it takes to build a learning community where youth and adults share without fear, an environment where young people are safe to be, to hear, to question, and to tell" (Soep & Chavez, 2010, p. 6). For us, not only is it important to open up expressions of hope and possibility and nurture the imagination (Vasudevan & DeJaynes, 2013) but to understand youth's engagement in reading, writing, speaking, performing, creating, and photographing. Thus "the product of art is not the work of art" in and of itself (Gadsden, 2008, p. 31). Instead, we embrace the distinction between what Goodman (2003) calls the "story making process" and "the story producing process." The process is critical to building community based on trust, relationships, and empathy, one that enables youth to develop a strong sense of belonging, identity, and an agentive self.

The overarching concern motivating the chapters in this book centers on the ways in which schools and other community spaces are equipping all students with the capacity to reach their highest potential as citizens in a democracy. Are youth learning to be reflective, empathic individuals who understand their own convictions and have the know-how to act on those convictions? Are they learning to see that raising questions is as important as trying to find answers? Are they learning to pursue equity and practice

6 Introduction

democracy in the face of injustice and inequality? We would argue that unless researchers and educators, alike, begin to see the world through our students' eyes and listen to their stories, we will "fool ourselves into believing we are looking through a window when instead we are looking into a mirror" (Purcell-Gates, 1997, p. 6).

Youth Voices, Public Spaces, and Civic Engagement focuses on the following themes informed by critical theories (e.g., Freire, 1998) that examine youth's social practices, their use of multiple literacies (e.g., art, play, digital storytelling, performance, and Photovoice) in both in-school and out-of-school spaces (e.g., Hull & Katz, 2006; Hull & Nelson, 2005), the extent to which democratic engagements can foster youth voices, agency, and empowerment and ways that socially just practices enable underrepresented youth to change inequities in the spaces they inhabit (e.g., Fox et al., 2010):

- The extent to which multiple literacies such as play, photography, art, mapping, digital storytelling, performance, and writing affect youth's identity, agency, and voice
- How youth have used multiple literacies to claim a space in their neighborhoods to create positive change through civic engagement
- The ways multiple literacies can help educators and researchers reframe our understanding of youth, the assets in their neighborhoods, and the conditions under which youth flourish
- How spaces youth occupy not only allow for multiple affordances but become affordances themselves where youth build relationships based on trust, care, and collaboration
- How schools can become community spaces where a commitment to authentic democracy can be restorative, humanizing, and liberating
- The ways educators can engage youth in socially just practices that challenge a school-to-prison pipeline through collaborative and participant action research
- How community-university partnerships illuminate and provide the conditions for meaningful change in communities and youth development, growth, and change
- The ethical principles of research with youth that ensure youth are respected and their views and perspectives gathered and reported with integrity
- Theories of change associated with youth empowerment and youth voice
- Community-based research and service learning spaces that cultivate youth voice and youth empowerment by providing alternative learning practices

More specifically, the chapters in this volume focus on youth's perceptions of what they believe civic engagement means based on their own experiences; the ways educators can create humane, participatory spaces that foster community-based and intergenerational dialogue, critical thinking, and authentic literacy practices; educational policies that promote civic engagement and investments in public education; and the ethics of working with youth as researchers, not as the objects of adults' research. Research is vital to understanding how we can improve children's lives and create a better future for all. As others have pointed out, "Methods of research involving children are expanding rapidly and changing the way we think about children and what they have to tell us about issues relevant to their lives" (http://childethics.com). We are committed to ensuring ethically sound approaches to research that treat children with respect by conveying their views and perspectives (Christensen & James, 2000; Phelan & Kinsella, 2013).

Similarly, Paris and Winn (2014) engage the question of what it means to do ethnographic research with youth and communities that are traditionally marginalized due to certain identity markers. Thus one of our goals is to highlight methods that transcend the boundaries between "subject" and "researcher" with a particular focus on creating various forms of text (Paris, 2011). We ask what we believe is an important question: For whom is this research being done and, just as important, with whom? As James (2007) points out, "giving voice to children is not simply or only about letting children speak; it is about exploring the unique contribution to our understanding of and theorizing about the social world that children's perspectives can provide" (p. 262).

Our collective stories can help us reimagine school, even as we write about opportunities for learning taken in spaces outside of schools. School can serve as a bridge between the struggles students experience in the spaces they inhabit and the vision for community they offer with their stories. As Goodman (2003) points out, reimagining the school day for urban kids "can create opportunities to connect and bring relevance to their varied experiences of school, mass media culture, and community life" (p. 100). Schools provide a logical starting place for reinvesting time and energy in opportunities for relationship building with children. Relationships are a necessary precondition, we learned, for creating space for counter-narratives to be told and heard safely, for fostering connections to community, and for cultivating an ethic of civic engagement and a sense of common good.

For all too many children in the U.S., schools are no longer places of relationship building or community connection. Efficiency and accountability-based education policies have moved schools further and further away from being sites where civic and community identities are fostered; instead, environments of competition, exclusion, and suspicion have become the norm (e.g., Lipman, 2011). Schools are increasingly not in the neighborhood especially in under-resourced, low-income, minority neighborhoods, and teachers are often unable to find time or energy to interact meaningfully with students given the all consuming culture of assessment (Darling-Hammond, 2010). Teachers no longer "know" students. They "test" them.

In the end, the authors in *Youth Voices, Public Spaces, and Civic Engagement* value youth's experiences as sources of knowledge for identifying forces of oppression; they shed light on the assets youth possess rooted in community cultural wealth (Yosso, 2005); and they embrace a transformative view of social action and racial justice (e.g., Delgado Bernal, 2002; Ladson-Billings & Tate, 1995; Solórzano & Yosso, 2002). When youth take ownership of their own stories, they can be in a position to empower themselves and a community to change inequitable conditions that deny people access to material resources, knowledge, and skills to function within a democratic society. Agency and empowerment can provide the ground from which to think strategically about how to live productively in the spaces youth occupy or to transform those spaces for the common good. For Jennings, Parra-Medina, Messias, & McLoughlin (2006), agency encompasses the "critical awareness of processes, structures, social practices, norms, and images that affect youth so that they can determine how to live productively within those social spaces or, better yet, how to change them for the benefit of all" (p. 50). Goffman (1981) and Ahearn (2001) reinforce the importance of Jennings et al.'s notion of agency as "critical awareness" of the linguistic, cultural, social, and structural aspects of participatory frameworks.

What remains unclear, however, is how critical awareness as an outgrowth of civic engagement influences youth differentially. How does increased agency, as Jennings et al. describe it, challenge or encourage youth to communicate about or work on ameliorating structural problems? For that matter, how can we most effectively work as partners with youth so that they can be agents of change as they move on in life?

Unfortunately, educational opportunities are not distributed equitably, and recent efforts to reform education mask racist and deficit ideologies. Such an approach not only favors privileged students who have adequate support but also results in tests that serve a "gatekeeping function, reflect[ing] the social stratification of language and wealth in the United States" (Baugh, 1999, p. 26). Indeed, No Child Left Behind, Race to the Top and, most recently, the Common Core have undercut the goals of democracy, equity, and social justice by narrowing the curriculum to accommodate increased testing and accountability. The result is that some youth do not have opportunities to engage in a wide range of opportunities. Moreover, the ways assessments are used have perpetuated the stratification of schools by race and class, enforcing both the exclusion and containment of underserved students.

Together the authors in this volume provide a humane vision of education that values agency, rigor, civic responsibility, democracy, and the dignity of children. Such a view embraces literacy as a social practice that involves the ways in which youth use texts (e.g., writing, images, fashion, embodied literacies, and spoken-word poetry) for socially meaningful purposes within culturally meaningful activities (Street, 2003). Language and literacy are tied closely to the ideologies of a culture and, as such, what counts as literacy is associated with historical, cultural, and political values of a given community. That literacy is a social practice challenges the assumption that literacy embodies a set of neutral skills, separate from the ideologies of a culture and its practices. Particularly helpful is the distinction that Paris and Alim (2014) draw between heritage or traditional practices of students of color and community practices in teaching and their argument that educators ignore the "shifting and evolving practices of [students'] communities." They provide much insight into "culture as dynamic, shifting, and encompassing both past-oriented heritage dimensions and present-oriented community dimensions" and point out that "[t]hese dimensions in turn are not entirely distinct but take on different salience depending on how young people live race, ethnicity, language, and culture" (p. 90). Youth identities shift, and our approaches to teaching should, they recommend, reflect "the evolving relations between language, culture, race, and ethnicity" (p. 92) and encourage youth to develop a critical lens through which to understand the implications of their own literate practices.

To view literacy as embodying a set of neutral skills is to ignore Gee's (1996) concept of discourse as "ways of behaving, valuing, thinking, believing, and speaking" (p. vii) or his observation that to be literate is to negotiate successfully the sometimes conflicting ways of interacting in places like schools. Standardized tests work against students' own strategies for expressing themselves in multiple literacies in a wide range of educational spaces that include, for instance, parks, community centers, and the sidewalks in children's neighborhoods. Kids "interact with neighborhood spaces in different ways" (Nespor, 1997, p. 94), and, we would argue, spaces themselves not only allow for multiple affordances but become affordances themselves when they begin to reframe community spaces as educational opportunity zones. Thus limiting conceptions of literacy to the written word capture very little of what youth know and what they are capable of. Doing so is even more significant for youth who are positioned on the wrong side of the achievement gap. As Darling-Hammond (1998) has observed:

> For democracy to survive and flourish, those who have been silenced need to find their voices. Those who have been marginalized need to seek, create, and find a myriad of possible places for themselves in society. They must be able to find their dreams in the American landscape if our nation is to enact the democratic dream. (p. 91)

Such an education should equip youth with the tools they need to flourish as civically engaged citizens in a democratic society, promote rigor, foster youth's sense of empowerment, and give legitimacy to their lived experiences in forums where their voices and ideas are taken seriously. Here we distinguish between "schooling" and "education" in keeping with the idea that urban youth experience more schooling (i.e., socialization rules, policing, and surveillance) than rigorous learning opportunities that "support citizenship skills . . . by promoting questioning and critical thinking skills and teaching democratic values" (Shujaa, 1993, p. 15). An empowering kind of education also motivates us to attend to children in educational spaces and to see them as coresearchers. Caringi, Klika, Zimmerman, Trautman, and van den Pol (2013) remind us that we must not only create spaces for youth to speak but "spaces within ourselves and within our research where we can deeply listen. . . . We can only hope that youth will join with us as partners in the research process to guide, shape, and teach us about their lived experiences" (p. 1211). Doing so can help reconceptualize the purpose of education and foster deep conversations about the purpose(s) of learning in a democracy.

We begin the book with youth voices and then shift the focus slightly from student voices to the types of programs that have the potential to engage youth in fashioning their own identities and improving their communities. We then conclude by considering the roles that educators and community actors can play in creating spaces to foster youth's sense of agency as citizens in a democracy, particularly as youth learn to take on responsibilities as leaders in their communities in the interests of social justice.

The stories in the first section, "Understanding Youth Perceptions of Civic Engagement and Resistance," challenge the media's depictions of deficits and pathology in urban neighborhoods, images that remain quite powerful 50 years after Patrick Daniel Moynihan's publication, "The Negro Family: The Case for National Action," what is now simply referred to as the Moynihan Report. In this report, Moynihan (1965) described "the tangle of pathology" of African American families as a way to account for persistent inequality in the U.S. Unfortunately, the report shifted the focus from structural inequality—the effects of racism in the workplace, education, health care, and housing—to the individual family, placing blame and responsibility back on precisely those disenfranchised by forces of structural inequity.

In place of a dominant narrative promulgated by politicians and pundits alike about failing family structures, uncaring youth, and people of color lacking motivation and ambition (Farmer-Hinton, Lewis, Patton & Rivers, 2013; Steinberg, 2015), the stories in this first section allow us to witness the insights that African American youth bring to issues of citizenship, social justice, and equity; to navigate limiting, if not oppressive spaces, to identify sources of opportunity; to interweave image and text in ways that call up stereotypes while simultaneously providing narratives of persistence and strength; and create spaces that acknowledge their history with a sense of permanence in a re-storied past. The authors in this section, and throughout this book, urge educators to persist in asking whose stories matter and what stories have become part of the official histories that we tell ourselves and our students. In turn, they challenge us to consider what it takes to create spaces that acknowledge students' histories and families. How do their stories become the "official" history, as Timothy San Pedro puts it (Chapter 3, this volume), rather than an afterthought?

The authors in this first section challenge educators and other researchers to become ethnographers of their students and listen to their voices. Unfortunately, they point out, there is little sanctioned school space for youth to engage the community where they live and go to school or to create, design, experiment, or imagine alternatives as agentive people. And we are reminded that even attempts at diversity education may effectively reify divisions, ultimately limiting space for youth's transformation and growth. Finally, the authors foreground the ethical responsibilities of working effectively in local communities where students live and go to school, especially when that work involves youth. They remind us that, as researchers, we need to be cautious of the ways we portray youth in conveying their stories as part of our own narratives about school, power, agency, and the capacity of youth to create meaningful change. Building relationships is, therefore, very much at the heart of any work with youth as we listen to their stories and convey their stories with integrity.

Seen in this way, the Youth Participatory Action Research (YPAR) Anthony M. Pellegrino and his colleagues describe is very much in keeping with Valerie Kinloch's description of "engaged scholarship" as relational and humanizing. In Chapter 1, "Picturing New Notions of Civic Engagement in the U.S.: Youth-Facilitated, Visually-Based Explorations of the Perspectives of Our Least Franchised and Most Diverse Citizens," Pellegrino, Kristien Zenkov, Melissa A. Gallagher, and Liz Long tell the story of a Photovoice project that explores the civic experiences of young people, the concerns they see in their communities, and the means through which they believe their concerns might be addressed. We witness the evolution of youth's concepts of civics and their engagement in the community, paralleled by teacher candidates' growth in their abilities to elicit adolescents' perspectives, images, and words. Indeed, youth reveal their capacities for agency in ways that belie their mentors' assumptions about what youth think and believe. We can't help but acquire as teachers and teacher educators some important lessons for how we can work with youth and help them cultivate voices as citizens in their writing and photographic illustrations of community change and leadership.

In the second chapter, "Speaking Through Digital Storytelling: A Case Study of Agency and the Politics of Identity Formation in School," Rebecca L. Beucher sheds light on the ways multiple literacies can serve as the basis of activism and civic engagement by analyzing one high school senior student's provocative, if not subversive, approach to composing an autobiographical digital story by integrating music, image, and text for her Honors Senior Thesis English Language Arts class assignment. Beucher's rhetorical analysis brings into focus how this student, Farrah, juxtaposed traditional images of Muslim women, media representations of Muslim terrorism, and images of strong Muslim women in seemingly nontraditional roles to challenge a dominant narrative of Muslim culture. Farrah's counter-narrative also disrupts the local discourse captured in her perception of a salient peer discourse about people grouped under the "Middle Eastern" label at her high school. Farrah's use of the songs "My Soul" and "Terrorist?" by political activist and hip-hop artist Low Key enabled Farrah to use the song's lyrics to inform her politically charged discourse that challenges readers and listeners to reconsider Muslim identity, gender roles, and the ideology of who is a terrorist.

Like others in this volume, Beucher argues that critical educators must take advantage of the possibilities that multimodal composition offers youth. Beucher underscores the urgency to develop curricular tools that center youth practices and diverse voices while promoting critical engagement with multifaceted texts to reposition youth as change agents and critical thinkers.

In Chapter 3, "Truth, in the End, Is Different From What We Have Been Taught": Re-Centering Indigenous Knowledges in Public Schooling Spaces, Timothy San Pedro focuses on the ways indigenous youth reclaim school spaces by constructing visual counter-narratives that correct dominant versions of their Native American histories. These histories have been systemically silenced in schooling spaces; however, in a unique Native American literature course, students were provided opportunities to examine whose stories are told in schools and whose are ignored, silenced, or simply storied past. The teacher of Native American literature that San Pedro describes provides students with opportunities to reframe—not just re-center—stories of Indigenous paradigms created by a dominant culture. They do so through the multiple affordances of constructing timelines critically analyzing what is included and left out in "official" histories, and "restorying" these histories through posters filled with symbols and metaphors, an elaborate board game, and in researched essays. These affordances provide the ground on which youth let us hear their voices and create a space that acknowledges their history, family, and tribal knowledges. As such, their stories become the "official" history, rather than an afterthought.

San Pedro argues that youth need these kinds of critical spaces in school, but he also urges us to be mindful of the ways we portray youth in disseminating our own stories to ensure that we share our stories with youth as significant social actors as we listen to their stories. He nudges us to consider the ways we can help students move toward sustaining their motivation, engagement, and identity development inside schooling walls, especially when students have opportunities to restory memories of the past.

In the concluding chapter of this first section, Chapter 4, Valerie Kinloch situates engaged scholarship as a way to understand the ethical responsibilities of working effectively in local communities where students live and go to school. In "Publicly Engaged Scholarship in Urban Communities: Possibilities for Literacy Teaching and Learning," she describes community engagement and critical service learning projects that she undertakes with students, community members, and public school teachers. These are collaborative, reciprocal relationships that acknowledge the assets that each stakeholder possesses in an effort to create meaningful change. Whereas media often depict deficits and pathology in urban neighborhoods, readers cannot help but see the vibrancy of neighborhoods where students in particular begin to voice what they think and believe, where they learn as much about others as they do themselves, and where they acquire tools for democratic participation. It is not sufficient, Kinloch argues, to critique inequality; instead, the tools of critical service learning and community engagement must include strategies for dismantling inequitable conditions that place many young people and their families at a disadvantage politically, economically, and educationally.

However, inasmuch as community partnerships can and need to be inclusive, the teachers and young people Kinloch worked with questioned the model of inclusion that guided their projects. We learn that listening to teachers' struggles and naming the problems that need to be addressed can serve as opportunities, and not as roadblocks, to community engagement. Perhaps most importantly, Kinloch provides a window into the lives of community members, students, and educators to show the value of connecting students' community experiences with their school experiences.

The authors in the second section, "Creating Safe, Creative Spaces for Youth through Community Partnerships," focus on a number of themes that we explained in the introduction and that the authors in the first section have also taken up: the extent to which play, photography, art, mapping, digital storytelling, performance, dialogue, and writing affect youth's identity, agency, and voice; how youth use multiple literacies to claim a space in their neighborhoods to create positive change through civic engagement; the extent to which youth draw upon sources of community cultural wealth—aspirational, familial, navigational, resistant, and social—that educators, policy makers, and others may overlook easily by focusing on more privileged forms of social and cultural capital (Yosso, 2005). The authors use case examples to challenge the misperception that youth lack capacity or that the communities from which they emerge are depleted, impoverished, or hopeless. As Tuck (2009) points out, characterizations such as these

> frame our communities as sites of disinvestment and dispossession; our communities become spaces in which underresourced health and economic infrastructures are endemic. They become spaces saturated in the fantasies of outsiders. (p. 412)

Instead, the authors in the second section reveal the vibrancy and sense of care with which to cultivate youth voice and youth empowerment. Like San Pedro and Kinloch, they also foreground the ethical responsibilities of working effectively in local communities where students live and go to school, especially when that work involves youth.

In Chapter 5, "'We Want This to Be Owned by You': The Promise and Perils of Youth Participatory Action Research," Lawrence Torry Winn and

Maisha T. Winn document the ways educators can engage youth in socially just practices that challenge a school-to-prison pipeline through collaboration and YPAR. But their "loving critique" of YPAR also serves as a cautionary tale for educators and researchers who can easily mischaracterize the youth (and their circumstances) with whom they partner. Importantly, they make visible the conflicts that can emerge in the work that youth and their adult allies collaborate on in addressing a shared set of problems. As researchers and educators, we cannot escape the reality that youth are complex human beings and that the trajectories of researchers, educators, and students learning together will never be linear.

Using the framework of "humanizing research," they ask a fundamental question about the role(s) that adult allies and/or university coresearchers play in the lives of youth participants: what issues do youth in underserved and under-resourced schools and communities pursue when adult allies create a space for dialogue, debate, and action?

Addressing this question, Winn and Winn also grapple with the complexities and tensions of conducting YPAR with youth who have been exposed routinely to a standardized curriculum that lacks critical literacy skills such as questioning, critiquing, challenging, and creating.

Describing their relationships with youth, Winn and Winn also call attention to the potential value that university-school-community partnerships can play in the lives of youth in under-resourced neighborhoods. Similarly, Marcelle M. Haddix and Alvina Mardhani-Bayne describe in Chapter 6, "Writing Our Lives: The Power of Youth Literacies and Community Engagement," the adult allies who collaborate with youth writers and provide opportunities for young people to write, create, produce, and perform their stories. Although youth often have few opportunities to express themselves in authentic ways in schools, we see just how engaged students are when they have opportunities that reflect what they most want to accomplish. Describing "Writing Our Lives," a program serving youth in Grades 6 through 12, they highlight the experiences of urban youth writers, teachers, parents, artists, and community members who partner together to provide youth writers with opportunities to write, create, produce, and perform their stories and experiences in authentic ways and forms. As readers, we have the opportunity to hear youth voices and to witness the value of allowing youth to reflect, to come to terms with who they are and who they want to be, and to be part of a writing community in which these young people feel like they matter. Especially poignant are the opportunities for young women to share their experiences in ways that bring to light the possibilities of using writing as a tool for unmasking inequity and bringing about a more just world.

In Chapter 7, "'It Help[ed] Me Think Outside the Box': Connecting Critical Pedagogy and Traditional Literacy in a Youth Mentoring Program." Horace R. Hall and Beverly J. Trezek echo themes that Haddix and Mardhani-Bayne focus on. This is especially true when they describe a school-based mentoring program that takes a social justice approach to fostering critically literacy while simultaneously preparing future educators to do similar work in their own classrooms. In their work with youth, Hall and Trezek describe the ways they assist youth in building self-awareness through personal reflection, dialogue, and critique of institutional power in their day-to-day experiences (e.g., poverty and the overrepresentation of Black males in the criminal justice system), the media, and praxis.

Providing an account of City Youth Activists (CYA), Hall and Trezek also bring into focus the value of a university-school-community partnership based on critical pedagogy that has the potential to serve as a blueprint for other school-based mentoring programs that seek to foster agency and civic engagement. Such an approach can enhance youth's literacy skills and the adult participants' worldviews in ways that are both liberating and empowering. The authors remind us that dialogue is especially important because it provides youth with opportunities to express themselves—oftentimes their repressed or ambiguous feelings—and their thoughts and experiences. Having opportunities to share their lived realities and critiquing experiences, participants in the program not only achieve a sense of awareness and cultural identity but also knowledge of their peers and the import of connecting with them to help navigate shared in- and out-of-school spaces.

In the final chapter in this section, "Where Are They Now? An Intergenerational Conversation on the Work of the Llano Grande Center for Research and Development," Miguel A. Guajardo, Francisco J. Guajardo, and Mark Cantú bring to the fore the assets that children and families possess. These assets are the foundation of capacity building, personal development, and civic engagement, which allow for meaningful and human-centered civic engagement.

To tell their story, Guajardo, Guajardo, and Cantú draw upon an analytical framework that emphasizes the longitudinal nature of change and that underscores principles of identity formation, academic achievement, and the public good.

The stories that former students tell consistently bring forth the value of the local community as a source of wealth and that it is possible to create opportunities if people recognize one another as "natural assets." Their stories demonstrate the sense of agency that emerges from sharing power in making joint decisions, from the ways that people push one another to have a voice, and from leading in an authentic way. In the end, their collective stories reframe ideas about privilege. As one former student explains, privilege is more than having access to material goods. It is about participating in a caring community with people who make sacrifices to ensure that their children have better lives.

In the final section, "Literacies as a Civil and Human Right," the authors build on a similar set of themes, embracing an asset-based approach to working with and engaging youth in socially just practices. The implicit question in these chapters is how educators in the broadest sense might begin to reimagine schools as community spaces where a commitment to authentic democracy can be restorative, humanizing, and liberating for everyone involved. Again, we envision a theory of change that involves youth, researchers, educators, and the larger community.

In Chapter 9, "Black 'Youth Speak Truth' to Power: Literacy for Freedom, Community Radio, and Civic Engagement," Keisha L. Green describes a youth leadership development program, Youth Voices, committed to cultivating young Black community leaders and activists through radio production and community organizing. In particular, Green highlights the promise and complexities of youth civic identity and engagement among marginalized youth of color in out-of-school contexts. Much of what Green chronicles focuses on youth's response to local social conditions. However, broader historical, national, and global social justice issues also informed their engagement in their community. This attentiveness to a wider lens is a valuable aspect of this work. Youth became conscious of their role in a larger movement to make the world a better place, specifically for minoritized and marginalized communities.

Green argues that authentic engagement provides affordances for making meaning well beyond the kind of literacy learning Black youth in public schools experience or the expectations that teachers have for Black students. This means conceiving of literacy learning and teaching as "literacy for liberation," and Youth Voices fosters the kind of experience so emblematic of independent Black institutions, especially the importance of self-definition, self-determination, and self-reliance of Black communities amidst oppression (Winn, 2008). The young participants shed light on the ways Black youth and other youth of color enact radical forms of civic life and assign meaning to participating in a community citizenship and collective power.

In Chapter 10, "Bilingual Youth Voices in Middle School: Performance, Storytelling and Photography," Ruth Harman, Lindy L. Johnson and Edgar Escutia Chagoya describe the opportunities that bilingual youth have to tell their stories through poetry, photography, and performance. As we witness throughout this volume, youth's stories have the power to reframe how educators understand who students are, their relationships to family members and friends, and their journeys across racial, ethnic, and geographic boundaries. Importantly, in the YPAR project that the authors describe, we learn from Edgar, a middle school student, how he experiences the spaces of a traditional curriculum that often silence non-English-speaking students. This is particularly true when instruction fails to account for the rich linguistic and cultural resources that youth already possess. The authors use Paris's (2011) model of "culturally sustaining pedagogy" as a way to understand the power of incorporating the languages and cultures of students while also challenging dominant paradigms of language learning and teaching.

Edgar's commentaries throughout the chapter serve as an important lens through which to understand how Edgar and other youth use their multiple literacies to develop a sense of identity connected to their journeys across borders, how they experience a sense of place, and how they attach meaning to their friends, family, and community. In turn, we listen to Edgar's words as he speaks in front of an audience for the first time; takes photographs that represent the experiences he expresses in writing, performance, and art; and shares his work with others in ways that help him reimagine his own capacities for learning and agency. Writing and multiple modalities foster his and other youth's abilities to author their worlds and afford educators the opportunities to see through the eyes of young people. The effect is transforming for educators who begin to see the complexity of their students' lives and the effects of policy on immigrant communities that prevent children and families from becoming who they truly are.

The Bilingual Youth Voices Project that the authors describe in this chapter also sheds light on how educators can be activists who create spaces of resistance to formal education that limits and contains youth's capacities for learning. These are spaces of hope that privilege youth's experiences in and out of school, that allow youth to name these experiences, and that have much to teach us about social justice. Indeed youth have much to teach educators about the need to provide young people with the tools that can enable them to contribute to what the authors describe as "trusting communities of practice."

In the final chapter of this volume, Chapter 11, "When Words Fail, Art Speaks: Learning to Listen to Youth Stories in a Community Photovoice Project," Stuart Greene, Kevin J. Burke, and Maria K. McKenna also emphasize the activist role that multiple literacies across varied spaces can play in cultivating youth's civic life. The affordances of taking photographs, creating art, and writing provide lenses through which educators can understand more fully the insights that youth have about a community's assets, including its history, architecture, organizations, and people. Access to multiple literacies, place, and space underscore the existence of multiple educational opportunity zones that youth create in their interactions with one another and their adult allies. This is most evident in neighborhood walks that youth took with their undergraduate mentors; when youth spoke to local residents about abandoned houses and the extent to which city leaders ignored their concerns; the field trips youth made to local historical sites; and the art gallery where they learned about each other through their art, writing, and many conversations about how to build upon what they identified as assets to improve upon the da-to-day lives of the people they came to trust and care about.

The authors describe instances of youth's developing sense of agency to explain the extent to which democratic engagement with young people fosters youth voices, agency, and empowerment, with particular emphasis on ways that socially just practices enable underrepresented youth to change inequities in the spaces they inhabit (e.g., Fox et al., 2010). Often missing from models of youth empowerment is an understanding of how relationships, empathy, and collaboration contribute to developing the safe spaces that youth and adults co-construct for this work.

As researchers and educators, we may not always, or even often, be able to transcend differences of race, language, and culture, but Greene, Burke, and McKenna explain the extent to which they learn from their students that engagement depends on our extending an ethic of care, meeting youth's "shouts for affirmation" with dignity and achieving reciprocity in a dialogic relationship through asking questions, identifying shared experiences, and being open about differences. Such a view demands that we, as researchers, "claim identities and experiences" (Paris, 2011) in the ways we ask youth to express themselves. Consistent with Winn and Behizadeh (2011), they contend that the work of "youth-centered scholarship focusing on cultivating critical literacy skills for urban youth can generate possibilities for disrupting and dismantling" the single story that equates illiteracy with a failure of words.

* * * * *

This final section brings to mind questions that the authors in *Youth Voices, Public Spaces, and Civic Engagement* have sought to address and that remain unanswered:

- How can educators partner with young people to bring them out of the shadows that obscure who they are, what they value, and what they need to flourish in neighborhoods and schools that are affected by neoliberal reforms?
- As educators and researchers, how can we partner with youth in ways that humanize youth and acknowledge their capacity both now and in the future to make a difference in their communities?
- How can we collaborate with young people to ensure that resources are distributed more equitably via socially just practices in schools and in their communities?
- How can we reimagine schools as places where youth have opportunities to use what they know in creative, artistic, constructive ways to be participants in a democracy not only in adulthood but in their present time?
- How can we work with youth to ensure that they have the tools they need to challenge oppressive conditions and policies that reinforce a school-to-prison pipeline?
- How can we best cultivate youth civic engagement and empowerment? That is, how can our work with youth and the community shed light on the complexity of youth's identities, the assets they bring to their community, and the ecology of community change in ways that challenge a paradigm that insists on "fixing" communities (Tuck, 2009)?

REFERENCES

Ahearn, L. (2001). Language and agency. *Annual Review of Anthropology, 30,* 109–137.

Baugh, J. (1999). *Out of the mouth of slaves: African American language and malpractice.* Austin: University of Texas Press.

Bishop, E. (2015). *Becoming activist: Critical literacy and youth organizing.* New York, NY: Peter Lang.

Burke, K., & Greene, S. (2015). "I used to have a house in this neighborhood": Participant action research, youth voices and civic engagement. *Language Arts, 92,* 387–400.

Caringi, J. C., Klika, B., Zimmerman, M., Trautman, A., & van den Pol, R. (2013). Promoting youth voice in Indian country. *Children and Youth Services Review, 35,* 1206–1211.

Christensen, P., & James, A. (Eds.). (2000). *Research with children: Perspectives and practices.* New York, NY: Routledge.

Darling-Hammond, L. (1998). Education for democracy. In W. C. Ayers & J. L. Miller (Eds.), *A light in dark times: Maxine Greene and the unfinished conversation* (pp. 78–91). New York, NY: Teachers College Press.

Darling-Hammond, L. (2010). *The flat world and education: How America's commitment to equality will determine our future.* New York, NY: Teachers College Press.

Delgado Bernal, D. (2002). Critical race theory, Latino critical theory, and critical raced-gendered epistemologies: Recognizing students of color as holders and creators of knowledge. *Qualitative Inquiry, 8*(1), 105–126.

Farmer-Hinton, R., Lewis, J. D., Patton, L. D., & Rivers, I. D. (2013). Dear Mr. Kozol . . . Four African American women scholars and the re-authoring of *Savage Inequalities. Teachers College Record, 115*(5), 1–38. Retrieved July 14, 2015, from http://www.tcrecord.org ID Number: 16955

Fox, M., Mediratta, K., Ruglis, J., Stoudt, B., Shah, S., & Fine, M. (2010). Critical youth engagement: Participatory action research and organizing. In L. Sherrod, J. Torney-Puta, & C. Flanagan (Eds.), *Handbook of research and policy on civic engagement with youth* (pp. 621–650). Hoboken, NJ: Wiley Press.

Freire, P. (1998). *Teachers as cultural workers: Letters to those who dare teach.* Boulder, CO: Westview Press.

Gadsden, V. L. (2008). The arts and education: Knowledge generation, pedagogy, and the discourse of learning. *Review of Research in Education, 32*(1), 29–61.

Gee, J. (1996). *Social linguistics and literacies: Ideology in discourse.* New York, NY: Routledge.

Goodman, S. (2003). *Teaching youth media: A critical guide to literacy, video production, & social change.* New York, NY: Teachers College Press.

Goffman, E. (1981). *Forms of talk.* Philadelphia, PA: University of Pennsylvania Press.

Greene, S. (2008). *Literacy as a civil right.* New York, NY: Peter Lang.

Greene, S. (2013). *Race, community, and urban schools: Partnering with African American families.* New York, NY: Teachers College Press.

Greene, S., Burke, K., & McKenna, M. (2013). Forms of voice: Exploring the empowerment of youth at the intersection of art and action. *The Urban Review, 45,* 311–334.

20 Introduction

Greene, S., Burke, K., & McKenna, M. (2014). Re-framing spatial inequality: Youth, photography and a changing urban landscape. In H. R. Hall, C. Cole-Robinson, & A. Kohli (Eds.), *Shifting demographics: A cross-disciplinary look at race and class in 21st century America* (pp. 107–127). New York, NY: Peter Lang.

Hull, G., & James. (2006). Geographies of hope: A study of urban landscapes, digital media, and children's representations of place. In P. O'Neill (Ed.), *Blurring boundaries: Research and teaching beyond a discipline* (pp. 255–289). Cresskill, NJ: Hampton Press.

Hull, G., & Katz, M. (2006). Crafting an agentive self: Case studies of digital storytelling. *Research in the Teaching of English, 41*(1), 43–81.

Hull, G. A., & Nelson, M. E. (2005). Locating the semiotic power of multimodality. *Written Communication, 22*(2), 224–261.

James, A. (2007). Giving voice to children's voices: Practices and problems, pitfalls and potentials. *American Anthropologist, 109*(2), 261–272.

Jennings, L., Parra-Medina, D., Messias, D., & McLoughlin, K. (2006). Toward a critical social theory of youth empowerment. *Journal of Community Practice, 14*, 31–55.

Kim, R. H. (2013). "Never knew literacy could get at my soul:" On how words matter for youth, or notes toward decolonizing literacy. *Review of Education, Pedagogy, and Cultural Studies, 35*(5), 392–407.

Kinloch, V. (2013, April). *Expanding methodological horizons in critical race theory: Leveraging counter-narratives through art*. Annual meeting of the American Educational Research Association, San Francisco, CA.

Ladson-Billings, G., & Tate, W. (1995). Toward a critical race theory of education. *Teachers College Record, 97*, 47–67.

Lipman, P. (2011). *The new political economy of urban education: Neoliberalism, race, and the right to the city*. New York, NY: Routledge.

McLaren, P. (1999). *Schooling as a ritual performance: Toward a political economy of educational symbols and gestures*. New York: Rowman & Littlefield.

Moynihan, D. P. (1965). *The Negro American family*. Retrieved July 14, 2015, from http://www.dol.gov/dol/aboutdol/history/moynchapter2.htm

Nespor, J. (1997). *Tangled up in school: Politics, space, bodies, and signs in the educational process*. Mahwah, NJ: Lawrence Erlbaum Associates, Inc.

Paris, D. (2011). *Language across difference: Ethnicity, communication, and youth identities in changing urban schools*. New York, NY: Cambridge University Press.

Paris, D., & Alim, H. S. (2014). What are we seeking to sustain through culturally sustaining pedagogy? A loving critique forward. *Harvard Educational Review, 84*(1), 85–100.

Paris, D., & Winn, M. T. (Eds.). (2014). *Humanizing research: Decolonizing qualitative inquiry with youth and communities*. Thousand Oaks, CA: SAGE Publications.

Phelan, S., & Kinsella, E. (2013). Picture this . . . Safety, dignity, and voice—Ethical research with children: Practical considerations for the reflexive researcher. *Qualitative Inquiry*. doi: 10.1177/1077800412462987

Purcell-Gates, V. (1997). *Other people's words: The cycle of low literacy*. Cambridge, MA: Harvard University Press.

Roberts, R., Bell, L., & Murphy, B. (2008). Flipping the script: Analyzing youth talk about race and racism. *Anthropology & Education Quarterly, 29*(3), 334–354.

Rodriguez, D. (2006). Un/masking identity: Healing our wounded souls. *Qualitative Inquiry, 12*(6), 1067–1090.

Schein, R. H. (Ed.). (2006). *Landscape and race in the United States*. New York, NY: Routledge Taylor & Francis Group.

Shujaa, M. (1993). Education and schooling: You can have one without the other In M. Shujaa (Ed.), *Too much schooling, too little education: A paradox of Black life in White societies* (pp. 13–36). Lawrenceville, NJ: Africa World Press.

Soep, L., & Chavez, V. (2010). *Drop that knowledge: Youth radio stories*. Berkeley: University of California Press.

Solórzano, D., & Yosso, T. (2002). Critical race methodology: Counter-storytelling as an analytical framework for educational research. *Qualitative Inquiry, 8,* 23–44.

Steinberg, S. (2015). The Moynihan report at fifty: The long reach of intellectual racism. *The Boston Review*. Retrieved July 14, 2015, from http://bostonreview.net/us/stephen-steinberg-moynihan-report-black-families-nathan-glazer

Street, B. (2003). What's 'new' in new literacy studies? Critical approaches to literacy in theory and practice. *Current Issues in Comparative Education, 5*(2), 77–91.

Tuck, E. (2009). Suspending damage: A letter to communities. *Harvard Educational Review, 79*(3), 409–427.

Vasudevan, L., & DeJaynes, T. (Eds.). (2013). *Arts, media and justice: Multimodal explorations with youth*. New York: Peter Lang.

Winn, M., & Behizadeh, N. (2011). The right to be literate: Literacy, education, and the school-to-prison pipeline. *Review of Educational Research, 35*(1), 147–173.

Wright Edelman, M. (2012). *America's public schools: Still unequal and unjust*. Retrieved April 4, 2012, from www.huffingtonpost.com/marian-wright-edelman/public-schools-minority-students_b_1408878.html

Yosso, T. J. (2005). Whose culture has capital? A critical race theory discussion of community cultural wealth. *Race Ethnicity and Education, 8,* 69–91.

Part I
Understanding Youth Perceptions of Civic Engagement and Resistance

1 Picturing New Notions of Civic Engagement in the U.S.

Youth-Facilitated, Visually-Based Explorations of the Perspectives of Our Least Franchised and Most Diverse Citizens

Anthony M. Pellegrino, Kristien Zenkov, Melissa A. Gallagher, and Liz Long

> Justice don't mean shit to me . . .
>
> —Ana

As a part of this project, the authors of this chapter—a team of teacher educators partnering with veteran and preservice teachers (PSTs)—used "Photovoice" methods to ask Ana and her classmates at a public "alternative" middle school to write about and take pictures of their perceptions of citizenship, justice, and equity. To us, Ana and her peers were not just adjudicated and disenfranchised students; they were also *authorities* on their own schooling and civic experiences who might benefit from using Photovoice methods to activate their civic voices and move beyond the stark disconnection expressed by Ana in our opening quote. For this project, we called on the teacher candidates and these young people to work side by side as coresearchers to examine youth's perspectives and explore civic education pedagogies.

Our inquiries into adolescents' perspectives relied on visual sociology and Photovoice methods. Like others in this volume, we were also guided by a YPAR orientation to engaging with adolescents and novice educators across school, university, and community contexts (Cammarota & Fine, 2008). Supported by one-on-one mentoring relationships with our future teacher research collaborators, adolescents took dozens of photographs to explore their points of view and then met with the teacher candidates to discuss three primary questions: "What do you believe makes a good citizen?" "What is justice—in and out of school?" "What is equity—in and out of school?"

These young people eventually described and illustrated their perspectives on civics topics via multimodal presentations. Perhaps most importantly, these image-driven activities, propelled by youth experiences and perspectives, encouraged too-often disengaged adolescents to develop and share their ideas about what it means to be a citizen and how notions of justice manifested in their lives. Moreover, these activities fundamentally allowed these young people, the preservice teachers with whom they were working, and us to *forget* the extent to which these adolescents typically arrive in our classrooms as seemingly apathetic or disempowered citizens.

As teacher educators and veteran teachers primarily focused on social studies and literacy education, we have implemented photo elicitation projects with diverse youth in both U.S. and international contexts for more than a decade—using sustained dialogue to explore their perspectives on school, community change, literacy, and leadership. We also have worked in university- and school-based teacher education contexts, where effective clinical practices are increasingly recognized as vital to teacher preparation. In response, we have begun to involve PSTs in our project and consider the impact of these visual, sociological explorations of civic education on their teaching practices.

Therefore, in addition to reporting on youth's perceptions on these civics topics, in this chapter we include the pedagogical lessons these future teachers have taken from their co-facilitation of these curricular and research endeavors. We also discuss the implications of the "youths as experts" stance of this project for social studies and language arts instruction and for teacher education efforts that prepare racially and socioeconomically homogenous future teachers to work with increasingly diverse youth. We illustrate our intervention research methods, results, and practices with youth's pictures, descriptive drafts, and multimodal presentations as well as through preservice teachers' reflections. Specifically, the story we tell in this chapter is based on our efforts to address the following research questions:

1. How do the perceptions of citizenship, justice, and equity expressed by Ana and her peers evolve as they participate in a Photovoice project?
2. What are the challenges and insights about teaching gleaned from PSTs' work with these youth?

SITUATING THE WORK

We looked to a critical pedagogy framework as the foundation for our work serving diverse young people and a considerably less diverse population of future teachers. Our social studies and English language arts instruction and scholarship rely on the foundational assumption that educational practices—in schools and teacher education programs—should address how to construct institutional conditions in which the lived experience of empowerment for students and future teachers is a defining quality (Ayers, 2004; Freire, 1970/2000; Kincheloe, 2004; Sleeter, 2008). Such critical perspectives on young adults' and family and community members' relationships to school and our civic education practices frequently have been examined through the use of alternative, multimodal research methods (Gold, 2004; Morrell, 2007).

In an effort to understand diverse youth's perspectives on school and engage them in meaningful school activities, researchers are considering these students' points of view on our foundational educational and civic institutions (Easton & Condon, 2009; Yonezawa & Jones, 2009). These scholars' inquiries rely on the principal assumption of a "youths as experts" framework, which assumes young people can be participants in their own learning and discern ways that can help them navigate their academic and civic experiences. Many of these studies have utilized visually oriented media, revealing that image-based tools motivate students to develop an awareness of and share personal insights related to their school and community experiences (Cook-Sather, 2009; Doda & Knowles, 2008; Harper, 2005; Smyth, 2007; Zenkov & Harmon, 2009; Zenkov et al., 2012).

Many student voice inquiries that rely on these multimodal and visual techniques also are grounded in YPAR methods. These visually oriented YPAR techniques incorporate explorations of youth's perspectives that challenge teacher-centered pedagogies, convergent interpretations, and dominant myths to understand sociological phenomena (Bell, 2008; Fobes & Kaufman, 2008; Hibbing & Rankin-Erickson, 2003). YPAR is a recognized form of experimental research conducted within a participatory community with the goal of addressing an area of concern and identifying actions that can improve the quality, quantity, and equity of outcomes (Cammarota & Fine, 2008; Fine et al., 2007; Mediratta, Shah, & McAlister, 2009).

YPAR in these contexts often focuses on "critical youth engagement," helping young people—especially those from economically disadvantaged and immigrant communities—to understand and address conditions of structural injustice (Kellett, 2009; Zeller-Berkman, 2007). Unfortunately, few of these visually oriented YPAR inquiries have been implemented with—or *by*—the future teachers who will soon serve these diverse young people. We hypothesized that these methods might support both adolescents' development of civic identities and agency as well as future teachers' effective clinical preparation as social studies and English teachers who view student perspectives as central to our organization of curricula. We speculated that our teacher education and scholarly efforts should facilitate preservice teachers' experiences in classroom settings, where the voices of adolescents are integral factors in determining the nature of effective instruction, particularly related to civic education.

Finally, we are aware that teacher education programs must provide preservice teachers with the tools and experiences necessary to be successful in diverse, dynamic educational climates (Levine, 2006; Zeichner & Conklin, 2008). McIntyre (2009) asserted that "(i)f we want student teachers to learn to engage, as part of their normal professional practice, in an informed intellectual analysis of their teaching and of how it can be improved, they need to learn this during their professional education as something that they do in schools" (p. 606). "Success" then, in these contexts, might be defined by these new teachers' entrenched beliefs that schools should be places where all constituents—including youth and PSTs—are given opportunities to become researchers into their own schooling experiences and to develop clear senses of their identities as learners and civic agents.

CONTEXTS FOR STUDYING CIVIC EDUCATION

The community where we implemented this curricular research project represents the different present and the certain future of much of the U.S. and its schools. Our mid-Atlantic ex-urban city has experienced considerable demographic shifts in the past decade, moving from five percent to almost 35 percent English for speakers of other languages (ESOL) students while simultaneously seeing a substantial increase in immigrant youth. These families are arriving from as close as our major city's inner-ring suburbs—where housing costs are increasingly unaffordable—and from as far away as Guatemala, El Salvador, Korea, Russia, and many other nations.

These quick demographic changes all are illustrative of the shifts in constituents, their relationships to school, notions of civics, experiences with civic activity, and language and literacy capacities that virtually every U.S. teacher will face in the future (Cruz & Thornton, 2013; Lucas & Grinberg, 2008). School and its foundational language of "citizenship" and its most common expressions simply do not *mean* to these youth and their families what they do to so many of us, including the PSTs with whom we work. They reflect teacher demographics across the nation, almost universally White, native English speakers who were born in the U.S. (Sleeter, 2008). Perhaps the most obvious evidence of this large-scale shift in our communities' relationships to school is the fact that the high school dropout—or "pushout"—rate for English language learners (ELLs) consistently has hovered near 50 percent (NCES, 2009; Somers, Owens, & Piliawsky, 2009).

LITERACY AS A PRACTICE

These aforementioned phenomena ultimately relate to literacy issues—both in terms of traditional notions of reading and writing and in terms of what we count as youth's "fluencies," "proficiencies," or "funds of knowledge." "Literacy" in our world now means something different than it did for us—this chapter's authors—as K–12 students and the educational institutions where we are employed. Numerous scholars have documented the expanding nature of "literacy" in the early 21st century, where "texts" come in forms as diverse as an exploding array of social networking tools as well as video, music, and more traditional modes (Christenbury, Bomer, & Smagorinsky, 2009; Moje, 2008). This notion of "literacy" is also useful for us as social studies and English language arts teacher educators and researchers as it reminds us that all educators are responsible for the citizenship education of youth, regardless of our subject areas, and that civic education and engagements should include this similarly expansive range of forms.

Conscious of the potential utility of these multimodal texts for engaging youth in more candid and complex revelations of their ideas, we looked to "slam" poetry as our curricular medium. Such texts commonly are considered in language arts classrooms but perhaps underutilized in social studies contexts. Ultimately we chose this rich and accessible genre as the mechanism through which we tasked our middle school students to creatively express and interpret their understandings of what it means to be an American citizen. We began by familiarizing participants with slam poetry through reading slam poems and watching slam poetry performances, followed by the introduction of a brief history and description of the nature of slam poetry, particularly as it contrasts with the poetic forms with which most young adolescents are generally and unfavorably familiar.

We explained slam poetry as a derivative of performance poetry first developed in the 1980s, noting that this medium differs from traditional forms of poetry in its confrontational nature and dual emphasis on writing and performance (Glazner, 2000). Slam poems rely on emotion and draw from authors' prior experiences to stir questions, identify controversies, and contribute insights about topics ranging from the intimately personal to the distantly political (Gregory, 2007). Thus, slam poetry became an ideal component of our project and an intriguing tool for helping us meet our objective of promoting students' creative, more thoughtful, and alternative explorations of citizenship.

To further enact this multimodal theory in our instruction, we also challenged students to illustrate ideas visually that might manifest in their poems related to the concepts of citizenship, justice, and equity. These illustrations allowed young adolescents to creatively underscore what they believed were the most significant contents of their poems and to visually synthesize the key ideas they were expressing in writing. Again, these visual-traditional literacy bridges frequently are considered in language arts classrooms and seemed particularly promising for engaging our students with novel notions of citizenship. Ultimately, the combination of slam poetry and these image-oriented activities—which included students' eventual production of illustrated presentations using popular software (e.g., PowerPoint, Keynote, or QuickTime)—meshed quite seamlessly into artful, contemplative, and even controversial explorations of citizenship.

CIVIC EDUCATION: CONTEXTS AND CHALLENGES

The foundational connection between literacy and civics was embedded in this project. Like literacy, civics at its most elemental is omnipresent. Civic exchanges occur daily in our lives and come from traditional and more contemporary forms of literacy. Whether we are voting in a national election, neighbors are talking about local construction projects hindering their daily commutes, children are coordinating a soccer game at a local park, or activists are working to arrange protests of political oppression in a distant nation, we are involved in civic activity often and in a variety of capacities that involve elements of literacy. This involvement extends into what Young (2000) referred to as "civil society"—those interactions that occur in connection with but outside official structures of the economy and the state. Organizations such as neighborhood associations, cultural groups, and nonprofit service providers exist in this space and function as fundamental components of civic life (Amnå & Zetterberg, 2010; Putnam, 2000; Young, 2000). By this extension, our civic activities touch our lives in myriad ways. And in light of how prolific civic experiences are, the matters of how and to what extent we cultivate youth's civic knowledge, awareness, and dispositions—and teachers' ability to facilitate these—are of great import.

In spite of the ubiquity of civic experiences, and the importance of civic understanding as a primary directive of public schools, civics curricula and instruction traditionally have not captured the attention of students (All Together Now, 2013). This failure has been well documented and explored from a variety of perspectives. For example, normative, quantitative data have been presented to demonstrate students' lack of civic knowledge (All Together Now, 2013; U.S. Department of Education, 2011). Kanter and Geary Scheider (2013), for example, explored performance of U.S. students on civic exams and surveys and concluded that the "health" of civic education was "anemic" (p. 7).

Headline-grabbing evaluations have drawn similar conclusions based largely on assessment of student civic knowledge at the most basic level (U.S. Department of Education, 2011; Westheimer & Kahne, 2004). In terms of instructional practice, scholars have focused on what Parker (1996, 2008) called a "nominal" interpretation of civics. This view largely serves those seeking quantitative measurement of civic knowledge and consists of learning about national political and governmental structures and functions, often regarding voting as the apex of civic engagement (Westheimer & Kahne, 2004).

Others have noted that much of our existing civics education curricula favor frameworks that promote civic understanding from a myopically celebratory perspective, arguing that this paradigm discourages critical engagement with civic structures and conceptions of citizenship (Fahmy, 2006; Richey, 2011; Straughn & Androit, 2011). And while Parker (1996) saw these limited civics objectives as "woefully partial" (p. 3), Knight, Abowitz, and Harnish's (2006) review of civic education that did extend beyond civic knowledge and factual recall revealed that even these instructional efforts are most often ineffectual and disengaging as they failed to connect to student experiences even as they explicitly attempted to promote engaged citizenship. Levinson (2012) further lamented that although some civics education curricula do seek to include student perspectives, a persistent "civic empowerment gap" remains, disaffecting many youth who see no connection between their civic experiences and the civics curriculum they encounter in formal school settings. This challenge is exacerbated in working with youth who come from marginalized communities for whom civic engagement is likely less common (Ward & Webster, 2011).

Wyn and Dwyer (1999) have argued for the extension of such curricula to include both adults *and* young people wrangling with fundamental ideas related to how members of society live together and necessarily shape culture. Through this lens, we can envision activities in which students are challenged to grapple with complex ideas such as justice and fairness and generating conceptual understandings that draw on their own experiences and those of the adults with whom they work. The inclusive dimension of cultural citizenship, therefore, explicitly endeavors to bring civic participation into the space that youth inhabit and defines "civic literacy" as understanding one's own civic experiences as relevant and formative. These scholars support a future of civic education where the ways youth already are civically engaged and the value of those engagements are taken into account fully as teachers consider relevant and purposeful school-based education experiences.

A NOTE ABOUT METHODS

Through this YPAR-based Photovoice project, we hoped to help middle school students explore, expand, and illustrate their notions of citizenship, justice, and equity (Kress, 2006; Streng et al., 2004). Given our dual focus on effective "youths as experts" practices and guiding preservice teachers in explorations of these pedagogies, we involved both young people and teacher candidates in our project-based study. We worked with 10 diverse, mostly working-class middle school students in this ex-urban community for eight 1-hour morning sessions over the course of six weeks. "New Youth" Middle School (a pseudonym) operated with a contract-based, credit-recovery system, with the expectation that if students followed highly structured behavioral and community guidelines and made sufficient academic progress that they would be allowed to return to their "base" schools. We paired each youth with one or two future social studies or English teachers, who facilitated three rounds of photo walk and photo elicitation exercises over the—snow day-interrupted—several weeks of our project. These future teachers matched the profile of most new teachers across the U.S. in terms of race and class—the majority were Caucasian, middle class, and from our immediate region.

With teacher educators serving as facilitators, the teacher candidates led young people on photo walks in and around the school and its grounds.

Across three photo walk cycles, each youth participant took an average of 50 images in response to three project questions:

1. What do you believe makes a good citizen?
2. What is justice—in and out of school?
3. What is equity—in and out of school?

The teacher candidates then worked with students to examine, select, discuss, and write about their photos. They reviewed photographs with youth participants in one-on-one and small-group gatherings, discussing images as a part of the elicitation process—asking questions like "What do you like about this photograph?" and "What does this photo mean to you?" Our future teacher collaborators transcribed youth's oral reactions to images, helped them edit their reflections on the photos that they felt best answered the project questions, and eventually assisted young adults in writing slam poems addressing these queries and accompanying their chosen images.

To understand the youth's perspectives on citizenship, justice, and equity at the inception of the project, our preservice teacher partners conducted interviews with the students that first focused their ideas about school, a most proximal and relevant experience. Questions gradually moved toward more abstract notions of citizenship and justice (Appendix A). At the end of each of our project sessions, the preservice teachers completed anecdotal records (see Appendix B), reflecting on their experiences with youth, their impressions of these adolescents' notions of "citizenship," and the significance of the day's events for their teaching practices. We considered these records and youth's images, daily draft writings, and final poems and pictures as the data for this chapter. We engaged in a "waterfall" qualitative analysis process, with each of this chapter's first three authors individually considering these visual and written data for prevalent visual and descriptive themes (Patton, 2002; Rose, 2006) then successively sharing our draft findings with the other two authors (Pole, 2004; Van Leeuwen & Jewitt, 2001). We primarily consider the themes drawn from PSTs' reflections in the "Implications and Discussion" section of this chapter.

YOUTH'S EVOLVING NOTIONS OF CITIZENSHIP, EQUITY, AND CIVIC EDUCATION

Here we share the themes related to youth's evolving notions of citizenship, equity, and civic education that emerged from our waterfall analyses. We also begin to discuss the themes in our preservice teacher partners' reflections on effective civic education and general teaching practices that consistently appeared in our analysis notes. We tell our story of youth civic engagement through the lens of Ana[1] (pronounced Anna, as she corrected us on Day 1). We chose to share the results of this study through her perspective to emphasize the centrality of one-on-one interactions and relationships in the structure and the success of this project.

Additionally, her story best illustrated the primary civics notions—and the evolution of such concepts—that emerged from all the youth who participated in this project. We discuss findings from the other students along with those from Ana, highlighting both similarities and differences among the youth. Presenting our findings through Ana's lens venerates our "youths as experts" approach and supplies readers with an effective means through which they might read and recognize the insights drawn from our study. We also argue that such an approach appeals to the "trustworthiness" threshold of findings that is commonly an element of YPAR examinations (Fine et al., 2007). Such explorations aim for descriptive or illustrative findings, rather than generalizable results, with the goal of informing educators' practices and paying close attention to data drawn directly from youth's—young adults' and future teachers'—experiences (Mediratta, Shah, & McAlister, 2009).

In what follows, we respond to our first research question examining how youth's perceptions changed throughout the course of this project. To do this, we first examine their perceptions of citizenship, justice, and equity in the initial interviews during the activation phase of the project. We elaborate using the anecdotal records that preservice teachers completed throughout the duration of the project and then refer to youth's final poems and the PSTs' anecdotal records from their final day in the project. Sharing these perceptions as they emerged from the students' voices during the activation, in the midst of the project and at the end, allows us to discuss how these students' perceptions changed as a result of participating. After outlining these themes, we realized they aligned beautifully with the stanzas of Ana's final slam poem. We integrate her poem throughout the findings, including her titles and in the order in which it was written, and with her photos in an effort to best tie together the stories of these youth.

The second set of themes we share explores the preservice teachers' reflections on the challenges and insights they encountered as they worked with the youth. We also present teachers' reflections through Ana's experiences in our project and the challenges she presented to the preservice teachers with whom she worked. Combined, the reflections the two preservice teachers with whom Ana worked were illustrative of the difficulties and insights encountered by all the preservice teacher facilitator partners.

The American Dream.
By Ana

Living in a cramped apartment, working three jobs
Working, struggling,
Just trying to survive in this cold world
Things got better.
A new job meant more money.

Figure 1.1 The American Dream

COMMENCEMENT OF THE PROJECT

In the initial interviews PSTs conducted with our middle school participants, we asked these youth about their feelings and perspectives on school, civics, and justice. The students consistently expressed that they went to school because they had to and because they wanted to get back to their "base" (traditional) school. Ana was one of the most disenchanted with the entire schooling venture, stating, "School is boring. I don't like school. I'd rather be sleeping, eating, chilling. . . . If I did (go back to base school) it would mean I got my shit together and that's good."

When asked to elaborate about specific features of school that worked for them or did not support their success, many students talked about teachers who made them either want to go to school or dislike it even more. Ana described the importance of her relationship with her science teacher: "She's been there for me. She's seen all my sides. She can calm me down. I can trust her. I do good in her class and I normally never do good in science." Another student's response offered a marked contrast to Ana's: David expressed his disenchantment with the comment that "[b]ad teachers make me lose points, for no reason . . . let their anger out . . . makes me give up, not want to put in effort."

In response to our initial queries, students reluctantly described their notions of justice, equity, and citizenship. We were struck, but not surprised, by their rudimentary understanding of what these terms meant. Specifically, their concepts of justice seemed tied almost exclusively to the courts and the justice system, with which many of them had experience. For instance, Kendrick, described justice as "courts, jail, penalties."

When we and the preservice teacher facilitators and coresearchers nudged these youth in their one-on-one elicitation conferences to say more about these terms, the notions of citizenship to which they appealed were based on everyday acts of following rules and being helpful. Kendrick further described a citizen as one who "[f]ollows the rules or pays consequences like jail." But Ana, with her no-nonsense approach to life, which was clear from the outset of the project, perhaps detailed her perceptions of justice, equity, and citizenship most honestly, "Ever since Trayvon and Ferguson, [justice] don't mean shit to me."

Money.
Money makes the world go 'round.
Money buys you the American Dream.

Figure 1.2 "The American Dream."

IN THE MIDST

As the project progressed, preservice teachers kept anecdotal records based on their daily work with the students, specifically focusing on what they saw and heard students do as writers and as citizens (Appendix B). They also reflected on their own practice by responding to the following sentence starters: "Some things that were difficult for me as a teacher today . . ." and "Some new insights I gained about teaching today . . ." In analyzing the part of the records in which preservice teachers noted what they saw and heard students do over the course of the Photovoice project, many themes emerged. We have categorized in terms of how students described themselves, how students described citizenship and justice, and how students changed as writers.

> *Prosperity.*
> *A safe place to stay.*
> *No more worrying about getting stabbed or worse.*
> *No more being hungry*
> *Brand name clothes and shoes*

How students described themselves. As students worked on their Photovoice projects, talking through the photographs they had taken, one theme that emerged repeatedly was the idea of an internal struggle. For instance, Ana described herself as "savage, tough, and intimidating," but she also assured us that she was a nice, "good" person. Other students described struggles to express their ideas via writing, while using the conventions of writing, to find their place in society or to manage peer pressure to join gangs. For instance, after the second working session, Caroline, the preservice teacher who worked with Mateo, wrote, "He told me that he feels like he isn't good at writing and wouldn't be able to craft a good story because he 'gets commas and stuff wrong.'" Toward the end of the project, the preservice teacher who worked with Amari wrote that she heard him explain how he "[w]restle[s] with society and how he fits into it and what he can do to make a place for himself in the world." While internal struggles are common to youth at this age (Eccles et al., 1993), these quotations illustrate the intensity of these students' difficulties with avoiding issues that more enfranchised populations may not encounter: the need to be tough, to stay away from gangs, and to find their place in a society they are not sure accepts them.

These young people also described themselves in terms of what was important to them, including relationships with adults and the supports provided by home, school, and sports. Kendrick talked about a photo of himself and the school's principal as an illustration of his need for "backup" and someone who cared about his success. Several of the youth chose to take pictures with faculty at the school who were influential in their lives.

For example, Thomas discussed how having his family in the bleachers at one of his sports events to support him was very important to him because it made him feel more confident. He also expressed that he learned skills in basketball that were transferable to other aspects of life: responsibility, teamwork, and hard work.

Descriptions of citizenship and justice. The initial descriptions of citizenship and justice that students provided were conventional and reluctantly shared. The preservice teacher who worked with Ana noted that she had a "most basic understanding of what it means to be a good citizen." Kendrick initially described citizenship in terms of voting and getting involved in church. However, as time went on these descriptions became more nuanced and reflected more of a conceptual focus. For instance, Mark, the preservice teacher who worked with Kendrick, noted that he described "what a citizen does from the concrete (pick up trash, help elderly across the street) to the more abstract (take responsibility, get a job, make something out of your life)."

Yet students' references to the justice system and their experiences with it remained prevalent, as were their expressions of frustration with any sort of what they perceived as "unfair" treatment. Ana discussed these ideas of inequity often. On the first day of the project, Erica, the preservice teacher with whom she worked, recorded that Ana "doesn't believe justice is for her or people like her. . . . In her experience, she feels she has been unfairly punished at school, in the courts, etc." She continued to discuss these ideas the following week noting that her "attitude toward citizenship is best described as apathetic. Her limited experience with law enforcement has her convinced that she is powerless. . . . She has alluded to the idea that justice is tied to race and money in the United States." Ana's ideas of justice and unfairness also can be seen expressed in the lines of her poem.

Justice.
Better lawyers
Being seen as a normal girl not a juvenile criminal
No more being ignored by the judge and jury

How students changed as writers. Students' engagement in the project increased over time. Specifically we saw students who were initially reluctant to participate but eventually welcomed our visits and project sessions, gradually but clearly developing their writing skills, including their voice and self efficacy for writing over time. At the beginning of the project all the youth seemed to struggle with expressing themselves through writing and with thinking abstractly. They often equated their writing interests and abilities with their limited senses of writing efficacy, conflating their concerns that they were not good with punctuation with what they perceived as a reasonable restriction on the right to share their ideas. It was clear that these young people had come to associate writing success with writing formulas, to which they too often were not privy.

Early on, the preservice teachers often wrote that the youth were "reluctant," "not very confident," "hesitant," and "in [their] shell[s]." Suzanne, the preservice teacher who worked with Samuel, wrote that he had "some trouble bridging the step between a literal interpretation of his photos to a more metaphorical interpretation. Looking at the basketball hoops [from the school gym] . . . answering most interpretive questions with some variation of 'it shows I like basketball.'" However, as time passed, the preservice teachers noted that the youth started to "open up and enjoy this process more." In her anecdotal records from a session near the end of the project, Suzanne also wrote, "He has always been polite and pleasant, but he is really starting to trust us and this process." By the end, on numerous occasions the youth expressed excitement about the project, shared their pride in their poems, took ownership of their writing, and even wrote poetry independently. Kendrick even asked for a copy of the poem to show his mom.

IN THE END

The project culminated in a field trip for the students to our university, where they presented their poems to an audience of their peers, our team of faculty, doctoral students, and preservice teacher researchers, and interested professors and staff. This trip was not originally part of the project, but we discovered that only one student ever had visited the campus ("one time for a basketball game"). This was the case, even though the university plays a prominent part in the region.

The students not only presented their work in a university classroom space; they also toured the campus and enjoyed a university cafeteria all-you-can-eat buffet. One of the highlights of this time was a question-and-answer session with the researchers about university life. Students asked about majors, dormitory life, cost, financial aid, and a host of other topics. The presentation of the poems, however, was the featured event, and Ana's final verses, woven throughout this findings section, was just 1 of the 10 poems presented by students that highlighted their too-often negative experiences with justice and their desires to reach for a better life.

> *Equality.*
> *Let me surprise you.*
> *Give me a chance*
> *I'm not just a criminal*
> *I have goals and dreams.*
> *I want to design and build my own car*
> *Buy my mom a house, stop her struggles*
> *See and experience the world*
> *I can make it.*
> *Give me a chance.*

Figure 1.3 Dreams of Equality

Aspiring. While a few students described their goals and dreams from the outset of the project, most students did not share these until the project neared its end. It may be that students waited until they felt they could trust the preservice teachers with whom they worked to share these ideas, but once they had developed this comfort, they overwhelmed us with the vastness of their aspirations. After Ana's regular descriptions of her disenchantment with school and the justice system, she surprised the preservice teachers by choosing to write a poem about the American Dream as she wants to embody it, sharing with them her desire to design and build a car, and she continued to surprise us.

We noted early in this chapter that we have begun to involve preservice teachers in these visually based, YPAR considerations of youth's perspectives on school, citizenship, and justice. We have shared some of their insights throughout this chapter to further illustrate and extend our adolescent participants' perspectives on what it means to be a citizen and their evolutions as civic agents and writers. As we reviewed these future teachers' reflections on how this project had impacted them as teachers—in general and as social studies and literacy educators—we realized that the themes we drew from their anecdotal records reflected many of the implications that we had noted in our consideration of this project.

Challenges. These preservice teachers noted two main instructional challenges: (1) navigating the tension between providing youth with writing support and spoon-feeding them answers to our project's questions, and (2) overcoming low self-image or self-efficacy that manifested as defiance or disengagement. The preservice teacher who worked with Ana reflected on the tension surrounding how much support to provide: "I wasn't sure how to prompt her. I wanted to allow her to express her ideas completely, untainted by any thoughts I might project, however, there were times when she needed encouragement." The future teacher who worked with Samuel reflected on a decision he made to cut one of the best lines in his draft. She wrote, "Although I was sad, I had to realize that he aptly defended an artistic decision, and it was not my place to talk him out of his developing style." One of the preservice teachers who worked with Ana wrote about the "huge gap" she saw between Ana's intense dislike of school and her desire to be an engineer: "I don't know how to address the huge gap between those worlds. Is that the role of a teacher?"

Insights. Part of the impact of this work was the format that allowed preservice teachers to work with the same students over a period of weeks. From that work, relationships formed, resulting in different challenges and the development of a variety of ideas about teaching: (1) the importance of establishing relationships with students; (2) fostering engagement through creativity, choice, and relevance; and (3) the importance of perseverance, persistence, and flexibility. Mark, Kendrick's preservice teacher mentor, observed Kendrick's relationship with the principal and noted, "The very meaningful perception that [the principal] wants him to do well, cares about him, and helps him deal with stressful situations appear to come directly from relatively short interactions." In a subsequent session, Mark reflected that an insight he gained through this experience was, "The importance of getting to know each student. . . . [I] [n]eed to try to appreciate their view of the world . . . and how that may differ dramatically from what I see given my background, experience, and perspective." Erica, the preservice teacher who worked with Ana, also expressed that she had learned about the importance of building relationships with students, writing, "Students want to be heard. They want to feel like their thoughts, experiences, dreams, and ideals are real, valid, and important."

The preservice teachers also reflected on the importance of allowing students room to be creative, to have choice, and to experience relevant curriculum. Caroline, the preservice teacher who worked with Amari, added, "I also realized that I need to let my students take their writing in the direction they are inspired to instead of imposing my own ideas or inspirations on them." Andrew, another preservice teacher, wrote, "When kids feel like they are working on their own material it ignites something within them that can't be duplicated when they feel like they are working on someone else's idea." Toward the end of the project, Suzanne, who worked with Samuel, reflected on the importance of fostering choice and creativity by "hand[ing] over the reins and mak[ing] sure that you aren't spelling out what you want students to do, but rather asking valuable questions that help them to make informed, interpretive decisions." In one particularly moving reflection, Caroline, who worked with Amari, noted the following:

All of these students possess so much potential. In situations like this the teacher has such a large role in exposing the parts of the students that he doesn't realize about himself, the part that can succeed and do well. Sometimes it's challenging because your original methods don't work. It takes stubbornness and determination to break through their shells and get them to open up.

Veteran teacher involvement. As teacher educators, we are more conscious than ever that the greatest impact we might have on promoting effective and innovative civic education is likely through our involvement of preservice teachers in these unique Photovoice civic literacy curricular and research projects. But—again as teacher educators—we are more conscious than ever that the missing piece in the teacher education equation has long been the mentor teacher and veteran teachers in general. As a kind of afterthought—albeit leading to some important insights about the project— we appealed to Liz, the teacher who initially invited us to work with her students, to provide her thoughts on the project.

Her perspective, particularly as someone who continued to work with these students after the project was completed, proved valuable. She agreed to coauthor this chapter with us and offered a rich post-project reflection on the impact of these activities on each of the students. Like us, Ana's experience became most prominent and exemplified the project most broadly:

Ana was one of my first choices when selecting students to participate in this project. Previously, throughout the school year she consistently showed a yearning to tell a story. . . her story. With each writing prompt, she connected it to her roots as a daughter of a father who is currently behind bars. That image, as she shared, was engrained in her mind, and it seemed to me that she was reaching out to him through her writing. One of the class' first writing assignments prompted students to write what you know and Carolina began, "What I know most about is love and heart break."

When I learned this project encouraged students to be authorities on their views of civics and justice, I knew Ana's story needed to be shared and developed for both an audience and her growth as an adolescent and youth writer. As I observed her work with her mentor, I saw stages of growth. In the beginning, she hid behind her hoodie and blushed behind her fingers. However, as the sessions progressed, Ana began to break out of her shell. Her teacher mentor asked her about her photographs, and her opinions, and her ideas. Before long Ana was crafting a structured slam poem about her perspective of the American dream. After the sessions, Ana would stop by my classroom and ask, "When are those mentors coming back?"

During her dramatic presentation of her slam poem, Ana stood tall with her mentor as she detailed her ideas on justice. Her writer's voice was very apparent and purposeful. From an audience's perspective, we sat silently, as we were invited into her world. Her story finally took a shape in which she admitted she was proud of and willing and ready to share.

Liz's description of the impact of the project on Ana and her other students three months after the conclusion of the project highlights one of the key implications of this effort, that is, how involving all of the constituents in these school-university intervention and research projects—youth, future teachers, veteran teachers, and teacher educators—might lead to the greatest gains in disenfranchised adolescents' writing, school, and civic engagement. This insight again echoes the impact we as educators can have on "at-risk" youth by paying attention to their perspectives, validating their experiences, and offering them a chance to articulate and understand something more or something different about themselves as civic actors.

The ever-changing demographics of the American classroom, combined with the indefatigable likelihood of novice teachers to teach as they were taught (Lortie, 1975), necessitates a change in the way we prepare teachers to deal with our least franchised and most diverse citizens. The findings of this YPAR Photovoice project suggest that the preservice teachers who worked with these youth in this one-on-one setting were able to gain an understanding of the importance of building relationships; of fostering engagement through creativity, choice, and relevance; and of being persistent. We propose that the one-on-one interactions that are at the core of our project and study need to become daily structures in our schools and classrooms, particularly these serving disengaged youth and perhaps particularly with civic education activities. And we speculate that the most important and compelling new notions of civic engagement in the U.S. might be drawn via these intensive, intervention-oriented, collaboratively facilitated considerations of the points of view and experiences of young people who are arguably at the very fringes of our schools and society.

Appendix A
Project Questionnaire

Student Name: _____
Date: _____
Interviewer Name: _____

PURPOSES

1) Why do you come to school? What do you believe are the purposes of school? What do you believe will happen as a result of you doing well in school?

_____
_____
_____
_____

Interview Notes

_____
_____
_____

SUPPORTS

2) What do you believe helps you to be successful in school? What helps you want to come to school? What helps you in and out of school with your academic success?

_____
_____
_____
_____

Interview Notes

IMPEDIMENTS

3) What do you believe gets in the way of your ability to be successful in school? In and out of school? What gets in the way of you wanting to come to school? What would you like to change in your life so that you could do better in school?

Interview Notes

"JUSTICE" AND "EQUITY" AND "CITIZENSHIP"

4) What do you believe makes a good "citizen"? What is "justice"—in and out of school? What is "equity"—in and out of school? What does school have to do with helping you to be a good citizen?

Interview Notes

Appendix B
Preservice Teachers Anecdotal Record Keeping Form

Student's Name_____ Your Name _____ Date_____

As a writer...

👁 I saw my student   👂 I heard my student

As a learner...

👁 I saw my student   👂 I heard my student

Other observations about my student . . .

Some things that were difficult for me as a teacher today . . .

Some new insights I gained about teaching today . . .

NOTE

1 While all names are pseudonyms, the student did correct the pronunciation of her name from the Latino pronunciation we first assumed an Anglo version.

REFERENCES

All together now: Collaboration and innovation for youth engagement. (2013). The Report of the Commission of Youth Voting and Civic Knowledge. Medford, MA: Center for Information & Research on Civic Learning and Engagement.

Amnå, E., & Zetterberg, P. (2010). A political science perspective on socialization research: Young Nordic citizens in a comparative light. In L. R. Sherrod, J. Torney-Purta, & C. Flanagan (Eds.), *Handbook of research on civic engagement in youth* (pp. 43–65). New York, NY: Wiley.

Ayers, W. (2004). Embers of hope: In search of a meaningful critical pedagogy. *Teacher Education Quarterly, 31*(1), 123–130.

Bell, S. E. (2008). Photovoice as a strategy for community organizing in the central Appalachian coalfields. *Journal of Appalachian Studies, 14*(1–2), 34–48.

Cammarota, J., & Fine, M. (2008). Youth participatory action research; a pedagogy for transformational resistance. In J. Cammarota & M. Fine (Eds.), *Revolutionizing education: Youth participatory action research in motion* (pp. 1–12). New York, NY: Routledge.

Christenbury, L., Bomer, R., & Smagorinsky, P. (Eds.). (2009). *Handbook of adolescent literacy research.* New York, NY: Guilford Press.

Cook-Sather, A. (2009). *Learning from the student's perspective: A methods sourcebook for effective teaching.* Boulder, CO: Paradigm Publishers.

Cruz, B. C., & Thornton, S. J. (2013). *Teaching social studies to English language learners* (2nd ed.). New York: Routledge.

Doda, N., & Knowles, T. (2008). Listening to the voices of young adolescents. *Middle School Journal, 39*(3), 26–33.

Easton, L., & Condon, D. (2009). A school-wide model for student voice in curriculum development and teacher preparation. In A. Cook-Sather (Ed.), *Learning from the student's perspective: A secondary methods sourcebook for effective teaching* (pp. 176–193). Boulder, CO: Paradigm Press.

Eccles, J. S., Midgley, C., Wigfield, A., Buchanan, C. M., Reuman, D., Flanagan, C., & Mac Iver, D. (1993). Development during adolescence: The impact of stage-environment fit on young adolescents' experiences in schools and in families. *American Psychologist, 48*(2), 90–101. http://doi.org/10.1037/0003-066X.48.2.90

Fahmy, E. (2006). Social capital and civic action: A study of youth in the United Kingdom. *Young, Nordic Journal of Youth Research, 14*(2), 101–118. doi: 10.1177/1103308806062736

Fine, M., Torre, M. E., Burns, A., & Payne, Y. (2007). Youth research/participatory methods for reform. In D. Thiessen & A. Cook-Sather (Eds.), *International handbook of student experience in elementary and secondary school* (pp. 805–828). Dordrecht, The Netherlands: Springer Publishers.

Fobes, C., & Kaufman, P. (2008). Critical pedagogy in the sociology classroom: Challenges and concerns. *Teaching Sociology, 36,* 26–33.

Freire, P. (1970/2000). *Pedagogy of the oppressed*. New York, NY: Bloomsbury.
Glazner, G. M. (2000). *Poetry slam: The competitive art of performance poetry*. San Francisco, CA: Manic D Press.
Gold, S. J. (2004). Using photography in studies of immigrant communities. *American Behavioral Scientist, 47*, 1551–1572.
Gregory, H. (2007). The quiet revolution of poetry slam: The sustainability of cultural capital in the light of changing artistic conventions. *Ethnography and Education, 3*(1), 61–71.
Harper, D. (2005). What's new visually? In N. K. Denzin & Y. S. Lincoln (Eds.), *The Sage handbook of qualitative research* (pp. 747–762, 3rd ed.). Thousand Oaks: Sage Publications.
Hibbing, A. N., & Rankin-Erickson, J. L. (2003). A picture is worth a thousand words: Using visual images to improve comprehension for middle school struggling readers. *The Reading Teacher, 56*, 758–770.
Kanter, M., & Geary Scheider, C. (2013). Civic learning and engagement. *Change, 45*(1), 6–14.
Kellett, M. (2009). Children as researchers: What we can learn from them about the impact of poverty on literacy opportunities? *International Journal of Inclusive Education, 13*, 395–408.
Kincheloe, J. L. (2004). *Critical pedagogy primer*. New York, NY: Peter Lang.
Knight Abowitz, K., & Harnish, J. (2006). Contemporary discourses on citizenship. *Review of Educational Research, 76*, 653–690.
Kress, G. (2006). *Reading images: The grammar of visual design*. New York: Routledge.
Levine, A. (2006). *Educating school teachers*. Washington, DC: Education Schools Project.
Levinson, M. (2012). *No citizen left behind*. Cambridge, MA: Harvard University Press.
Lortie, D. C. (1975). *Schoolteacher: A sociological study*. Chicago, IL: University of Chicago Press.
Lucas, T., & Grinberg, J. (2008). Responding to the linguistic reality of mainstream classrooms: Preparing all teachers to teach English language learners. In M. Cochran-Smith, S. Feiman-Nemser, & D. J. McIntyre (Eds.), *Handbook on teacher education: Enduring questions in changing contexts* (3rd ed., pp. 606–636). New York, NY: Routledge.
McIntyre, D. (2009). The difficulties of inclusive pedagogy for initial teacher education and some thoughts on the way forward. *Teaching and Teacher Education, 25*, 602–608.
Mediratta, K., Shah, S., & McAlister, S. (2009). *Community organizing for stronger schools: Strategies and successes*. Cambridge: Harvard Education Press.
Moje, E. B. (2008). The complex world of adolescent literacy: Myths, motivations, and mysteries. *Harvard Educational Review, 78*(1), 107–154.
Morrell, E. (2007). *Critical literacy and urban youth: Pedagogies of access, dissent, and liberation*. New York, NY: Routledge.
National Center for Education Statistics. (2009). *The condition of education: 2009*. Washington, DC: National Center for Education Statistics/Institute of Education Sciences.
Parker, W. C. (1996). Advanced ideas about democracy. *Teachers College Record, 98*(3), 104–125.

Parker, W. C. (2008). Knowing and doing in democratic citizenship education. In L. S. Levstik & C. A. Tyson (Eds.), *Handbook of research in social studies education* (pp. 65–80). New York, NY: Routledge.

Patton, M. Q. (2002). *Qualitative research and evaluation methods* (3rd ed.). Thousand Oaks, CA: Sage.

Pole, C. (Ed.). (2004). *Seeing is believing? Approaches to visual research (Volume 7)*. New York, NY: Elsevier.

Putnam, R. D. (2000). *Bowling alone: The collapse and revival of American community*. New York, NY: Touchstone.

Richey, S. (2011). Civic engagement and patriotism. *Social Science Quarterly, 92*, 1044–1056.

Rose, G. (2006). *Visual methodologies: An introduction to the interpretation of visual materials*. Thousand Oaks, CA: Sage.

Sleeter, C. E. (2008). Preparing White teachers for diverse students. In M. Cochran-Smith, S. Feiman-Nemser, & D. J. McIntyre (Eds.), *Handbook on teacher education: Enduring questions in changing contexts* (3rd ed., pp. 559–582). New York: Routledge.

Smyth, J. (2007). Toward the pedagogically engaged school: Listening to student voice as a positive response to disengagement and "dropping out"? In D. Thiessen & A. Cook-Sather (Eds.), *International handbook of student experience in elementary and secondary school* (pp. 635–658). Dordrecht, The Netherlands: Springer.

Somers, C., Owens, D., & Piliawsky, M. (2009). A study of high school dropout prevention and at-risk ninth graders' role models and motivations for school completion. *Education, 130*, 348–356.

Straughn, J. B., & Androit, A. L. (2011). Education, civic patriotism, and democratic citizenship: Unpacking the education effect on political involvement. *Sociological Forum, 26*, 556–580.

Streng, J. M., Rhodes, S. D., Ayala, G. X., Eng., E., Arceo, R., & Phipps, S. (2004). *Realidad Latina*: Latino adolescents, their school, and a university use photovoice to examine and address the influence of immigration. *Journal of Interprofessional Care, 18*, 403–415.

U.S. Department of Education. National Center for Education Statistics (NCES) (2011). *The nation's report card: Civics 2010* (NCES 2011–466). Washington, DC: Institute of Education Sciences, U.S. Department of Education.

Van Leeuwen, T., & Jewitt, C. (Eds.). (2001). *Handbook of visual analysis*. Thousand Oaks, CA: Sage.

Ward, S., & Webster, N. (2011). Cultural relevance and working with inner city youth populations to achieve civic engagement. *Journal of Extension, 49*(5), 1–5.

Westheimer, J., & Kahne, J. (2004). What kind of citizen? The politics of educating for democracy. *American Educational Research Journal, 41*, 237–269.

Wyn, J., & Dwyer, P. (1999). New direction in research on youth in transition. *Journal of Youth Studies, 2*(1), 5–21.

Yonezawa, S., & Jones, M. (2009). Student voices: Generating reform from the inside out. *Theory into Practice, 48*, 205–212.

Young, I. M. (2000). *Inclusion and democracy*. Oxford, UK: Oxford University Press.

Zeichner, K., & Conklin, H. G. (2008). Teacher education programs as sites for teacher preparation. In M. Cochran-Smith, S. Feiman-Nemser, & D. J. McIntyre

(Eds.), *Handbook on teacher education: Enduring questions in changing contexts* (3rd ed., pp. 269–289) New York: Routledge.

Zeller-Berkman, S. (2007). Peering in: A look into reflective practices in youth participator action research. *Children, Youth and Environments, 17,* 315–328.

Zenkov, K., Fell, M., Harmon, J., Bell, A., Ewaida, M., & Pellegrino, A. (2012). Youth as sources of educational equity: Using photographs to help adolescents make sense of school, injustice, and their lives. *Education in a Democracy, 4*(12), 79–98.

Zenkov, K., & Harmon, J. (2009). Picturing a writing process: Using photovoice to learn how to teach writing to urban youth. *Journal of Adolescent and Adult Literacy, 52,* 575–584.

2 Speaking Through Digital Storytelling
A Case Study of Agency and the Politics of Identity Formation in School

Rebecca L. Beucher

> Certain lives will be highly protected, and the abrogation of their claims to sanctity will be sufficient to mobilize the forces of war. And other lives will not find such fast and furious support and will not even qualify as "grievable."
>
> (Butler, 1993, p. 24)

> Remember . . . when there was a tsunami in Japan? Right? They had like a moment of silence for them on International Day . . . But . . . when seventeen people died in my country [Afghanistan] [when] a US soldier went and killed the children and women nobody even said anything about it. How is that [even] fair to me? I'm not representing my country [at the school's International Day]. Just come here and be like, oh I'm so proud to be from there and be a big loser who just comes here and [doesn't] even say anything [when] seventeen people died back home. . . . I'm not going to . . . [April 9, 2012].

I begin this chapter with the words of philosopher and post-structural gender theorist Judith Butler and Farrah Azizi, a female refugee from Afghanistan and high school senior at Regional High. (All names in this chapter have been changed to pseudonyms.) These women's words speak to the inequitable treatment of human life that informs Farrah's approach to autobiographical digital storytelling as a form of civic engagement. Farrah was a student at Regional High, an internationally diverse school in the Rocky Mountain region of the U.S. On this particular day, Farrah, a senior in Dr. Kira Buchannan's Honors English Language Arts class, sat among a group of her female peers, who were also refugees from the Middle East and Africa, and planned out her autobiographical digital story. In the midst of talking about themselves and what story they wanted to tell of themselves to the class, the topic of International Day arose. Regional High celebrated its student body's international diversity in several ways, one of which was via International Day, a student-organized event that occurred annually. I begin with Farrah's expression of discontent with her school's implicit messaging about whose lives mattered and her plans to protest International Day by way of initiating a conversation about how Farrah's approach to digital storytelling offers a reframing of youth civic activism within the school context.

Farrah's refusal to take the stage and hold the Afghani flag as a representative of her home country demands pause and consideration for how public school spaces can function in relation to afforded opportunities for youth to engage civically in school spaces. Rather than view taking the stage as an opportunity to speak up about the devaluing of lives she witnessed within her school, she understood her taking the stage in the manner it was being offered—as an act of betrayal to the people "back home." Farrah stated that standing silent on the stage would be an act of betrayal and implied that she had something to say. In this chapter, I showcase Farrah's story as an exemplar of an adolescent youth who took it upon herself to compose an autobiographical digital story as an act of civic activism within a school context wherein she leveraged an opportunity to speak her mind.

Farrah composed her digital story,[1] from which this paper draws, as a part of a class assignment, called the Digital Media Project (DMP). The classroom teacher, Kira Buchannan, asked the students to "write" multimodal digital identity narratives as one of several culminating projects for the class. The requirements for the digital story were that the movies span two to five minutes, communicate a story of the self, and include music, text, and images. Kira emphasized to the students that while they were sharing this project with the class, it was meant to be a reflection of themselves and feature what they wanted others to know about them. She also required all students to submit an "I am" poem as a prewriting activity. For this poem, students wrote five statements about their past (where I've been), present (where I am), and future selves (where I'm going). This chronological ordering informed the where I've been, where I am, and where I'm going plot structure used by many of the students, including Farrah.

I investigated the following research question in the study informing this chapter: How do non-dominant youth in Honors Senior Thesis English Language Arts negotiate subjectivities in relation to and contestation with macro and micro discourses across conversational and compositional contexts when digital storytelling? Through my analysis of Farrah's DMP, I demonstrate how telling her personal story necessarily involved responding to school discourses that conflicted with her own sense of self. In my analysis of her storytelling, I illustrate how she astutely layered modes (music, text, and images) to challenge assumptions she felt her peers and school members made about her as a Muslim woman. Here, I discuss how, through digital storytelling, Farrah skillfully interwove hip-hop music with images of herself, her family members, and Afghani women to tell a subversive personal story and perhaps shift her peers' perspectives about herself and about Muslim women. This chapter builds on previous work centered on the agentic affordances of digital storytelling while contributing to the conversation about how digital storytelling affords feminist civic activism within the classroom space. I discuss these implications for practice in the conclusion.

SITUATING THE WORK

In what follows, I discuss Farrah's approach to digital storytelling and how this approach to digital composition can be located within the New Literacy Studies (NLS) tradition. I argue that this theoretical underpinning enables a logical mapping to critical literacy practices (Freire, 1993; Freire & Macedo, 1987; Giroux 1983; Giroux & McLaren, 2014; McLaren, 1989) necessary to promoting youth agency within the school context. In this way, NLS practices such as digital storytelling importantly deviate from rigid school literacy practices that arguably constrain possibilities for subversive storytelling, a necessary component of agentic authorship. As long as mainstream literacy practices maintain a dominant cultural position, educators must continue developing instruction that facilitates access to the "culture of power" (Delpit, 1988, p. 24) while crafting humanizing educational spaces that sustain and nurture students' cultural practices (e.g., del Carmen Salazar, 2013; Paris & Winn, 2014) in ways that make sense to the students themselves.

While digital storytelling affords critical literacy practices, it does not necessarily unfold as a critical literacy practice. Moreover, youth, well aware of multiple school discourses, astutely negotiate multiple storylines within the school context when composing digital narratives of the self that will be shown to a peer audience; thus, how youth perceive their audience informs the story they tell (Beucher, 2015). I also argue that feminist post-structural theory enables a critical reading of discourse and subjectivity resonant in the digital composition. Such a perspective offers nuanced insight into the multiple discourses a youth author engages and negotiates when digital storytelling with a peer audience in mind. To study the critical literacy practices that Farrah employs within this particular school context required critical discourse analysis (CDA) (Fairclough & Wodak, 1997; Luke, 1995). CDA allows for a close, *critical* reading of the digital text. In other words, CDA provides a means for illustrating how Farrah refigures the Islamophobic language of terrorism resonant in a post 9/11 world (Puar & Rai, 2002; Zaal, 2012). In its place, Farrah proffers a storyline through which she characterizes Muslim women as powerful, agentic, intelligent, and beautiful all the while nodding toward the oppressive practices and narratives that fuel a dehumanizing and flattening inscription of terrorist labels on Muslim bodies.

Digital Storytelling: An Agentic Opportunity

Alternative to mainstream literacy practices that follow a one-size-fits-all model, NLS, which digital storytelling falls within, challenges dominant notions of what it means to be "fully literate" in documenting the diversity of localized, situated meaning-making practices (Hull, 2003). Literacy, Gee

(2010) writes, "is integrated with different ways of using oral language . . . acting and interacting . . . ways of knowing, valuing, and believing; and . . . of using various sorts of tools and technologies" (p. 2). NLS, in large part due to its theoretical underpinnings, which focus on local literacy practices in context, maintains a commitment to disrupting the mechanisms perpetuating the oppression of historically marginalized cultural communities in and out of schools. These commitments can be heard in calls for educators to design learning experiences that harness literacy and language practices engaged by diverse youth (Gutiérrez, Bien, Selland, & Pierce, 2011; New London Group, 1996).

Research on digital storytelling with nondominant youth has begun to establish how digital storytelling, a multimodal, digital composition tool, affords agency for youth authors. Within this body of work, researchers argue that by leveraging youth knowledge, experience (Halverson, Lewenhaupt, Gibbons, & Bass, 2009; Vasudevan, 2006), and mediated cultural literacy practices (Nixon & Gutiérrez, 2007), youth authors are positioned to construct self-images that resonate with their life experiences, identities, and desires to be understood and known in particular ways (Gibbons, Drift, & Drift, 2010); constructing these self-images provides the ground for agency on the part of the author (Hull & Katz, 2006). Researchers have further documented how youth whose identities are constructed as nondominant have taken it upon themselves to consciously author narratives in which they challenge the mainstream discourses that rationalize acts of discrimination and violence on nondominant people (Bing-Canar & Zerkel, 1998; Curwood & Gibbons, 2010; Hull & Katz, 2006) and, more broadly, as an educational tool to facilitate an awareness among those unfamiliar with the author's cultural practices (Lavia & Moore, 2010).

However, as digital storytelling grows in popularity and becomes an increasingly salient school practice, the implications for the practice to school and classroom culture are still being negotiated. Educators are positioned uniquely to inform the possibilities for what multimodal composition can offer classroom discourse and particularly how this tool can promote adolescents' civic activism within school. From a critical feminist perspective, I argue here for the necessity to consider not only what youth authors' multimodal composition processes accomplish for their own sense of self but also how artistically producing counter-narratives can effectively transform classroom and school discourse, consequently making visible what dominant discourse censors and silences. How we read these narratives informs what we take from them. In this respect, I contend that there is an important distinction to be made between understanding student-generated texts as accomplishments of individual voice verses creative and agentic instantiations of discourses that challenge oppressive ideologies—that are in part formed in response to youth's perception of audience in the form of predominant messaging within a given context.

Feminist Post-Structuralism, Subjectivity, and Agency

Post-structural feminist theory can further help us understand Farrah's story and her agentive potential as her ability to appropriate language and other means of signification. This appropriation allows her to refuse subject positions that do not serve her while forcing new positions through reworking what was previously unrelated in dominant discourse (Davies, 2000). The stability of any constructed category resides within a delicate balance between what it is and what it is not. Indeed, one's identities are fragile, constructed through the power of others to define who we are. Yet, as people perform subject positions across a multiplicity of discourses, they affect what discursive practices within any discourse signify; in other words, people's discursive practices transform discourse. Agency involves coming to know non-dominant discourses that provide individuals access to previously unknown ways of being. By taking up new subject positions in conversation, through writing, and through bodily movements individuals can act agentively to dislodge, disrupt, and reject the hegemonic discourses that leave limited and constrained options for subjectivity (Davies, 2000). Choice, or agency, is realized through the dislodging of self from hegemonic narratives, making it possible for the speaking subject to "discover the possibility of *auth*or*ity* [where she understands herself as] . . . a protagonist inside the storylines she is living out" (p. 67).

Applying a post-structural reading to Farrah's DPM builds on Nelson and Hull's (2005) work, wherein researchers illustrate how semiotic pairings of multiple modes enable new forms of signification while additionally enabling a reading of subversive feminist discourses resonant where binaries are disrupted and discourses are refigured toward agentic ends. This stance rejects a humanist discourse, which understands the person as a free agent autonomously choosing who he or she is and accessing that self from within (Davies, 2000) in favor of viewing people as occupying and performing multiple subject positions or subjectivities. Further, feminist post-structural theory understands subjectivity as fluid, always changing, and always in process, thereby leaving possibilities for agentic movement away from what does not serve one toward empowered constructions and performances of oneself.

A NOTE ABOUT METHOD

The digital story examined in this chapter is taken from a yearlong ethnographic study of four high school English language arts classes taught by the same teacher, Dr. Kira Buchannan. In the spring of 2012, I conducted a pilot study in Kira's two Senior Honors Thesis English Language Arts (SHT) classes. Farrah's digital identity story was created during this time. Much of my time during class sessions involved me assisting students with navigating the storytelling technology. I audio recorded student digital story planning sessions, interviewed several students following the project completion, took field notes, and collected all completed student digital stories. I selected Farrah's digital narrative among her peers because it stood out as an especially powerful example of resistance and negotiation of gendered and racialized discourses.

My analysis loosely builds on Nelson and Hull's (2008) findings that multimodal production enables new forms of meaning making that would not be otherwise possible should the modes be separated. I made the following observations via narrative description based on an attempt to document signals of race and gender discourse (values, beliefs, and culture).[2]

- *Image*: For photographs and other images of people, I described body positioning, eye gaze, hand placement, location of the people in the shot, amount of space the figure took up in the shot, colors, number of people in the photograph, and the people's orientation in relation to one another as well as facial expressions, skin tone, hair length, clothing, and colors in the shot.
- *Text*: I recorded the author's written words and quoted text in addition to the words' colors, font, and placement on the screen.
- *Music*: I recorded the song lyrics, whether they were sung, spoken, or rapped as well as information about tone.

After making these observational notes in a transcript for Farrah's digital narrative using the qualitative coding software, Transana, I noted within the transcript thematic elements (e.g., family, self, Muslim, and women) that gave rise to discursive categories that I explored in more depth in the analysis. Through reading modes in relation to one another within each frame first and then across, I determined salient discourses present in Farrah's DMP that arose through the modal juxtapositions.

The following analysis illustrates how Farrah's use of hip-hop music in relation to other modes (image and text) enabled her to effectively challenge the oppressive language of terrorism that perpetuates inequitable treatment of human lives. Viewing the digital story as an opportunity for sharing her sense of Muslim identity and femininity opened the possibility for Farrah to harness the multimodal components specific to digital storytelling to challenge dominant discourse about terrorism and subjugated Muslim women, which she detected among her peer and school audience. Using her life journey as an example, Farrah presents a complex picture of a Muslim woman navigating the complex terrain of remaining connected to her geographical and national cultural roots while envisioning a future life trajectory in which she becomes an international health-care worker alongside other strong Afghani women. Farrah's approach to digital autobiographical storytelling illustrated her resistance to the ways others systematically erase human life among those whom she identified as "her people." Coupling her words with Low Key's lyrics in the two songs "My Soul" and "Terrorist?" and images of people in her immediate life as well as those whom she identified with ethnically and in nationality, Farrah's story was both personal and political in its rejection of Islamophobic discourse. Her efforts to humanize Muslim people were reflected in how she countered oppressive discourse captured in Low Key's lyrics and in her drawing on personally and politically meaningful examples. Ultimately she proffered an agentic counter-narrative of powerful, educated, beautiful Muslim women who were supported by Muslim men and many of whom made it their life's work to help people.

Farrah's rhetorical moves invite a conversation for coalition building wherein peer and educator audience members may be called upon to both examine their own perpetuation of systemic inequities impacting their peers' lived experiences as well as develop a shared sense of injustice about these oppressions. In the final section of this chapter, I discuss how educators can build strategically upon youth's seized opportunities for civic action and coalition building within the classroom context.

"I Am Farrah Azizi"

Farrah's story, while unique to her cultural, national, and ethnic identities and subversion of Islamophobic discourse, followed a similar plot structure to her peers' stories. The family storyline captured in the first eight frames arises as Farrah introduced individually the members of her family. While Farrah likely distinguished herself in calling attention to her national identity (she was according to her friends the "only" Afghan student in the school), she simultaneously normalized her and her family members' subjectivity in describing them through familial roles recognizable to a Western audience. At the same time, she immediately inserts Low Key's lyrics, thereby calling attention to how her family members are oppressed within Western discourse.

Farrah began her DMP with bold text written in white lettering set against a black background. The words appearing on the screen, "I AM FARRAH AZIZI," were written in white and in all caps. British Pakistani hip-hop artist Low Key's voice was heard saying, "No souls for sale here, mate." The discourses resonant in the opening frame established a salient theme for the story. In keeping with the assignment, Farrah began the story with her name, telling the audience that this was a story about her, but the particular framing was captured in Low Key's words, "No souls for sale here, mate." The presentation of the words in white contrasted to the black background conveyed a tone that built throughout and worked to establish the fierce conviction of a bold author who had an important message to relay about herself and, more broadly, Muslim and Afghani women, the cultural and gender groups with whom she identified. She established here that she belonged to a subjugated group of people who refused to be erased.

Farrah next explicitly linked her subjectivity to her national identity and geographic point of origin. The screen turned black and transitioned to a meandering mountain valley glowing with emerald, rich forestry. The valley seemed to continue endlessly into unfolding mountains. The photograph was marked with a red date in the bottom right corner, "20.7.2004," meaning this photograph was about 8 years old and had been taken when Farrah was around 10 years of age. The text written in white inscribed in the center of the screen read, "This is where it all started, in Laghman, Afghanistan, where my dad was born. The reason I am alive today." Using the words, "This is where it all started," in reference to where her father was born indexed a patriarchal lineage through which Farrah traced and located her point of origin to her father's birthplace. The beautiful imagery she presented in this frame sharply contrasted with the dusty, war-torn Afghanistan frequently shown on mainstream media (Hackett, 2014). Against a soothing beat, Low Key's deep voice, marked with an English accent, was heard saying, "They say, the fool thinks himself to be a wise man." Low Key's words, "They say the fool thinks himself to be a wise man," immediately countered the ignorance that has marked Muslim and Arab people as terrorists (Hackett, 2014; Patel, 2014; Puar & Rai, 2002) and set the tone for the counter-narrative, which unfolded throughout Farrah's DMP.

Following the presentation of her patriarchal lineage, Farrah introduced her father in the next frame. He was smiling and standing casually with his hands in his pockets. Behind him people gathered together sitting facing one another. They sat in front of two-story buildings draped in multicolored cloths and the lush green vines of hanging plants. In the center of the image toward the bottom, white text labeled the image, "My Amazing dad!" Low Key rapped, "But the wise man knows himself to be a fool. I say that to say this. You might take my life . . ." In an allusion to Shakespeare's As You Like It, Low Key employed chiasmus, reversing the meanings for wise man and fool to illustrate that the fool was he who claimed to know all, or the so-called wise man. While Farrah located her origins in a patriarchal lineage, she celebrated her father as being "amazing," and while her intentionality could not be known in the absence of her own expressed rationale, the modal pairings between image and lyrics characterized her father as a "wise fool."

Farrah followed the image of her father with an image of her mother. Farrah's mother stood straight-faced and tall against a dark background. She wore a graduation cap and gown. The yellow tassels draped over the right side of her cap glowed brightly in contrast to the dark background. Her hands were clasped at her waist. Calling attention to both location and discrimination imposed upon Muslim women that transcended borders, the text written in white labeled this image as Farrah's mother and read, "My wonderful mother AKA the greatest woman in the world. Who struggled to get her M.D. in Afghanistan but can't practice medicine here." Using the word "here" indexed Farrah's attention to her present physical location, her current home country, the U.S. "Here" was where she lived and where she and her mother's identities were being erased.

The text paired with this image relayed the reality that Farrah's mother suffered as a refugee in the U.S. Despite being a trained physician, Dr. Azzizi was unable to practice in her new home country. This counter-narrative drew attention to the consequences of a liberation discourse fueling the U.S.'s war efforts in the Middle East specific to the so-called liberties afforded to Afghani women (see Abu Lughod, 2002). At the same time, Farrah's written words, "My wonderful mother AKA the greatest woman in the world. Who struggled to get her M.D. in Afghanistan," attend to the inequities present for Afghani women in Afghanistan pursuing higher education. These semiotic pairings illustrated the complexities involved in negotiating multiple discourses toward subversive efforts. In other words, Farrah's mother, while educated as a physician, struggled in Afghanistan to earn her degree and struggled to practice in the U.S.; these struggles reflected the continued discrimination she faced despite her scholarly accomplishments. Low Key rapped, "But you can't take my soul. You might take my freedom, but you can't take . . ." Low Key's words, "You might take my freedom," challenged the notion of liberties gained by Farrah's mother in making the move to the U.S. and rather underscored what was lost, her ability to practice medicine. At the same time, the repetition in Low Key's lyrics, of what would not be taken, one's soul, reflected the tone of resistance to oppression.

Offering another example of a powerful female influence on her life, Farrah next included a picture of her older sister, whom she described in white text centered at the bottom of the image as, "My older sister who has been like a mother, a best friend, a classmate, and a person to look up to and learn from." Reflecting feminine beauty, Farrah's sister was pictured wearing a magenta dress with long sleeves adorned in delicate, multicolored, decorative flowers that matched the front of the dress. Her long, brown hair curled past her shoulders; her lips were painted in pink gloss, and her right hand sat firmly on her right hip. She offered a slight, closed-lipped smile to the camera. While Farrah wore hijab, neither her mother nor sister wore hijab in these images. Low Key rapped, "You can't take my soul, no you can't take my soul. You might take my life, but you can't take my soul . . ."

Following the picture of her sister, Farrah introduced her brother, Habib, as a smiling child who "brightens everyone's day!" and Aamir, an adolescent male pictured against a natural backdrop as "the person [Farrah loved] the most but never [showed] or [who showed her] love through fight;" this image was followed by a picture of Farrah wrapping her arms around Aamir's waist in a picture labeled "Siblings :)." Labeling the picture with a smiling face emoticon of the sister lovingly hugging her brother further demonstrated the happiness she associated with this relationship. She followed these images with a picture of her sister Saleh, a short-haired, young woman in a plaid shirt "who can be really mean sometimes but [was] the smartest kid in [her] whole family," according to the words written at the bottom of her photograph. Yet, Low Key's provocative lyrics continued to play as Farrah introduced her siblings. Over the aforementioned images, he rapped,

"You can't take my soul. You might take my freedom. But you can't take my soul. No you can't take my soul." The juxtaposition of text across these images proffered a normative family discourse inclusive of sibling love/hate relationships. Yet, coupling these images with Low Key's lyrics reveals how Farrah and her family used love as a way to resist their oppressed positioning and maintain their humanity.

Following the images of her family, Farrah presented two starkly different images of herself. The first showed a young woman clothed in black, a black hijab covering her hair; dark shadows circled her eyes; her chin rested firmly on her raised fist and covered most of her mouth, and the knuckle of her left closed fist stopped just below her nose. She looked directly at the camera. The text appeared as white letters, was centered inches below her fist, and read, "ME!" A woman's voice chanted, "na, na, na, na," and Low Key, in a rhythmic voice proclaimed, "So, we must ask ourselves, what is the diction[ary]—."

In the brief exchanges I captured on audio when Farrah and her friends were first planning their digital stories, Farrah and her friends astutely located the ways in which their subjectivities within the school context were constructed via an Islamophobic discourse echoed in Low Key's lyrics. In the following frame, Low Key's lyric finished as he expressed the word, "terrorism." Here, in calling on his audience to revisit the "dictionary definition" of the word "terrorism" he was challenging the imposition of the terrorist label on Muslim, Middle Eastern, Arab, Afghani bodies, such as Farrah's. Farrah's deadpan stare coupled with the label "ME!" invited the audience to confront their own assumptions about terrorism and terrorists. Here, the audience was asked to both consider the dictionary definition and the legitimacy of its application to Farrah's body.

Visually echoing earlier imagery of female beauty, the DMP transitioned to a profile image of Farrah, sitting on a raised ledge in what appeared to be a park; her arms were covered by a white sweater stretched out in front of her; her head leaned down, a silken red scarf laced with golden threads covered her forehead, and cascaded down her face, but was pulled back just enough to show her cheeks, painted lips, closed mouth, and a hint of a smile. Her eyes were brushed with mascara; a blush color painted her eyelids and complemented the colors of the scarf. In the foreground, the audience encountered glowing, emerald-green grass with lush trees rising up from the ground. The sunlight, filtered through tree leaves, cast delicate shadows across her back, and a streak of light caught the gold on her scarf. The same rhythmic voice of Low Key completed the inquiry, [dictionary] definition of 'Terrorism.' The systematic use of . . . ."

Using images and words, Farrah masterfully juxtaposed song lyrics, the sounds in the song, and the images and words on the screen to illustrate the absurdity of inscribing Muslim bodies, her family members, with the label of terrorism. In no way do the aforementioned images suggest anything akin to the violence or destruction reflected in the dictionary definition Low

Key shared with his audience. Rather, Farrah drew on a Muslim discourse to establish for her Western audience that Muslim and Afghani subjectivity was peaceful. Following this notion with graceful and multicolored dancers, she evoked imagery of feminine beauty and grace that paralleled the imagery in Farrah's senior picture (the image of herself pictured in the park) and further attached this agentic discourse to her subjectivity through the words, "I am an Afghan."

"Islam Is Peace"

Starting with a familiar plot structure and storyline worked toward establishing common ground among a diverse peer audience. Such a common ground enabled Farrah's DMP to make an agentic turn in its transition to offering the audience a new definition for Muslim people—peaceful. She asserted this counter story line through presenting images of her community at large—diverse Muslim and Afghani people and then specifically Afghani women representing feminine beauty, strength, and pride. In juxtaposition to these unalarming images, Low Key's lyrics conversely describe "the real terrorists."

Farrah begins this next section sharing an image of her immediate community members (in addition to her family). Starting with her local school context, Farrah included a picture of her peers. Three young women and a young man stood close together smiling at the camera. From left to right: the first, a light-skinned young woman with a face the color of delicate porcelain, wore a black hijab covering her hair and long black [dress] with a white stitched collar that followed around her neck and down the front of her dress; the second, a male student with short brown hair and caramel-colored skin who wore a low-cut shirt and jeans and crossed his arms across his chest. Next to him, a young woman with an olive complexion wore a multicolored pink head scarf, covering her hair, that flowed to her waist and complemented her light-blue, long-sleeved top with red threads, which flowed over a black skirt. Next to her, a young woman, with a dark coffee complexion wore an auburn, long-sleeved jilbāb that formed a hood over her head; she wore a black cloth, or under scarf, under the hijab tight to her head and covering her hair; her arms were covered in long black sleeves, and she held her hands clasped at her waist. The picture was framed with a black border, and below the figures, words in white text read, "The friends that have taught me true meaning of friendship and have always been there for me." Low Key rapped, "[The systematic use of] terror especially as a means of coercion."

Farrah followed the picture of her friends with a picture of Arabic script of the words "ISLAM IS PEACE" written below the Arabic. Across the image, Farrah had typed in black text, "I am a Muslim." Low Key rapped, "But what is terror [a gun loading and being shot off is heard in the background]? According to the dictionary I hold in my hand—."

The project transitioned to the image of two lines of dancers, five people deep. People sitting at tables surrounded the dancers. Large windows opened up into courtyards filled with green glass. The dancers danced on a beechwood floor; a black line intersected the room. The dancers, as though caught between movements, raised right arms and hands in unison. Their backs were to the camera; they faced an audience of viewers sitting at tables cloaked in blue and yellow. The dancers wore multicolored clothing—blue, teal, purple, and red scarves decorated their heads and were tucked neatly around the dancers' faces; the scarves cascaded down their backs and seemed to lift with the wind created by their movements. The dancers' bodies were garbed in bright cloth—blues, reds, oranges, teal, and yellow—that lifted from their bodies, filled with air, and flowered out, like upside-down flowers that bloomed with the dancers' movements. Their legs were covered, green and blue stems showing when the cloth bloomed up in their movements. The text, in black, as though printed across the beechwood floor announced, "I am an Afghan." Low Key rapped, "Terror, is violent or destructive acts such as bombing committed by groups in order to intimidate a—."

Farrah next included images of powerful, civically engaged Afghan women, whom she characterized as both serving the people of the world and their home country while standing up for their rights to follow their chosen career paths. The first image showed a room of straight-faced, uniformed women wearing hijab and sitting in red chairs. Three light-skinned women were framed in the front center of the image; behind them were rows of women and then men. The text centered at the bottom of the screen, written in white lettering, read, "Love and respect to the women that serve their countries despite the cultural stereotypes." Low Key rapped, "Population, or government into granting their demands, so—."

In her text, Farrah acknowledged the subjugated positioning of Afghani women in Afghanistan but underscored their power and fortitude to serve in the Afghan military despite "cultural stereotypes" that previously had kept women from doing so. Here Farrah complicated the notion of terrorism in presenting empowered female members of the Afghani military who were there exercising their right to serve. Moreover, she circumvented a terrorist inscription on these women by offering her own "love and respect" for them, and as though in response to Low Key's lyrics defining terrorists as those who used intimidation tactics to coerce a government into granting their demands, she implicitly framed these women as civil rights activists who were enacting their rights to serve their country. She further established a civil rights discourse in the text of the following slide, labeling the next picture of women in the forefront, who were likely Afghani, with the words, "Proud of the women who are standing up for their rights in parliament." Low Key continued to rap, "So, what's a terrorist? They're calling me a terrorist, like they don't know who the terror is."

"Outside the Kitchen"

The next frame anticipated Farrah's future career as a health-care worker. The woman wearing a green hair cap and white shirt leaned over another woman and pressed a cone-shaped object against the pregnant woman's stomach as though listening for signs of life. The text in white read, "Women that are educated and help others "OUTSIDE THE KITCHEN . . ." Low Key continued, "When they put it on me I tell them this, I'm all about peace and love, peace and love. When they calling me a terrorist . . ." Establishing education as a pathway to a career, Farrah pointedly responded to a discourse that assumed that all Muslim women were tethered indiscriminately to a life of domestic labor.

Further anticipating her career as an international health-care worker and subverting the notion that all Afghani women were relegated to a life bound to the home, Farrah included a picture of a white, sandy beach surrounded by trees. The text in white read, "I love traveling. One of my dreams is to [visit] Palestine, (?), Jamaica, Australia, England, Turkey, and Malaysia because I love the beaches, the culture, and the accents of these countries! :)" Low Key continued, "Like they don't know who the terror is, insulting my intelligence. Oh how these people—."

Farrah continued her DMP with two images that from the labeling Farrah provided, appeared to have been taken in Afghanistan. Low Key's music continued to play throughout. Farrah's DMP ended with her anticipating her future career as an international health-care worker. The image showed a small room that appeared to be inside of a tent housing a multiracial group of men and women. A woman wearing a white coat with a blue collar faced a small child; the two appeared to be in conversation across a table. Next to the pair was another table with two people, one in a white overcoat and a person in a multicolored outfit across from her. Several people gathered toward the back of the tent. A sign against the wall read, "CONTRA EL SIDA," which in English translates to "Against AIDS." Low Key rapped, "Tell me, what's the bigger threat to human society BAE Systems or homemade IED's? Remote controlled drones."

Finally, returning to the overarching subversive story line, Farrah concluded her digital project with images of Low Key, whom she identified as a British rapper who had profoundly influenced her. Over his picture in black lettering, she wrote, "The Amazing British rapper that inspires me and my dreams. The person who taught me to defend my religion and culture and break the;" the text unfortunately cut off at the end. The remaining slides revisited Farrah's stated career ambitions and revealed photographs of Low Key as Low Key continued rapping.

The final screen was black. Credits rolled up from the bottom of the page in the center. Text white read, "CREDITS: Farrah Azzizi; Thank you for watching :) STARRING My family, friends, lowkey, and the Afghans :) MUSIC Lowkey." Low Key continued, "Irrelevant how eloquent the rhetoric peddler is. They're telling fibs, now tell us who the real terrorist is." The chorus picked up, "They're calling me a terrorist. Like they don't know who the terror is. When they put it on me, I tell them this I'm all about peace and love. They're calling me a terrorist. Like they don't know who the terror is."

IMPLICATIONS: THE SPACE BETWEEN UNREST AND ACTION

Closely examining Farrah's digital media project in relation to her articulated sense of inequitable treatment of human life within her school context indicates that Farrah's approach to digital storytelling exceeded composing for the purposes of completing an assignment. In the final section of this chapter, I discuss two salient implications related to context and coalitions that I view as areas to be leveraged and built upon as we work collectively to create the conditions that enable youth to create, resist, and act.

The classroom context, while not a focal point of analysis, was a space that Farrah seized upon to speak up and out against dehumanizing discourses. Kira, a veteran teacher in public urban education, created a culturally responsive space wherein she positioned her culturally, ethnically, and linguistically diverse students as knowledgeable learners and teachers. As a teacher of juniors and seniors, Kira encouraged self-directed, autonomous learning among her students. Thus, sitting in self-selected groups, as Farrah and her peers were when discussing their digital stories, reflected normal classroom practice. Kira explained that her primary objective was to prepare her students for life. This philosophy was reflected in how she aligned her instructional goals with her students' interests and plans for their own futures. She incorporated this knowledge of students into her unquestionably rigorous academic instruction.

Kira embraced and invited diverse perspectives. This diversity was reflected in the literature she included on the course syllabi, the guest speakers she invited to her class, and the ways in which she approached facilitating class discussions. She often emphasized that this was a place to speak one's mind, to share one's life experiences, and to respect the diversity in the space. At the same time, Kira consistently demanded that students engage respectfully with each other, and she defined the parameters of conversation from the critical equity framework she brought to bear in their approaches to text analysis. It was in this classroom context that Farrah seemed to find ease and comfort in sharing her political message. Yet, Farrah deliberately missed class on the day that we shared her digital story in class; she later told me that she felt embarrassed. Her embarrassment, I believe, reflects a felt sense of division between herself and many of her peers (see Beucher, 2015). Particularly in diverse classrooms, educators play an important role in helping students come to know one another lovingly and through new viewpoints like those reflected in Farrah's DMP.

Feminist scholar and activist María Lugones (2003) reminds us of the ways in which people shape discourse and subject intelligibility. In this way, she argues that one's power to effect transformation in oneself and in others lies in people's ability to see one another differently. She writes, "We are fully dependent on each other for the possibility of being understood and without this understanding we are not intelligible, we do not make sense, we are not solid, visible, integrated; we are lacking" (p. 86). While digital storytelling offered Farrah an opportunity to bring visibility and a new storyline to how Muslim female subjectivity might be read, authoring the story merely opened the door to the conversation. Educators can take the lead in guiding their students through. At the same time, this work is always a collective endeavor that requires the work of all community members. Given the sensitive nature of personal storytelling, I advise that teachers start with a discussion of student music selection as a way to lead into conversations about salient discourses among student digital autobiographies.

Scholars have argued extensively for harnessing urban youth hip-hop culture in the English language arts classroom (Mahiri, 1996, 1998, 2006; Morrell, 2002; Morrell & Duncan-Andrade, 2002; Paris & Alim, 2014). On this point, Morell (2002) asserts, "Popular culture can help students deconstruct dominant narratives and contend with oppressive practices in hopes of achieving a more egalitarian and inclusive society" (p. 72). Farrah's use of hip-hop music in her DMP worked toward this ambition.

Beginning a class discussion about inequity, oppression, resistance, and action in relation to digital storytelling could start with analyzing the discourses in the music students select for their projects. Through collectively deconstructing lyrics first, students could develop their critical media literacy practices while growing their consciousness of how discourses function to perpetuate and challenge inequities in relation to how people come to know one another through discursive messaging. Such an approach would position students alongside teachers as knowledgeable experts in the classroom as they colead the discussion about their selected songs. Teachers and students then could move deeper into more sensitive parts of the analytical discussion. Questions for conversation might include: (1) Why did you select this particular music? What was the intended effect? (2) What messages within the music resonated personally with the story that you wanted to tell about yourself? (3) Why these images, these words, and so on? What was the intended effect? As the conversation evolves, teachers can move the questioning to a more critical line of questioning (see Luke, 1995) that would allow youth to interrogate the discourses they have engaged in their work and discuss the implications of these choices for how people, including themselves, are situated in the world. In this way, youth and educators can move closer into one another's worlds toward developing deeper understanding of one another's social positioning and experiences and through coming to know one another anew to work collectively to create, resist, educate, and transform the world.

NOTES

1 Farrah's story is part of an ethnographic study that spanned the Spring 2012–Spring 2013 school year in which I was a participant observer and qualitative researcher in four high school English language arts classes taught by the same teacher in a linguistically, culturally, ethnically, nationally, and racially diverse urban high school in the Rocky Mountain region of the U.S. The entire data set included 135 students. Farrah's class (Spring 2012), Senior Honors Thesis (SHT), had 35 students (43 percent male; 57 percent female; 31 percent White; 29 percent Latina/o; 11 percent African; 9 percent Black or African American; 14 percent Middle Eastern; 6 percent Vietnamese).
2 Students like Farrah built their DMPs by image forming the first layer with other modes, like text and music, following. I elected to privilege the visual mode of image to define the boundaries for each unit of analysis. I made this choice because I felt that it would allow me to analyze the film from the perspective that I observed most students creating their digital narratives—by first selecting the image and then choosing the music and text to match. Selecting image first was largely on account of how the software functioned. To add music to the story, it has to be paired with another mode such as an image or a background color. To create the transcript for Farrah's video, I logged the time each image was on the screen as well as made note of specific observations about each mode (image, text, or music).

REFERENCES

Abu Lughod, L. (2002). Do Muslim women really need saving? Anthropological reflections on cultural relativism and its others. *American Anthropologist*, 104(3), 783–790.

Beucher, R. (2015). *Negotiating black masculinity and audience across high school contexts: A feminist post structural analysis of three non-dominant students' multiliteracy composition practices during digital autobiographical storytelling* (Unpublished doctoral dissertation). University of Colorado, Boulder.

Bing-Canar, J., & Zerkel, M. (1998). Reading the media and myself: Experiences in critical media literacy with young Arab-American Women. *Signs*, 23(3), 735–743.

Butler, J. (1993). *Bodies that matter: On the discursive limits of "sex."* New York, NY: Routledge.

Curwood, J. S., & Gibbons, D. (2010). "Just like I have felt": Multimodal counternarratives in youth-produced digital media, *Formulations and Findings*, 1(4), 59–77.

Davies, B. (2000). *A body of writing: 1991–1999*. Sydney: Hampton Press.

del Carmen Salazar, M. (2013). A Humanizing pedagogy reinventing the principles and practice of education as a journey toward liberation. *Review of Research in Education*, 37(1), 121–148.

Delpit, L. D. (1988). The silenced dialogue: Power and pedagogy in educating other people's children. *Harvard Educational Review*, 58(3), 280.

Fairclough, N., & Wodak, R. (1997). Critical discourse analysis. In T. vanDijk (Ed.), *Discourse as social interaction* (pp. 258–284). London: Sage.

Freire, P. (1993). *Pedagogy of the oppressed*. New York, NY: Continuum Press.

Freire, P., & Macedo, D. (1987). *Literacy: Reading the word and reading the world.* South Hadley, MA: Bergin & Garvey.

Gee, J. P. (2010). A situated-sociocultural approach to literacy and technology. In E. Baker (Ed.), *The new literacies: Multiple perspectives on research and practice* (pp. 165–193). New York, NY: Guilford Press.

Gibbons, D., Drift, T., & Drift, D. (2010). Whose story is it? Being Native and American: Crossing borders, hyphenated selves. In J. Fisherkeller (Ed.), *International perspectives on youth media: Cultures of production and education* (pp. 172–191). New York, NY: Lang.

Giroux, H. A. (1983). Theories of reproduction and resistance in the new sociology of education: A critical analysis. *Harvard Educational Review, 53*(3), 257–293.

Giroux, H. A., & McLaren, P. (Eds.). (2014). *Between borders: Pedagogy and the politics of cultural studies.* New York, NY: Routledge.

Gutiérrez, K., Bien, A., Selland, A., & Pierce, D. (2011). Polylingual and polycultural learning ecologies: Mediating emergent academic literacies for dual language learners. *Journal of Early Childhood Literacy, 11*(2), 232–261.

Hackett, R., & Fraser, S. (2014). *Understanding media in the age of terrorism.* Hershey, PA: International Science Reference.

Halverson, E. R., Lowenhaupt, R., Gibbons, D., & Bass, M. (2009). Conceptualizing identity in youth media arts organisations: A comparative case study. *eLearning, 6*(1), 23–42.

Hull, G. A. (2003). Youth culture and digital media: New literacies for new times. *Research in the Teaching of English, 38*(2), 229–333.

Hull, G. A., & Katz, L. M. (2006). Crafting an agentive self: Case studies of digital storytelling. *Research in the Teaching of English, 41*(1), 43–81.

Hull, G. A., & Nelson, M. E. (2005). Locating the semiotic power of multimodality. *Written Communication, 22*(2), 224–261.

Lavia, J., & Moore, M. (Eds.). (2010). *Cross-cultural perspectives on policy and practice: Decolonizing community contexts.* London, UK: Routledge.

Lugones, M. (2003). *Pilgrimages/Peregrinajes: Theorizing coalition against multiple oppressions.* New York, NY: Roman & Littlefield Publishers, Inc.

Luke, A. (1995). Text and discourse in education: An introduction to critical discourse analysis. In M. Apple (Ed.), *Review of Research in Education, 21,* 3–48. Washington, DC: American Educational Research Association.

Mahiri, J. (1996). Writing, rap, and representation: Problematic links between text and experience. In P. Mortensen and G. Kirsch (Eds.), *Ethics and representation in qualitative studies of literacy* (pp. 228–240). Urbana, IL: National Council of Teachers of English.

Mahiri, J. (1998). Streets to schools: African American youth culture and the classroom. *The Clearing House, 71*(6), 335–338.

Mahiri, J. (2006). Digital DJ-ing: Rhythms of learning in an urban school. *Language Arts, 84*(1), 55–62.

McLaren, P. (1989). On ideology and education: Critical pedagogy and the cultural politics of resistance. In H. Giroux & P. McLaren (Eds.), *Critical pedagogy, the state and cultural struggle* (pp. 174–202). Albany, NY: State University of New York.

Morrell, E. (2002). Toward a critical pedagogy of popular culture: Literacy development among urban youth. *Journal of Adolescent & Adult Literacy, 46*(1), 72–77.

Morrell, E., & Duncan-Andrade, J. (2002). Toward a critical classroom discourse: Promoting academic literacy through engaging hip-hop culture with urban youth. *English Journal, 91*(6), 88–94.

Nelson, M. E., & Hull, G. A. (2008). Self-presentation through multimedia: A Bakhtinian perspective on digital storytelling. *Digital storytelling, mediatized stories: Self-representations in new media.* New York, NY: Peter Lang.

New London Group. (1996). A pedagogy of multiliteracies: Designing social futures. *Harvard Educational Review, 66*(1), 60–92.

Nixon, A. S., & Gutiérrez, K. (2007). Digital literacies for young English learners. In C. Genshi & A. L. Goodwin (Eds.), *Diversities in Early Childhood Education: Rethinking and Doing* (pp. 121–135). New York, NY: Routledge.

Paris, D., & Alim, H. S. (2014). What are we seeking to sustain through culturally sustaining pedagogy? A loving critique forward. *Harvard Educational Review, 84*(1), 85–100.

Paris, D., & Winn, M. (2014). *Humanizing research: Decolonizing qualitative inquiry with youth and communities.* Thousand Oaks, CA: Sage Publications, Inc.

Patel, S. (2014). Racing madness: The terrorizing madness of the post-9/11 terrorist body. In L. Ben-Moshe, C. Chapman & A. Carey (Eds.), *Disability incarcerated: Imprisonment and disability in the United States and Canada* (pp. 201–216). New York, NY: Palgrave MacMillian.

Puar, J. K., & Rai, A. (2002). Monster, terrorist, fag: The war on terrorism and the production of docile patriots. *Social text, 20*(3), 117–148.

Vasudevan, L. M. (2006). Making known differently: Engaging visual modalities as spaces to author new selves. *E-Learning, 3*(2), 207–216.

Zaal, M. (2012). Islamophobia in classrooms, media, and politics. *Journal of Adolescent & Adult Literacy, 55*(6), 555–558.

3 "Truth, in the End, Is Different From What We Have Been Taught"
Re-Centering Indigenous Knowledges in Public Schooling Spaces

Timothy San Pedro

Visual representations within urban schools, historically and currently, construct damaging deficit perspectives for students of color (Johnson, 2014; Morrell, 2008; Tuck & Yang, 2013). Johnson (2014) states: "From the building, to the signs and symbols associated with school culture and learning, to the people within its walls, school as place is an important factor in the shaping of the educational experiences of students" (p. 1). To provide an example of such disconnects from the lived realities of Native American students outside of school to the visual representations of themselves—their cultures and histories—inside of schools, I restory my visual journey into one particular high school located in the urban Southwest U.S.

Engraved in the concrete above Desert View High School's (DVHS)[1] front doors is the school's seal—a balance, scroll, feather pen, and flying shoe surrounding a torch. The seal is plastered onto the side profile of a cartoon-like Native American face. The nose is disproportionately large as are the bulging eyebrows. Braided hair is bound by strings and feathers. The word "LOYALTY" hangs like a heavy earing. Every school day, students walk underneath this seal, this symbol, and perhaps after a while they no longer notice it; maybe it was never noticed at all. Many of these students—about 10 percent of the school's population—are from multiple tribal nations both far and near, predominantly Diné (Navajo), Hopi, Akimel O'odham (Pima), and Xalychidom Piipaash (Maricopa), giving Desert View High the largest population of Native American[2] students attending an off-reservation school in this city. This is due, in large part, to its physical proximity to a Native American reservation (composed of Pima and Maricopa peoples), located just two miles away.

I walk underneath this seal, through the doors, and into the hallways of DVHS on my way to a unique course titled Native American Literature.[3] Despite this major Southwest city's proximity to multiple native nations, this is the *only* course devoted entirely to the teaching of literacies and histories of Native American peoples in any of the city schools, a notable accomplishment considering that the creation and implementation of this course came during the banning of ethnic studies courses in Arizona.[4] As I wait for the

"Truth, in the End, Is Different From What We Have Been Taught" 69

Figure 3.1 Seal and Symbol on the Outside Wall of DVHS Depicting a Stereotypical Native American

second-period Native American Literature class to begin, I roam the empty hallways. Moving through these hallways, a space shared by all students, I am aware of new student-created posters hanging on the walls outside of classrooms. I take note (as well as pictures) of the visible stories being told in the common spaces of the school.

I come upon one particular classroom—a required junior level "American" history course. The posters on display outside this class have titles like "Explorers in America!" and "America Discovered!" One particular poster depicts ships sailing from Europe to North and Central America, red and black arrows chart their general westward route. On the left side of the same poster is a 4' by 5' table chart. Three heroes and explorers are listed: Cortes, Cartier, and Cabot. Underneath each of the names, boxes depict

Figure 3.2 Hallway Intersection at DVHS

the goals, accomplishments, and interactions of each explorer. For Cortes, students list the goals: "To find gold/wealth." For the accomplishments, students wrote: "Took over Aztecs, Got a lot of Gold!" And for the interactions, they mentioned: "Left sickness."

In seeing these visible storied narratives, I flash back to moments in my K–12 schooling experience in western Montana, where as a Filipino American who grew up on the Flathead Indian Reservation, I became aware of the drastic separation between school and community. This sharp contrast between community and school knowledge led me to question why the stories, knowledges, and perspectives shared by my Native American (Salish, Kootenai, and Pond d'Oreille) friends and their families were not making their way into my school's curriculum. As I walk through these halls at DVHS today, I am also walking through my storied memory in the hallways of my high school. While slowly walking closer to the Native American Literature classroom and away from the "American" history class, I continue to ask questions that emerged so long ago for me when I was in high school. These questions have become more nuanced for me, but I can hear their genesis in the conversations I continue to have with students taking this Native American Literature course:

- Whose stories are visible in schooling spaces? And in their visibility, validated? Concurrently, whose stories are invisible? And in their invisibility, invalidated?
- In what ways might educators reinforce or counter the visual representations in schools that regulate students and communities of color while reinforcing the dominant White, Eurocentric narratives in schools?
- In what ways were students storying (Kinloch & San Pedro, 2014) the in/validation of being in/visible in the school's curriculum?

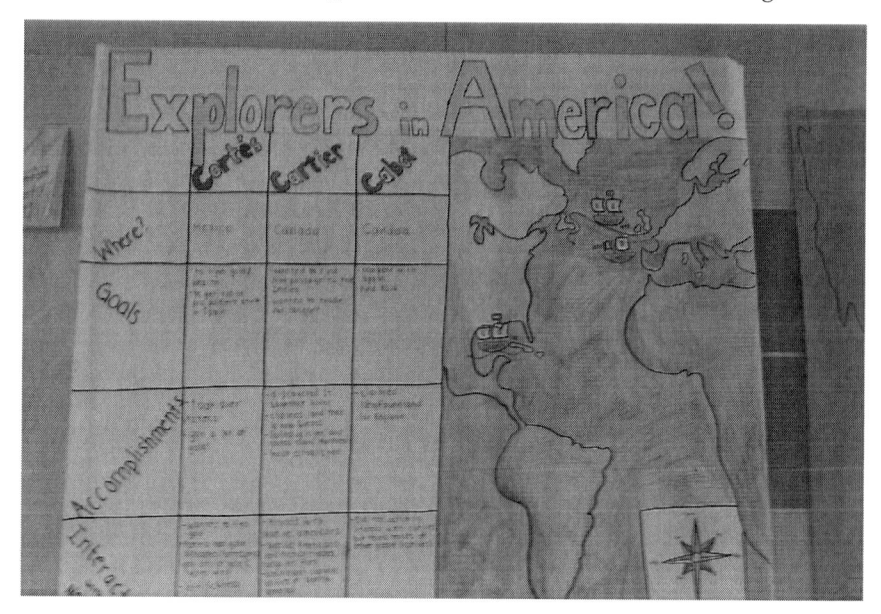

"Truth, in the End, Is Different From What We Have Been Taught" 71

Figure 3.3 A Poster Titled "Explorers in American!" Taped Along the Outside Wall of an "American" History Course

RELATIONSHIPS AND PRAXIS: SITUATING THE WORK

According to Wilson (2008), Indigenous Research Methodology are rooted in the construction, maintenance, and sustenance of relationships through the sharing of our stories. In employing these methods as understood by Wilson and others (Grande, 2004; Kovach, 2005; Smith, 2012), I developed and sustained humanizing relationships (Kinloch & San Pedro, 2014; Paris & Winn, 2014) with students and the classroom teacher, Ms. Bee, in a longitudinal, humanizing, and ethnographic study from 2010 to 2012.

Through these relationships (many of which still continue during the time of this writing), I continue to be welcomed into this classroom to learn along with the students and to provide any assistance Ms. Bee needed in planning and development. The class I focus on in this chapter comprised of students who self-identified as the following:

- Eighteen Native American students from seven different tribes (Navajo, Apache, Zuni, Muscogee Creek, Hopi, Pima, Tohono O'odham)
- Five Hispanic students
- Two African American students
- Two White students
- Three biracial students: two self-identified as Navajo and African American, while one said Pima and Hispanic

By engaging in a longitudinal and ethnographic study using grounded theory (Charmaz, 2006), I was afforded multiple opportunities to overlap meaning from similar lesson plans delivered in all three of the years I participated in and observed the course (Emerson & Pollner, 2003; Paris, 2011). The three main sources of data collected were: (1) digitally recorded whole- and small-group discussions in class and accompanying field notes; (2) semi-structured and dialogic interviews (two per participant); and (3) written artifacts, which were mostly copies of participants' written work. In addition, through sustaining relationships with participants beyond the scope of the research setting, I was able to share stories with them and they with me about the situations happening in this classroom. For example, Elijah Carlos[5] was a student during the inaugural year of this course during the fall of 2010. We worked together during his time in the class, but then he graduated from high school and attended Arizona State University, which I was also attending as a PhD student at that same time. We continued developing our relationship as we entered into a multicultural mentor/mentee program called SHADES. Through our continued relationship, we discussed the happenings in the course. During one such meeting, Elijah invited me to a coffee shop to discuss an idea Elijah had in relation to the course. In that exchange, Elijah spoke with me about starting a community-based discussion group with current and prior students of Native American Literature (San Pedro, Carlos, & Mburu, in review). Soon thereafter, Elijah and I were engaged in weekly discussions with students at coffee shops, pizza parlors, and community parks. Through these interactions, our stories continued to emerge with others as we worked to understand how to continue to develop our collective critical conscientização (Freire, 1970; Smith, 2003) in spaces that might not be accepting of the perspectives and lenses we were coming to understand.

FOCUS AND DIRECTION: COUNTERING "AMERICA DISCOVERED!"

For this chapter, I focus on one lesson plan taught in all three years that attempted to shift or counter the dominant, Eurocentric visual narratives in the shared hallway spaces of DVHS. Critical place pedagogies as understood by Johnson (2014) helps frame this move by Ms. Bee to counter dominant narratives while re-centering Native American histories and knowledges through art. Johnson (2014) states, "Critical place pedagogies address shared experiences, problems, languages, and histories that communities rely upon to construct a narrative of collective identity and possible transformation of oppressive spaces" (p. 2). Furthering critical place pedagogies, this lesson asked students to consider and reflect upon whose perspectives (paradigms) were taught in their school and whose were ignored. Through this critical reflection, students took action: They countered the

"America Discovered!" type of visible narratives with posters of their own that re-centered the stories of Indigenous people in relation to their painful and forced history with the U.S. government.

In restorying this lesson, I argue that through transformative praxis, students were able to alter the very nature of the visible narratives in their shared hallway spaces by reframing—rather, re-centering—the official, academic stories upon Indigenous paradigms, epistemologies, and ontologies. Transformative praxis promotes "validity and legitimacy of . . . language, knowledge, and culture" of Indigenous peoples while taking into account "unequal 'power relations' between dominant / subordinate" communities and promoting positive changes for Indigenous peoples and communities as defined by them (Smith, 2003). For many students, this reclamation of school space gave them opportunities to move past forced silences by storying and re-centering their placement in the American landscape (Darling-Hammond, 1998; Kinloch & San Pedro, 2014; Kirkland, 2013; Smith, 2012)—a landscape inclusive of their family, community, and tribal knowledges.

In developing relations with students based on mutual trust, shared stories, and listening, I relied on *storying* as a methodology. Storying (Kinloch & San Pedro, 2014) is the convergence and interaction of theory, method, and practice that "push us to listen to the questions we [collectively] raise and vignettes we offer" (p. 22). Further, I am envisioning storying not only in the ways we root our research in the stories shared and subsequent relationships developed but also in the ways we share those stories with others (see *accessibility*, hooks, 2000). As such, vignettes, narratives, and the construction of story all provide access to larger audiences, including those youth who shared their stories with me (and I with them) so as to continue the giving and telling, receiving and hearing, of stories with others to create and sustain humanizing relationships built upon trust and respect for one another.

TEACHING HISTORY AS PERSPECTIVE, NOT AS FACT: A LESSON PLAN[6]

Early in the semester, Ms. Bee delivered a fundamental lesson that she continued to build upon throughout the year. This lesson introduced how our shared "American" history has been taught from a particular lens or perspective and that to see a more inclusive picture of our past, we need to see it from multiple perspectives. She mixed things up for this lesson: When students entered the classroom, they noticed that Ms. Bee rearranged the desks to create three groups of 12. The circled desks all faced and were equal distance from a stool in the middle of the group. After students chose a seat, Ms. Bee asked them take out a pen or pencil as well as tear a piece of paper in half and share it with someone next to them. When ready, Ms. Bee walked to each of the groups and carefully placed a stuffed animal on the stool located in the center of each of the groups. As she did so, she explained that they were to write for five minutes about the factual details they saw on the stool in front of them. Before they began writing, she discussed a couple rules:

1. They were not allowed to touch or reposition the animal.
2. They could not move from their seated positions while they wrote.

They agreed with these rules and began writing. Pens and pencils captured what they saw. Some students paused, put pencil to lip, and began writing again.

After time was up, Ms. Bee asked prearranged questions to specific students in the groups. One group had a stuffed animal that appeared to be a dog in sitting position. She asked Stephanie, a student sitting directly in front of the stuffed animal, to share her writing with the class. Stephanie read from her list: one eye open, blue nose, finger up its nose. After Stephanie exhausted her list, Ms. Bee asked a simple question: "What is the dog's name?" This was a detail Ms. Bee knew was out of Stephanie's line of sight.

"Uh . . . I don't know," Stephanie said, which was met with an exasperated reply from Ms. Bee: "What? The dog's name is right there! Why can't you answer this simple question?"

Figure 3.4 Front View of the Stuffed Animal Used in History as Perspective Lesson Plan.

"Truth, in the End, Is Different From What We Have Been Taught" 75

The class was shocked by Ms. Bee's reaction, except for the students sitting opposite of Stephanie, who could clearly see the dog's collar that had its name on it. These students laughed with the satisfaction of having the knowledge that the others did not. Ms. Bee asked one of the laughing students, Michael, if he knew the name of the dog.

"Of course," Michael said confidently. "Its name is Digger. It's right there on the collar." Ms. Bee quickly turned the questioning on Michael this time and asked him about a detail that Stephanie did not mention: "What color is Digger's jaw?"

Michael's confidence cracked as he shrugged his shoulders. "I don't know," he said.

Ms. Bee matched her exasperated reply that she had for Stephanie a minute ago but now directed it at Michael: "What? The dog's jaw is right there! Why can't you answer this simple question?"

Ms. Bee then turned back to Stephanie and asked: "Stephanie, do *you* know the color of Digger's jaw?"

"Of course," Stephanie said replicating Michael's discourse. "Digger's jaw is grey. It's right there!"

Students laughed at the exchange as they made sense of the lesson Ms. Bee was delivering.

Figure 3.5 Behind View of "Digger" the Dog, the Stuffed Animal Ms. Bee Used in a Perspective Lesson Plan.

In a similar questioning fashion, Ms. Bee moved to the other groups to make sure all students had the opportunity to internalize the lesson's message. After the last group, she asked the whole class: "What does this activity attempt to help us understand?" Collectively, students realized that based on their perspective, they could only provide a limited amount of information about something even as simple as describing a stuffed animal. To better understand a historical event, they need to look at it and understand it from multiple perspectives.

Ms. Bee asked further prompting questions: "What about describing an event or a way of life that is different from your own? What about information that is passed down from generation to generation? How do perspectives change? How do biases work their way into the perspectives? How does this activity apply to your learning in other classes?"

The discussion seemed hushed. Few students verbally volunteered their opinion. Noticing this, Ms. Bee asked them to reflect their thoughts on paper. Immediately, pens flew across pages. Some students wrote about how they had never taken into consideration the perspectives of other groups, particularly in school:

> The perspective activity showed me how something can easily be misread or left out depending on how you look at it. It related a lot to what I have, or more importantly, have not learned in my history classes growing up.
> ~Will, White[7]

> You can only see this tiny little angle. An angle that you may not have a say in if you want to see more. . . . [W]e as students do not realize what is not being taught.
> ~Mary, Hispanic

> This activity showed me how much I DO NOT know about Native American history. . . . It also showed me that our history classes do not really tell us the whole story, just parts of it. So in my opinion I do not think we are being educated how we should. Native Americans played a huge part in the U.S. history.
> ~Erin, Hispanic

A few Native American students wrote about how validated they felt to see their fellow classmates realize what many of them had known all along: that *all* perspectives must be told if we are to better understand our shared history:

> The history of Native Americans . . . is simply ignored in our history classes. . . . The stuffed animal . . . showed us that the truth in the end is different from what we have been taught. It's nice to have one class where more students realize this too.
> ~Ivan, Native American (Pima)

"Truth, in the End, Is Different From What We Have Been Taught" 77

RE-CENTERING SHARED ACADEMIC SPACES: "TRUTHS MY TEACHER DIDN'T TELL ME"

The next day, Ms. Bee repositioned the desks back into the normal spots. Without the students knowing, she passed out two different 26-page timelines with important Native American historical events listed. She asked them to circle at least 20 events that they felt should be included in history lessons. Students shuffled through the pages, circling. After some time, she asked students from opposite sides of the room to pair up (so as to have the two different timelines in one group) and discuss which events they chose. They also were asked to dwindle down their 40 total events to 20 that they both felt were important. As students began this work, confusion ensued.

Keene said, "Ms. Bee, we have different timelines."

"Oh, I may have given you two different packets," she said. "So that means you have 26 pages of history, and *you* have 26 pages of history. Total, each group has 52 pages of collective history. That's a whole lot of Native American history that you have not learned over the past 18 years. Are you guys starting to see the enormity of what you need to be taught?"

Students then formed larger groups and were invited to construct timeline posters to teach others the lessons and events important to include into understanding a more complete portrait of American history. Over the next three days, they moved into the hallways to construct their posters on the ground as they shared in conversation sometimes on topic, sometimes off. It was there that they reframed and re-centered historical events inclusive of Native American histories. Multiple groups invited me to join and help with the coloring and writing they were doing. As they constructed these posters, they discussed these events in greater detail while also learning more about each other and about me. The stories shared while co-constructing artistic representations of their timelines led to moments of student-led learning as they shared their developing understanding of these events often left out of their traditional academic spaces.

In understanding the generative space co-constructed through the telling and hearing of stories while constructing art, I use the term "visual storying" (Pedro, T., Koo, A., & Barton, M., in review). Visual storying is a way of building meaningful relationships and understandings through the experiences of creating and storying visual images, leading to expansive storied spaces where individual's stories begin to interweave with others' stories. In this process, collective meaning is made through the conversations shared while co-constructing and interpreting art. In this way, art as envisioned in visual storying becomes an important form of literacy as students engage in generative spaces of understanding both their worlds and the worlds of another.

Each group created elaborate posters with a lot of symbols and metaphors, which sparked deeper conversations for us. Keene and Eileen's group discussed their drawing of a heart that was breaking in half, and in between the breaking was a light shining through. Keene said this represents Native

78   *Timothy San Pedro*

hearts breaking, and yet a shimmer of hope is seen in the light. In his description, I realized that the heart was not breaking; it was mending.

Another group led by Shila created an elaborate board game, where the square board spaces that the traveler or person playing the game landed on were the historical events they decided to include as a group. At the start was a teepee, from which a two-way road emerged. Travelers had choices all along the way as to which direction to move next. Some routes led to dead ends. Others led to roundabouts. In the background, handprints from group members—composed of multi-tribal and multicultural students—represented that this was their shared story. As they pressed their hands to paper, Shila said, "Tim, you should put your handprint on here too." Having been invited, I gladly obliged.

I found it interesting that the final space on the board game was a two-story house with the word "stop" underneath it. It did not say "finish" or

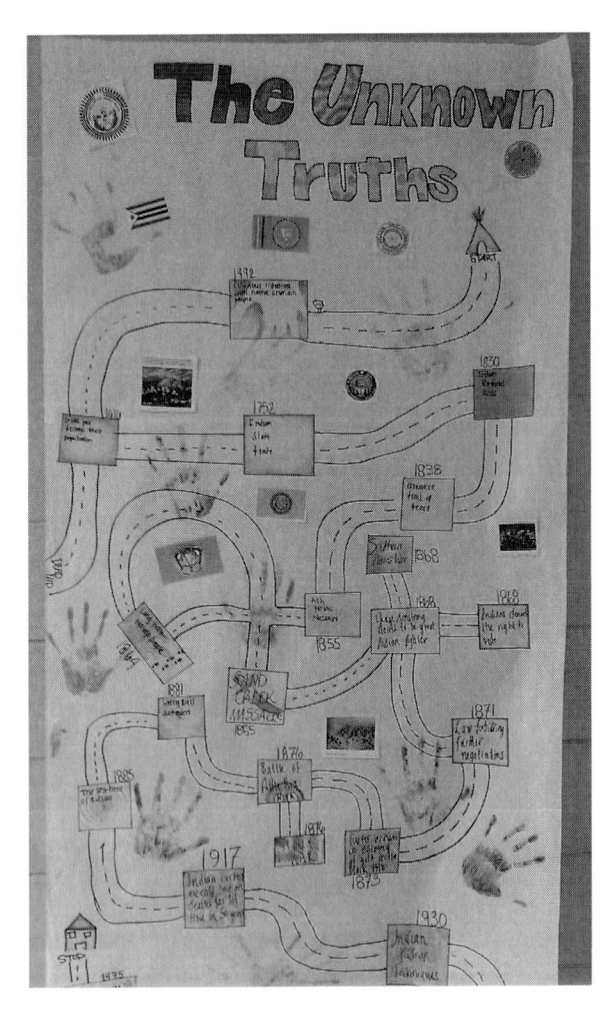

Figure 3.6 Timeline Poster Constructed for the History as Perspective Lesson Plan

"end" or "final destination." Although I didn't ask at the time, I now wonder if this was to represent that the goal of the game was not necessarily to reach the "end," thus the inclusion of two-way streets that led to and from the "start" and "end."

Poster titles included:

- Truths My Teacher Didn't Tell Me
- The Untold Story
- The Unknown Truths
- The Hidden Truth
- Walk in the Moccasins of a Native
- Truth Be Told
- Today's Sorrow From Past Hearts

Once completed, Ms. Bee invited the groups to tape their posters up throughout the school. Whether intentionally or not, the group with the poster titled "Truths My Teacher Didn't Tell Me" taped theirs up on the outside wall of the required junior-level "American" history course. It was at this moment I realized that students who chose to take this senior-level, English-elective Native American Literature course were enrolled, the year before, in the required "American" history course; they were asked to create posters similar to the "America Discovered!" and "Explorers in America!" ones. On that particular day, they re-centered the "truths" that Ms. Bee *did* teach them in a shared hallway space that had historically invalidated their histories, their stories, and their truths.

Once taped up throughout the school, Ms. Bee led a silent viewing of these posters, asking students to take note of the similarities and differences between the posters. They spent about three minutes in quiet contemplation of each piece. Many students noticed that the titles all referenced that which was not taught in their prior education. They were extending their critical questioning and reflections of whose stories were taught as factual in school and whose were silenced and storied over. Just as crucial, they were doing something about it. They added Indigenous histories and knowledges alongside "official" knowledges in their public schooling space. In doing so, their knowledges became part of the official academic knowledge, not simply on the periphery of it. Gruenewald (2003) might argue that this process of praxis these students engaged in *is* decolonization or the unlearning of "dominant culture and schooling . . . and [the] learning [of a] more socially just and ecologically sustainable ways of being in the world" (p. 9). They engaged in decolonization through praxis and, for some anyway, revealed that they were changed by it. In reflecting about their action, students wrote:

> I look back on the years I have history or any class. This is the only class I know I'll get full information on the events of my ancestors or on all tribes who went through so many hardships.
>
> ~Nisha (Zuni and Apache)

80 *Timothy San Pedro*

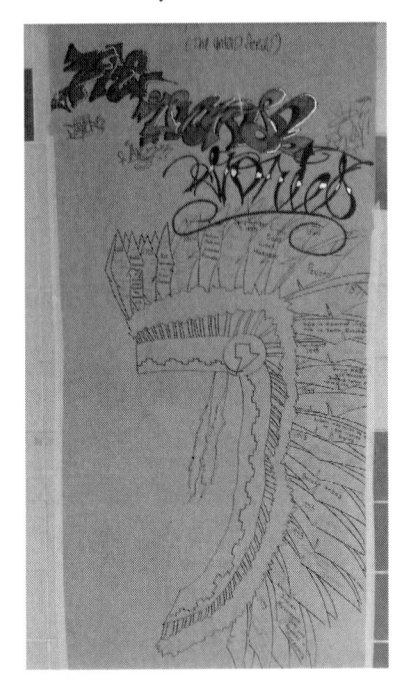

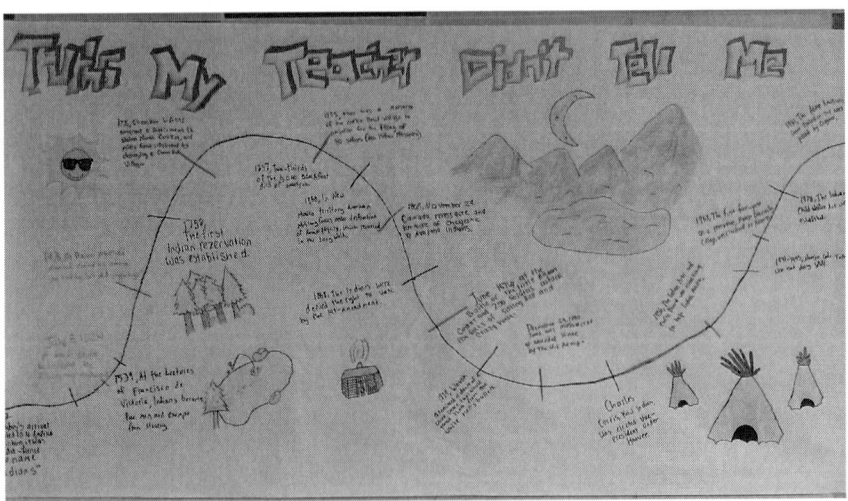

Figure 3.7.1, 3.7.2, 3.7.3 Timeline Posters Constructed for the History as Perspective Lesson Plan

>History classes will quickly talk about [us] and will give some info on the tribe but the information they give will be incorrect. . . . But I do believe that students are not learning enough about the great Native American tribes in the U.S.
>
>~Damon (Hopi and Navajo)

> Today a lot of Native American teens struggle living in the city, because there is still racism that happens to this day. In the history of Native Americans, we were tortured, tricked and taken from her homeland, and young natives should know what has happened to their tribe and others as well. But in school, "it is written European version of history . . . [and] is widely accepted as true history." We are not able to choose what we learn but we can go beyond our reach and explore the true events that have happened.
>
> ~Shila (Navajo)

In hearing the power in Nisha, Damon, and Shila's reflections, it is not hard to hear their desire to take further actions to learn more about themselves and their tribes and have their teachings taught to others. For Nisha, the lessons helped her realize that she wanted to learn more about her tribes. For Damon, it was the belief that students who are not Native American also benefit from this knowledge. And for Shila, she learned the ways her education had intentionally been limited in schools; however, she no longer saw this as a limitation but as a call to action to "go beyond our reach and explore the true events" of her and others' tribal histories and stories. Collectively, these students were engaged in praxis—the back-and-forth process of reflection and action (Freire, 1970; Smith, 2003).

For transformative praxis to flourish, I would argue that it is imperative for anyone working with youth—teachers, researchers, community members—to codevelop fertile and safe spaces with youth to make sense of our emerging critical realities through processes of reflection and action. While students are developing the capacity to become critically aware of power dynamics and injustices that surround them and their communities, they also need to see that this crucial work has a space *inside* schools. They need to know that their struggle and ideological becoming are worthy of inclusion into academic and authoritative spaces. They need to know that their knowledges are a crucial part of the official curricula and the pedagogical decisions made to include them as producers of culture, knowledge, and language (Alim & Reyes, 2011; Paris, 2012; Paris & Alim, 2014). To illustrate this point, I offer two brief examples of the importance of praxis inside schooling spaces.

PRAXIS #1: REFLECTION, ACTION, REFLECTING UPON THAT ACTION, ACTING AGAIN

> We are not able to choose what we learn but we can go beyond our reach and explore the true events that have happened.
>
> —Shila

Shila's words continue to impact me. Within one sentence, she was coming to understand how the tentacles of colonization were reaching far into her academic spaces: "We are not able to choose what we learn." As she acknowledged this power, she no longer saw it as an impossible limitation but an opportunity to struggle for self-determination: "[W]e can go beyond our reach and explore the true events that have happened." Here, Shila was reflecting upon the action the class took collectively: to construct stories that challenged and complicated dominant discourses in the school's shared hallway spaces. And in this reflection, she found a need to take further action.

While I had originally thought of praxis as simply reflecting and then acting, I am realizing the fluid movement of it. Praxis moves back-and-forth between reflection and action. I pause to explain: We often take actions (however small or large) to better ourselves, our families, and our communities. We reflect upon our successes and failures, our positions and choices, made in that action. Based on those lessons learned through reflection, we alter our actions moving forward to build upon the successes and to turn failures into successes. Freire (1970) discussed two dimensions of praxis: Whereas *reflection* asks us to contemplate our realities—to be critical and conscious of it—*action* attempts to change that reality: "To exist, humanly, is [not only] to *name* the world, [but also] to change it" (Freire, 1970, p. 69). Garcia and Shirley (2012) add: "This process [of praxis] must be inclusive of a *dialectical* experience that offers opportunities for individuals and communities to engage in analyses, critiques and dialogues in order to recognize, unpack and resist notions of power and dominance" (p. 80). Graham Smith (2003) calls this process "consciousness-raising," "conscientization"—and later "Indigenous transforming praxis" (2004)—and is a transformation that must be "won on at least two broad fronts; a confrontation with the colonizer and a confrontation with 'ourselves'" (2003, p. 2). Such a confrontation with "ourselves," Linda Smith (2012) states, is the location where the "struggle for self-determination" (p. 8) begins. Shila began this struggle—sparked by the history as perspective lesson plan—by going "beyond" the limitations of her schools' narrowed curriculum and Eurocentric paradigms by "exploring . . . true events" that are often silenced, ignored, and storied over in courses like "American" history.

PRAXIS #2: REFLECTION, ACTION, REFLECTING UPON THAT ACTION, ACTING AGAIN

As we help to co-construct safe and fertile spaces with youth to make sense of our realities, it is essential to acknowledge that such spaces are rare for most students. When they leave the fertile spaces we are attempting to co-create, the world continues to function as per usual. However, as we encourage their development of a critical consciousness, they are beginning to see the world through a new lens, ones that bring into focus systemic inequities, pain, and suffering that may seem insurmountable and, thus, their actions to change their world hopeless. The question I then pose is: What does their "struggle for self-determination" though praxis look like in other spaces that continue to denounce and deny pluralistic realities? I offer the following closing vignette to illustrate answers forming to this question.

In talking more about this perspective and timeline lesson plan with Eileen in the school's library, she says she is in a unique situation: Because she chose *not* to learn the lessons in her "American" history class the year prior, it led to her failing and having to retake it again this year (see San Pedro, 2014). Because of this, she is the only student[8] in the Native American Literature course who moves directly from Native American Literature to the "American" history course.

Eileen mentioned that she's thought a lot about the perspective and time line lesson plans, particularly in relation to her "American" history course. She said, "[Very few students] in the American history class knows about [the histories taught in the Native American literature class], like it's basically European history . . . and [justifying] what they did to Native Americans [as good]." Her reflection upon this situation led her to act: Instead of *refusing* to write a biography paper like she did the year before, she decided to write a paper about one of those "noble conquerors" but from a Native American perspective. She felt she needed to do this because students in the "American" history class didn't "know what really happened in detail because no one said anything about it." To Eileen, it is not their fault for not knowing; they are also products of larger systems of colonization. However, now that Eileen has learned a new perspective to history, one that values her understandings, she is armed with the knowledge to right this wrong by teaching others: "I can easily put [the assignment] together and give them the bigger view of what really happened."

Eileen did just that. She wrote that paper—a paper that never came to be the year before. It included facts often discarded and silenced: the rape, theft, sickness, and genocide of Indigenous peoples at the hands of the so-called "heroes" and "noble conquerors." As she shared her paper with the class, students were interested in what she was saying; however, they were in disbelief that what she was saying could be true. Some students turned to the teacher and asked if what Eileen said had any factual basis. The teacher, knowing enough of "American" history, knew it to be true and could not dispute Eileen's contribution; Eileen's lesson, which taught her truth to U.S. history, re-centered her own knowledges and histories in a space that invalidated her paradigms in the past (San Pedro, 2014).

Through Eileen's reflecting with me about the impacts of the history-as-perspective lesson plan, she decided to act in other infertile spaces. As she struggled for her self-determination in spaces that denounced and silenced her knowledges, she relied on the fertile and safe spaces developed in the Native American Literature course to help her construct and teach her perspectives, her ideologies, and her truths elsewhere. As she struggled for self-determination, she taught, and students learned.

As she shared this lesson within her "American" history class, on the other side of the wall, a poster titled "Truths My Teaching Didn't Tell Me" was taped up alongside a poster titled "America Discovered!"

YOUTH ACTIONS, MY REFLECTION

As we work to take actions that "reframe who [students] are and what they want for themselves," teachers, researchers, community members, must also provide spaces to "pause" (Patel, 2014) with students and the participants we work with. We must take moments to reflect on the actions we are taking together, the risks involved for both of us, and the transformation happening within all of us (see Paris & Winn, 2014). Such pauses become important moments to plan how we might act in different ways to create more meaningful transformations for ourselves and for those around us through future actions. This is praxis. And, as we reflect through analyzing and writing about the situations students helped us to see, we must also be aware of the way we share and disseminate that message to others.

Who is listening? Who is receiving the words we write here in the chapters of this book as we restory the impact youth had upon our lives, our understandings, and our realities? To answer, I put into focus the fundamental purpose of this book: To "reframe . . . the purpose of education [by] . . . seeing youth as significant social actors." If we do, in fact, believe they are "significant social actors," shouldn't they be our primary audience so as to benefit from their own stories? If so, how can we employ more inclusive languages to reach broader audiences?

Kinloch and I (2014) began to develop partial answers to these questions when coming to understand the importance that listening had upon us and the youth with whom we worked. We theorized that a certain reciprocal and dialogic power was occurring when we provided spaces to listen critically (San Pedro, 2013) to the stories of others as well as build upon those stories by connecting and offering our own stories in relation to theirs (Wilson, 2008). This giving and receiving of stories co-constructs spaces between people where meaning can be made with one another. We used the term "storying" (San Pedro, 2013) to denote the fertile spaces where theories, methods, and practices converge and intersect to further the development of relationships (Kinloch & San Pedro, 2014). So as to prevent the disconnection of our shared and emerging stories, we must recognize how our academic discourses may be severing youth's stories from those who created them. In our analysis and subsequent retelling of their stories in relation to our own, we must recognize them as significant social actors who can propel their words into the world. We must be aware of how our message is received and how our words and discourses chosen either limit who is able to engage in storying with us or expand and extend the stories to greater spaces and to more peoples, including the youth with whom we work.

As such, I offer "storying-as-literacy," which attempts to give access and invite those very communities and youth who helped us co-construct and codevelop our shared stories herein. Within such a literacy, the power of stories—the emotions, the feelings, the inclusion of self, and relationships—fuels the writing so as to attempt greater connections. So, as I construct this chapter, I think back to the conversations and stories generated while engaging in visual storying through the creation of the timeline art pieces. The lessons heard and stories shared with those students with whom I worked fuel this article; because their knowledges and understandings were weaving and connecting with my own, I write with the intent to reconnect with those students who helped expand my understanding. Further, storying-as-literacy provides fertile spaces between the telling and hearing of stories and knowledges. If we are simply writing for each other (i.e., higher education audiences), and not with those who helped us see, I argue that we continue to mute, silence, and story over youth words, which is the very antithesis of this book. If, however, we reveal our shared story through literacy, our work teaches, just as Eileen taught students in an infertile "American" history space.

As we pause and reflect on the ways we—those working with youth and the youth themselves—come to and make sense of the multiple spaces we occupy, we must also devote the lessons learned to those who helped us see. In this way, the stories we share continue to be "our" stories as we work to become "authentic chroniclers" of youth praxis (Kinloch, 2013, p. 111) using storying-as-literacy (and as an extension visual storying-as-literacy so as to include art as a generative space to be and become in our worlds).

Storying can be a literacy by constructing narratives inclusive of youth voices and the situations they found themselves. Just as we are never separate from the spaces we occupy, I do not pretend to be an objective observer but someone who impacts and is impacted by the stories, contexts, and situations students storied with me. Because their words continue to impact me and connect with my experiences, I write to them and with them. They are my audience, and because they are my audience, I recognize them as significant social actors who can propel their message forward with me through storying-as-literacy.

> [We] share a commitment to engaging [with] youth in ways that give them opportunities to develop their voices, to "change the nature of the conversation" in schools and communities, to reframe who they are and what they want for themselves, and to participate in the decisions that affect youth so that they [and we] can begin to "find a myriad of possible places for themselves in [a pluralistic] society."
>
> (introduction to this volume).

NOTES

1 School names and participant names are pseudonyms to protect anonymity.
2 In a conversation with students, Ms. Bee asked them what students from tribal nations prefer to be called collectively. Students agreed that Native American should be used. As such, I comply with their preference.

3 During the time of the telling, this course was still being taught in the same school by the same teacher.
4 Arizona's House Bill 2281 states that school districts are not allowed to include any (non-White) "ethnic" studies program of instruction because, according to those drafting this legislation, such courses: "Promotes the overthrow of the United States government. Promote resentment toward a race of class of people. Are designed primarily for pupils of a particular ethnic group. Advocate ethnic solidarity instead of the treatment of pupils as individuals."
5 While other participants' names are pseudonyms, Elijah Carlos, while coauthoring an article together asked that I include his real name. Through proper documentation and signature, this was arranged.
6 This is an adaptation of a lesson plan found in Harvey and Harjo's (1998) book *Indian Country: A History of Native People in America*.
7 I include the term students used to self-identify themselves.
8 Erin was another student who had a similar movement between courses a year prior but was a teacher's aide, not a student, in the "American" history course.

REFERENCES

Alim, H. S., & Reyes, A. (2011). Complicating race: Articulating race across multiple social dimensions. *Discourse and Society, 22*(4), 379–384.

Charmaz, K. (2006). *Constructing grounded theory: A practical guide through qualitative analysis*. Los Angeles, CA: Sage Publications.

Darling-Hammond, L. (1998). Education for democracy. In M. Greene, W. Ayers & J. L. Miller (Eds.), *A light in dark times: Maxine Greene and the unfinished conversation* (pp. 78–92). New York, NY: Teachers College Press.

Emerson, R. M., & Pollner, M. (2003). Constructing participant/observation relations. In M. R. Pogrebin (Ed.), *Qualitative approaches to criminal justice: Perspectives from the field* (pp. 27–43). Thousand Oaks, CA: Sage Publications.

Freire, P. (1970). *Pedagogy of the oppressed*. New York, NY: Continuum Publishing Co.

Garcia, J., & Shirley, V. (2012). Performing decolonization: Lessons learned from Indigenous youth, teachers and leaders' engagement with critical Indigenous pedagogy. *Journal of Curriculum Theorizing, 28*(2), 76–91.

Grande, S. (2004). *Red pedagogy: Native American social and political thought*. Oxford, UK: Rowman and Little Field Publishers.

Gruenewald, D. A. (2003). The best of both worlds: A critical pedagogy of place. *Educational Researcher, 32*(4), 3–12.

Harvey, K., & Harjo, L. (1998). *Indian country: A history of native people in America*. Golden, CO: Fulcrum Publishing.

hooks, b. (2000). *Feminism is for everyone: Passionate politics*. Cambridge, MA: South End Press.

Johnson, L. P. (2014). The writing on the wall: Enacting place pedagogies in order to reimagine schooling for Black male youth. *Discourse: Studies in the Cultural Politics of Education*. doi: 10.1080/01596306.2014.909968.

Kinloch, V. (2013). Difficult dialogues in literacy (urban) teacher education. In C. Kosnik, J. Rowsell, P. Williamson, R. Simon, & C. Beck (Eds.), *Literacy teacher educators: Preparing teachers for a changing world* (pp. 107–120). Rotterdam: Sense Publishers.

Kinloch, V., & San Pedro, T. (2014). The space between listening and story-ing: Foundations for projects in humanization. In D. Paris & M. Winn (Eds.),

Humanizing research: Decolonizing qualitative inquiry with youth and communities (pp. 21–42). Thousand Oaks, CA: SAGE.

Kirkland, D. E. (2013). *A search past silence: The literacy of young black men.* New York, NY: Teachers College Press.

Kovach, M. (2005). Emerging from the margins: Indigenous methodologies. In L. Brown & S. Strega (Eds.), *Research and resistance: Critical, Indigenous, and anti-oppressive approaches* (pp. 19–36). Toronto: Canadian Scholars' Press/Women's Press.

Morrell, E. (2008). *Critical literacy and urban youth: Pedagogies of access, dissent, and liberation.* New York, NY: Routledge.

Paris, D. (2011). 'A friend who understand fully': Notes on humanizing research in a multiethnic youth community. *International Journal of Qualitative Studies in Education, 24*(2), 137–149.

Paris, D. (2012). Culturally sustaining pedagogy: A needed change in stance, terminology, and practice. *Educational Researcher, 41*(3), 93–97.

Paris, D., & Alim, S. (2014). What are we seeking to sustain through culturally sustaining pedagogy? A loving critique forward. *Harvard Educational Review, 84*(1), 85–100.

Paris, D., & Winn, M. (Eds.). (2014). *Humanizing research: Decolonizing qualitative inquiry with youth and communities.* Los Angeles, CA: Sage

Patel, L. (2014). Countering coloniality in educational research: From ownership to answerability. *Educational Studies: A Journal of the American Educational Studies Association, 50*(4), 357–77.

San Pedro, T. (2013). *Understanding youth cultures, stories, and resistances in the urban southwest: Innovations and implications of a Native American literature classroom.* Dissertations Abstracts Internationals. (UMI No. 3558673)

San Pedro, T. (2014). Internal and environmental safe spaces: Navigating expansions and contractions of identity between Indigenous and colonial paradigms, pedagogies, and classrooms. *Journal of American Indian Education, 52*(3), 42–62.

San Pedro, T., Carlos, E., & Mburu, J. (In Review). Critical listening and storying: Fostering respect for difference and action within and beyond a Native American literature classroom.

Smith, G. (2003). *Indigenous struggles for the transformation of education and schooling* [PDF document]. Retrieved from Keynote Address to the Alaskan Federation of Natives Convention online website: ankn.uaf.edu/curriculum/Articles/GrahamSmith/index.html

Smith, G. (2004). Mai I te maramatanga kit e putanga mai o te tahuritangi: From conscientization to transformation. *Educational Perspectives Journal of the College of Education, 37*(1), 46–52.

Smith, L. T. (2012). *Decolonizing research: Research and Indigenous peoples* (2nd ed.). New York, NY. Zed Books.

Tuck, E., & Yang, K. W. (Eds.). (2013). *Youth resistance research and theories of change.* New York: Routledge.

Wilson, S. (2008). *Research is ceremony: Indigenous research methods.* Winnipeg, MB: Fernwood Publishing.

4 Publicly Engaged Scholarship in Urban Communities
Possibilities for Literacy Teaching and Learning

Valerie Kinloch

> Many teachers working in our schools in this neighborhood don't know the neighborhood enough to help our young people develop a pride about where they come from and see that there is good in their neighborhood.
>
> (donna Hicho, with a lowercase "d")

I open this chapter on publicly engaged scholarship in urban communities by sharing important insights from donna Hicho, a close friend, a critical community educator, and the executive director of the Greater Linden Development Corporation (GLDC), a nonprofit organization on the south side of Columbus, Ohio. The organization's primary purpose is to collaborate with local residents to revitalize the community by focusing on five initiatives: housing, business and economic development, community development, planning and coordination, and community safety and beautification. In addition to partnering with others to strengthen the community, the organization also collaborates with teachers, students, parents, and researchers to design and implement high-quality educational opportunities inside and outside schools. Thus, it was not surprising to the group of nearly 30 public school teachers, teacher educators, graduate researchers, and me that she graciously welcomed us into the GLDC's first-floor conference room to talk about our responsibilities to work effectively in local communities.

Hicho's sentiments are central to the diverse ways in which we (e.g., educators, school administrators, and community partners) collaborate *with* students, listen to students, see students as agentive beings, and intentionally seek to learn about the communities where students live and attend schools. After she surveyed the room, stopping only momentarily for a brief pause and to exchange a warm smile, Hicho said, "You know, all those words that you talked about—diverse and developing and whatever... My hope is that when you're in a neighborhood, wherever it is, that eventually you see words like loving, vibrant, cultural, fun, noisy, crazy, loud, whatever." She continued:

> That you see beyond the missing pieces to what's really beneath and under there—spiritual, familiar, close knit. All of those positive things

about neighborhoods that our media hides, that first impressions hide. It's just like meeting a person. You know, the first time you meet somebody you judge just by the appearance on the outside. But after you get to know them you learn so much more about their background and their history and their likes and their dislikes and their challenges and their loves. And it is the same way you need to approach a neighborhood like Linden or any of the other neighborhoods that you might be working in.

I share her sentiments here because they encapsulate the type of engaged scholarship I am committed to—the type that "see[s] beyond the missing pieces to what's really beneath and under there," or what Hicho also refers to as "spiritual, familiar, close knit." This type of scholarship, which pushes me to understand neighborhoods in my quest to understand and work with young people, includes a variety of stakeholders. From community elders, organizers, families, and nonprofit leaders to students, teachers, principals, superintendents, school board members, and teachers' union presidents, everyone plays a vital role.

More specifically, and for the purposes of this chapter, Hicho's words are fundamental to how I teach my critical service learning and community engagement courses for preK–12 public school teachers and education support professionals in the district. In fact, her words are reflective of our ongoing conversations about diversity, reciprocity, community, and engagement as these things relate to the work we are doing *with* students in urban contexts. Our wonderings have led to some "difficult dialogues" (Kinloch, 2013) and provocative questions such as: Do we teach by caring about students, listening to what they tell us, and helping them as they also help us navigate challenging situations in schools and neighborhoods, all while working with them to achieve academically and socially? As teachers, what do we mean when we say affirm student differences in classrooms? How, who, and what are we affirming, and how do we intentionally move beyond affirming and into criticality?

Additionally, how are we deeply engaging students in teaching and learning in ways that invite them to deeply engage us in these same processes? What does that engagement look like outside schools? Do we know about the communities in which our students live? Is our work relevant to students? Is it relevant to their familial communities? Is it reciprocal? Mutually engaging? Mutually beneficial? Humanizing? Real? Truthful? Relevant? Inclusive? Is there space for vulnerabilities? Is it grounded in critical listening? Advocacy? Social justice? Is it guided by care, compassion, and love? If so, then for whom, by whom, and with whom? If not, then why? And, if not, then what are we doing working with young people?

So, what?

For the last four years, I have participated in similar wonderings with more than 85 preK–12 public school teachers, teacher educators, and education support professionals across the district, to include English, Spanish and language immersion, history, science, mathematics, and art teachers as well as guidance counselors, occupational and speech therapists, social workers, parent coordinators, and principals. Our conversations, which began within the context of a university-level critical service learning course that I taught, always begin with a focus on the academic and community engagements of students who attend schools that are depicted as "marginal," "on the fringes," "underperforming," and as "not meeting adequate yearly progress." Just over two years ago, the district was confronted with scandals about school personnel altering students' attendance records and changing their grades in an effort to impart a standardized, one-size-fits-all image of progress to critics. It is not surprising that this accusation, which has been investigated, has not been situated within a larger discussion about the material and financial resources that are not provided to many "underperforming" urban schools in the U.S. Then, a year and a half ago, the district, along with the mayor's office, the teachers' union, social service organizations, elected officials, and clergy collectively supported the bond issue and tax levy that came to be referred to as "Issues 50 & 51." They argued that 50 & 51 would provide sorely needed funds to renovate school buildings, modernize technology, upgrade obsolete computer systems, finance preschool for all children, replicate high-performing schools in the district, and among other things, fund an independent auditor to examine district data and finances.

On November 5, 2013, Issues 50 & 51 failed, with 31% of the voters supporting it and 69% of the voters rejecting it. Regardless of where the voting population in the city stood on this bond issue and tax levy, one cannot deny the larger implications of underfunded public schools in urban districts. According to Rhonda Johnson, former President of the Columbus Education Association, the largest teachers' union in the state of Ohio, and current Director of Education for the City and the Mayor's Office, "the failure of 50/51 says something about the failure to put at front and center urban teachers and students. It's a failure to address big issues staring at us. It's a failure to act because we're saying no to putting resources into eradicating big issues impacting us, especially students." When I inquired into those "big issues," Johnson listed: "Hunger, health, socio-emotional needs, air-conditioned buildings where students aren't forced to learn in classrooms that climb to 100 degrees . . . functioning technology in schools, quality and available preschool for every kid." She concluded, "When we stop one upping each other and focus on what's best for students and teachers, we can see clearly and work together to fill in the pieces that shouldn't be missing in the first place." Johnson's directive about what we need to do in relation to urban schools—"stop one upping each other;" "see clearly;" "fill in the pieces"—echoes Hicho's plea about what we need to do with regard to urban communities—identify "positive things", "see words like loving, vibrant, cultural", and "see beyond the missing pieces." Additionally, their directives speak to the need for engaged practices and opportunities that do not re-inscribe competitive, individualistic, and racist beliefs that privilege some people (e.g., those in positions of financial power; those who benefit from white privilege) over others (e.g., those who have been historically disenfranchised; those who are marginalized by structural oppression).

Relying on Hicho and Johnson's plea that we see urban communities in positive and loving ways, I describe the types of activities (e.g., community engagement and critical service learning partnerships) high school students are participating in—with the support of teachers, principals, and community partners—during school and nonschool time. Their activities serve to critique larger narratives of failure that circulate about their lives and academic engagements, on the one hand, and about this urban school district and its local communities, on the other. As I enter into this discussion, the following claims are important to highlight:

- We must listen to and learn from the perspectives of young people as we work with them inside schools and local communities. Youth lives and literacies cannot be ignored in our continuous, yet flawed and failed, attempts to understand the changing dynamics of urban environments and the growing concerns of urban youth. In fact, we must admit that educational reform efforts will not work when done in isolation of the desires and needs of children, youth, families, educational practitioners, and community groups (see Campano, 2007; Kinloch, 2010).
- There is never an excuse to use deficit-driven approaches, especially when working with young people. Instead, we need to adopt humanizing theoretical and methodological perspectives in our teaching, research, and community collaborations (see Irizarry & Brown, 2014; Paris, 2010; Willis et al., 2008).
- Engaged activities, or scholarship, should be activist oriented and should, as Johnson describes, "put at front and center urban teachers and students" and, I would add, community partners. Thus, a paradigmatic shift is needed, one that is no longer grounded in individualism, competition, and inequality but in collaboration (e.g., ongoing exchange of ideas and collaboration as respectful and reciprocal), empathy (e.g., that results from critical listening and a discourse of care), and humanization (e.g., freedom, conflict, vulnerabilities, and respect) among diverse people (see Freire & Macedo, 1987; Kinloch & San Pedro, 2014; Nemeth et al., 2014).

In the remainder of this chapter, I take up these claims. I highlight relevant literature as a way of explaining my deliberate choice to refer to this work as community engagement and critical service learning. Then, I describe some of the visual and print narratives of students who are participating in a community-engaged and critical service learning project at Truth High School in the U.S. Midwest. I pay attention to what these narratives tell us about teaching, learning, and engagement in urban schools and communities. It is my hope that these narratives can contribute to a wider conversation about the importance of working *with* youth and working *within* schools and communities in ways that are collaborative and that center engagement among people—students, teachers, principals, community partners, and others—who come to see, as Hicho does, "beyond the missing pieces to what's really beneath and under there."

COMMUNITY ENGAGEMENT AND CRITICAL SERVICE LEARNING

To meaningfully reflect on the aforementioned sentiments from Hicho and Johnson, I turn to scholarship in community engagement and critical service learning. I do so for specific reasons. First, the body of literature on community engagement accounts for the dynamic interactions among people in a variety of contexts, including but extending beyond the space of schools. In fact, the New England Resource Center for Higher Education (n.d.) defines community engagement as "collaboration between institutions of higher education and their larger communities (local, regional/state, national, global) for the mutually beneficial exchange of knowledge and resources in a context of partnership and reciprocity." Relatedly, the literature that I am drawn to in critical service learning relies on a social justice approach that connects classroom instruction to community engagement. Not only can critical service learning "strengthen partnerships among schools, universities, and communities," but it can also foster "collaborations among students, teachers, researchers, administrators, parents, and community groups" around shared goals (Kinloch, 2015, p. 1). For the purposes of this chapter, it is necessary that I explain the perspectives I rely on when talking about community engagement and critical service learning.

Community Engagement

In their definition of community engagement, the Carnegie Foundation goes a step further with their insistence that:

> The purpose of community engagement is the partnership of college and university knowledge and resources with those of the public and private sectors to enrich scholarship, research, and creative activity; enhance curriculum, teaching and learning; prepare educated, engaged citizens; strengthen democratic values and civic responsibility; address critical societal issues; and contribute to the public good. (New England Resource Center, n.d., para. 11)

There are many scholars who share this understanding of community engagement. Israel, Schulz, Parker, and Becker (1998) define community-engaged scholarship as community-based participatory research (CBPR). They see it as a partnership in which community members and researchers "contribute their expertise to enhance understanding of a given phenomenon and to integrate the knowledge gained with action to benefit the community involved" (p. 173). Koné et al. (2000) refer to this work as community partnerships and insist that such partnerships require a movement away from traditional research methods to approaches that value diverse perspectives in the facilitation of community members' participation in research. They discuss the results of "community-researcher collaborations" in Seattle, Washington, that sought to develop "appropriate public health research strategies that address [urban] community concerns" (p. 243).

In relation to community-engaged research and health care, Michener et al. (2012) believe that researchers must first learn about the community's history, culture, and demographic trends and economic, social, and political structures. As they learn about these things, they should demonstrate genuine respect for members of the community by involving them in all phases of the research. In so doing, Michener et al. encourage researchers to acknowledge the reality and impact of power differentials as they work at "developing meaningful and genuine partnerships" and having "open and respectful discussion[s]" with community partners (2012, p. 5).

The focus on collaboration, respect, and recognition of power differentials is crucial to the work of community engagement. Equally important is the need for "respectful dialogue and a clear commitment to maintain relationships for a matter of years rather than weeks" (Mulligan & Nadarajah, 2008, p. 81). In writing about globalization, community-engaged research methodology, and sustainable community relationships, Mulligan and Nadarajah (2008) contend that this work should include "spaces for engagement" and incorporate "a range of research methods (including surveys, story collection, strategic conversations, photo-narrative techniques, and research journals)." This approach can "generate rich data to be used . . . by both community-based and university-based researchers. The research methods are linked to forms of analysis that relate local experiences to broader social processes" (p. 81).

So, what might these understandings of community engagement mean for work that involves young people in urban contexts? To consider that question, I turn to Chelsey, an 18-year-old, White female student-participant-collaborator from one of the community engagement and critical service learning projects at Truth High School. During a summer planning and reflection session, she talked about the benefits of being a long-term participant (four years in high school and two years post-high school) in an urban garden initiative located adjacent to the school. Chelsey described community-engaged work as "bringing people together who might not have ever been together before. Now we're family. Through this garden project, we're [youth] working with lots of people." She continued, "We're changing how people see us and, well, how we see them, and we're dealing with a community issue by helping residents have fruits and vegetables. We're engaged in what's going on and doing something to help."

Much like Chelsey, I understand community engagement as directed, intentional, and purposeful collaborations involving various people—students, teachers, researchers, families, neighbors, community representatives, members of school districts and local businesses, and others—who engage in problem-posing and problem-solving to address identified community concerns. I believe engagement signifies reciprocal, collaborative partnerships *with* and *in* communities around social, civic, educational, and political issues. Such partnerships are long term—in relationships that are formed, the commitment to the work that has been identified, and the action that arises.

Critical Service Learning

In our edited collection on service learning and literacy education, Smagorinsky and I (2014) write, "The learning that results from direct engagement with community members and in dialogue with . . . the academic curriculum often contributes to profound changes in students' (and our own) views of demographics that they (and we) may not have had previously learned to respect" (p. xxii). We believe it is necessary to focus on "the relational nature of such efforts and the degree to which they have needed to be flexible, compromising, understanding, respectful, and engaged" with community partners. An emphasis on "the relational nature" of this work leads me to Mitchell's (2015) claim that critical service learning is "an approach to civic learning that is attentive to social change, works to redistribute power, and strives to develop authentic relationships" (pp. 20–21). Elsewhere, Mitchell (2008) writes, "critical service-learning programs encourage students to see themselves as agents of social change, and use the experience of service to address and respond to injustice in communities" (p. 51). There are other scholars who believe in the relational nature of critical service learning and its potential to address social, political, economic, and educational forms of injustice.

Ginwright and Cammarota's (2002) social justice and social awareness approach to critical service learning emphasizes "community problem solving through critical thinking that raises questions about the roots of social inequality" (p. 90). They advocate for projects that are steeped in social awareness, that motivate people "to examine and influence political and economic decisions" (p. 90), and that work to eliminate inequalities, such as homelessness, hunger, and poverty. They believe that socially just, critical service learning projects will not only motivate people to investigate pervasive sociopolitical issues but will also encourage them to examine how institutions and systems "could better serve their own communities and initiate strategies to make these institutions responsive to their needs" (p. 90). This approach intentionally seeks to disrupt, critique, and eradicate "inequitable systems that impact learning and participation across multiple contexts" (Kinloch, Nemeth, & Patterson, 2015, p. 41).

Ginwright and Cammarota's (2002) suggestion that critical service learning projects should help participants question how institutions respond to human conditions paves the way for Wade's (2008) belief that such projects should address local needs and be framed within a social justice perspective. Referring to this perspective as "social justice-oriented service-learning" (SJSL), Wade believes it must be: (1) student centered; (2) collaborative; (3) experiential; (4) intellectual; (5) analytical; (6) multicultural; (7) value-based; and (8) activist-oriented (p. 57). Those who use an SJSL approach should have a commitment to examining oppression, inequity, democracy, and citizenship. Relatedly, Battistoni (1997) argues, "when service is understood as an educational tool for our students to learn about democracy and citizenship, parents and organizations in the larger community can be approached as partners in education rather than as clients to be served" (p. 140). Battistoni's attempt to rethink labels—*clients* to *partners*—fosters "an understanding of community . . . not as those with problems but as the group to which we all belong" (p. 140).

Rethinking labels and recognizing the many different ways we belong to communities can move us closer to being responsive and responsible people dedicated to combating inequitable educational, social, and political conditions. A social justice and social awareness approach to critical service learning can lead to "building diverse coalitions, tapping unheard voices, and creating a culture for social justice and social change" (Calderón & Cadena, 2007, p. 75). Or, as Rendell, an 18-year-old, Black male student-participant-collaborator in one of the critical service learning projects at Truth High School, describes, "Service-learning taught me to work with people I probably would never talk to. . . . I see not everything's right in the world. . . . [I]t takes people wanting to improve what's wrong."

For me, critical service learning represents "selfless collaborations . . . of people who are committed to both addressing identified community issues and seeking ways to eradicate forms of social inequalities that impact one's economic, educational, social, and political choices" (Kinloch, 2015, p. 1). While this uptake of critical service learning sounds hopeful, I am aware that service learning, itself, has a negative connotation, hence, my purposeful move away from traditional iterations of service learning to "critical service learning" and "community engagement." I believe this move encapsulates collaborative activities of people who seek to critique and dismantle inequitable systems or, as Rendell suggests, "improve what's wrong."

LISTENING TO AND LEARNING WITH EACH OTHER

The previously referenced literature speaks to the types of engaged activities occurring in many schools and communities throughout the city. For example, in one project titled Latinos y CSIA: Construyendo Puentes de Salud (Latinos and CSIA: Building Health Bridges), second graders in

Brenda Nieves-Ferguson and Michelle Fye's class researched healthy habits, explored ways to take care of their bodies, and examined how nutrition and exercise can improve overall health. After students researched Latin@ health issues in the city, they wrote an ABC health book with illustrations in Spanish to inform other children about healthy habits. They donated their books to two local community organizations that serve as partners on their project and that work with large populations of Latin@ and African American residents.

In another project, Reading Mentors, the student council at a middle school, along with a special education reading group, partnered with a neighboring elementary school in the district to implement a reading-mentoring-buddy program. As mentors, middle schoolers participated in a critical service learning experience in which they listened to, talked with, read to, and mentored elementary-age students. They reinforced to them crucial literacy skills and practices. Working with their guidance counselor, Erica Grimes, across two academic years, participating middle schoolers acquired specific strategies for "teaching" reading, and subsequently, they enhanced their own literacy skills and leadership capacities.

Another example of a critical service learning and community-engaged project is *Beyond the Black Berry Patch*, a project that involved a small group of high school students who partnered with their teacher, Johnny Merry, as well as local activists and community groups to research and collect data on a historic African American neighborhood in the city—one that has been undergoing gentrification and revitalization. Students collected oral histories from current and past residents of the neighborhood and published a journal that contains historical research, reflections, poems, visual art, and photographs about the area. They also learned how to interview residents, how to analyze interviews as texts, how to use Adobe InDesign publishing software, and how to engage in social justice efforts to preserve the community.

These projects (and many others) created "spaces for engagement" (Mulligan & Nadarajah, 2008) for students, teachers, and community partners. Within these spaces, participants asked questions about identity, accessibility, and equity (see Nemeth et al., 2014); about naming "positive things" that exist in urban communities (see Hicho); and about "what's best for students and teachers" (see Johnson). To capture their questions and document the projects that resulted from them, I first invited teachers from the district to take a newly designed university course with me on critical service learning and community engagement. The course was designed as a semester-long cohort experience and consisted of three different groups of approximately 30 teachers each. Weekly, we had classes at different community sites (e.g., settlement houses, community pride centers, YMCAs, the United Way, schools, a historical society), and we talked with representatives from each site about their engaged activities. In addition to classes, we also participated in community visits and interview sessions. I sat in on teachers' inquiry groups, visited their classes, collected their written reflections and other project artifacts, noted their shifting dispositions related to community engagement and critical service learning, and met with them in small monthly research groups after the university course concluded.

Second, I witnessed how teachers purposefully included students and community members—as partners and collaborators—in decisions about the design, purpose, implementation, and sustainability plans for their emerging community-engaged and critical service learning projects. For their respective projects, which served as a final capstone assignment for the course, teachers asked students to generate ideas that could materialize within their classroom, school, or out-of-school community, and they took a backseat to how students wanted to approach the work with community partners. Many of the teachers noted that students wanted to learn more about the community; thus, they invited community groups and organizations into their classes to talk about their needs, desires, and hopes. Collectively, teachers, students, and community partners agreed that it was important to see, as Hicho reminds us, "beyond the missing pieces" for community-engaged and critical service learning initiatives to really thrive in collaborative ways.

I also noticed how some teachers struggled with the idea that community-engaged and critical service learning initiatives must be inclusive of the perspectives of all participants. In fact, I often struggled to model this inclusive approach in my own teaching. As a teacher researcher, I turned to mentor texts for inspiration. I reread Campano's (2007) *Immigrant Students and Literacy: Reading, Writing, and Remembering*, and I held on to his belief that teacher researchers must "make more porous commonplace distinctions between academic theory and the everyday theorizing of urban life, between the intellectual work of teaching and the labor of research" if we are to "come to a deeper appreciation of our own cultural work and its potential contributions to the field of education" (p. 9). Then, I sat with Cochran-Smith and Lytle's (1999), "Teacher Research Movement" and Cochran-Smith and Lytle's (1993), *Inside/Outside: Teacher Research* as I contemplated how to make this work more visible, more inclusive, and more central to how we teach, research, and interact with others in school and community spaces. I listened to Richardson (2000) in "Writing: A Method of Inquiry," who reminded me that "the more different voices are honored within our qualitative community, the stronger—and more interesting—that community will be" (p. 959). In addition to these readings, I also returned to Bartolomae's (1994), "Beyond the Methods Fetish: Toward Humanizing Pedagogy," in which she encourages us to establish "pedagogical spaces that enable students to move *from object to subject position*" (p.177).

From these texts, I realized that our struggles—to be inclusive, collaborative, and not always in charge—were not uncommon and did not have to serve as roadblocks to the work we all sought to pursue. Naming our struggles allowed us gradually to let go of them as we came to understand

98 *Valerie Kinloch*

that the power of collaboration lies, in part, with the ability to work with others to determine the purpose, nature, and potential significance of community-engaged and critical service learning projects. In fact, the more we named our struggles and fears, the more we learned to embrace the opportunity to listen to, learn with, and work alongside students and community partners.

NOT IGNORING YOUTH LIVES AND LITERACIES

Example #1

To illustrate this work, I share examples of students participating in a community-engaged and critical service learning project at Truth High School, a Title 1 urban public school in the district that, at the time of this study, had 47 certified teachers and nearly 800 students in 9th through 12th grades. Students have sponsored school- and community-wide disability awareness campaigns, donated fresh vegetables to food pantries, volunteered at nonprofit organizations, and participated in philanthropic activities. Additionally, they have presented on their academic engagements and community involvements inside university classes, at local meetings for district principals, and at national conferences. Their commitment to their project and to improving school-community relations is obvious when one

Figure 4.1 The Good Seed Community Garden

visits their initiative, "The Good Seed Community Garden," a wheelchair-accessible fruit and vegetable garden adjacent to the school. This initiative was created as a partnership among students at the school; Ms. Washington, a Black woman who is a 17-year veteran English teacher in the district; and members of a local church. The garden signifies a social justice approach to the forms of learning and doing that can result when groups of people collaborate to address a shared concern.

One of the class sessions on community engagement and critical service learning that I facilitated with teachers and education support professionals was held at Truth High. As 4:30 p.m. quickly approached, which was the time when class began, 30 preK–12 teachers gathered into the school's library. They were greeted by students who handed them pamphlets covered with pictures of various students working in the garden. For this particular session, we discussed how to be purposeful and intentional with inviting, including, and centering students in our projects. To frame the conversation, we previously had read articles by Abravanel (2003), "Building Community Through Service-Learning: The Role of the Community Partner," Adejumo (2010), "Promoting Artistic and Cultural Development Through Service-Learning and Critical Pedagogy in a Low-Income Community Art Program," and Maybach (1996), "Investigating Urban Community Needs: Service-Learning From a Social Justice Perspective." Also, we had engaged in a variety of activities, such as completing topic-specific group presentations on possible project ideas, talking with representatives from community organizations, and writing performance pieces on "Who I Am and Where I'm From." What better way to have a discussion on partnering with students in community-engaged and critical service learning projects than by listening to actual students who were already doing this work?

After students introduced themselves, I explained the purpose of our session—for everyone gathered in the library to talk with students about who they are, their school-community engagements, and their reasons for being involved in the project. Ms. Washington then explained, "We've got a large variety of students working on putting things together for [the project] and I think that's kind of neat when lots of students feel included in something." Jonathon, a 17-year-old Black male student-participant-collaborator, agreed with Ms. Washington before making connections between what he was studying in his science class and what he was learning from participating in the project:

> Something that stood out to me was the environmental science course offered here and I thought back to Ms. Washington's [English] class and how much fun it was to actually help not only the community, but also the environment. So, I figured I might as well work at this [science class], too.

His comments reiterate a central goal of critical service learning initiatives—that they are intentionally structured in such a way that students are able to make direct connections between what they are studying, debating, questioning, and writing about inside their classes with what they are thinking about and doing inside the community. For Jonathan and his peers in the room, this connection produced new and expansive ways for them to see themselves as community members, community problem solvers, and to borrow a phrase from Rendell, dedicated "community learners."

Another student, Hailee, a 17-year-old Black female student-participant-collaborator, explained how she and her peers designed a poster about the project. The poster, which sat atop a table in the library, was filled with pictures of people working in the garden in collaborative and supportive ways. Hailee shared, "We named it 'All It Takes Is One Hand' because we've decided that, like, it actually does take one hand to help someone in need or to actually just give help . . . if someone's in need or not. Just be generous." Hailee's explanation of the poster and her use of the phrase, "All It Takes Is One Hand," ignited questions from teachers, such as these:

- *What does this project mean to you?*
- *How did you get involved?*
- *Do you engage students who don't participate?*
- *Where'd you learn that much about being generous?*
- *You work with community partners?*
- *Who gets to have a say in the project?*

These questions were followed by student responses, including these:

- *This project means a lot because I get to be part of a group.*
- *I got involved because Ms. Washington asked us on the first day of school to write a journal about if we'd want to be involved, why, and what we'd do.*
- *I get to make decisions with others.*
- *I work with people I never even talked to.*

After these responses were shared, Mr. Alston, a Black male who serves as the school's principal, stood up, surveyed the room, and commented, "You have to allow people to think outside the box because the larger picture, the greater picture here is: How will students be affected? Will they want to be engaged? Will we improve relationships?" He continued by talking about the importance of building relationships with students:

> And those things, when you want to teach students, those things are more important than trying to, to stick to the curriculum. And we can probably go further in the curriculum if we establish the relationships and we make sure students are engaged in what they're doing, and then we can find the connections to the curriculum . . . and students can get a much deeper understanding.

Figure 4.2 All It Takes Is One Hand

Mr. Alston's comment, "allow people to think outside the box," and Hailee's phrase, "All It Takes Is One Hand," are central components of community-engaged and critical service learning initiatives. Their sentiments speak to the important role of forging partnerships or, as Mr. Alston names it, "relationships," among students, teachers, and community members at Truth High School and in the surrounding community. They also point to what can result from critical service learning and community-engaged initiatives: "connections to the curriculum" and engaged students who "can get a much deeper understanding" of "what they are doing."

Example #2

These sentiments also point to how students have begun to see themselves as engaged members of their high school and local community. In her essay titled "Self-Discovery," Chelsey, an 18-year-old White female student-participant-collaborator, described how she used to be "the girl who sat in the very back of the classroom . . . [who] hardly ever talked or interacted with peers and teachers." She recalls the time Ms. Washington invited students "to write a journal entry about being a part of a Design Team for a community garden project." The Design Team is a group of cross-grade-level students who colead the project with their teacher and community partners. They help determine the readings, activities, and directions as well as present on the project at school, in the community, and throughout the district. For Chelsey, this opened up an opportunity for her to reflect on her family—"I thought, wow, I love to garden with my mom and grandpa"—and to get to know others while contributing something to the community—"I wanted to be part of the project because . . . I did not know a lot of students at the school, but I was eager to get to know people and see how I could give back to the community." She was invited to participate in the project, and in doing so, she worked with students to plan activities, raise awareness of disabilities (more than 20 percent of the students at the school used mobility devices), and form partnerships with community groups.

Chelsey was not shy about describing her desire to work in and with the community. She writes that another student who was invited into the project volunteered much of his nonschool time at "a nonprofit organization that serves as an assisted living center for physically disabled adults." After joining the project, this student "suggested we take a field trip over to visit the assisted living center." According to Chelsey,

> [w]hen we visited, we were able to take a hands-on approach to learn about the everyday lives of residents in wheelchairs. It was this visit that influenced the Design Team to think about having cement pavers in the garden so students in wheelchairs at the school could access the flowerbeds. The visit really opened our eyes and helped us . . . think about how the challenges some high school students face (worrying about being part of social groups, being popular, wanting the latest fashion, demanding independence) aren't that important in the larger scheme of things. What's important . . . our relationships with people in the community and making sure they have safe spaces and equal chances.

In the same essay, Chelsey writes about working alongside her teacher, peers, and community partners from the local church to plan the garden, clear the land, design flowerbeds, plant fruits and vegetables, and a few years later, design and install the cement paver. Her involvement with the project helped her to become "a different person." She "see[s] the value of improving the school and community, not just the physical space, but the culture . . . when we're working with people in the community, we do meaningful work. We learn these issues, like hunger and poverty, are *our* issues." She continues: "They won't be solved if we don't come together, regardless of who we are.

Publicly Engaged Scholarship in Urban Communities 103

How we look and where we live don't matter . . . [W]e don't ever see those as negatives. That's what we've learned."

Her point clearly echoes Ginwright and Cammarota's (2002) insistence that critical service learning projects should emphasize social justice and social awareness, should be dedicated to "community problem solving," and should encourage participants to examine "social inequality" (p. 90). Additionally, her sentiment speaks to perspectives forwarded by scholarship in community engagement. Chelsey understands that sociopolitical issues "like hunger and poverty, are *our* issues" and that they do not belong or get assigned to any one person. Thus, her involvement in the project reflects her growing awareness of the value of "mutually beneficial" and "reciprocal" partnerships that "address critical societal issues" (New England Resource Center for Higher Education, n.d.).

In the closing paragraph of her essay, Chelsey recalls her time in the project, beginning "in 2009 when I was a freshman" through "my completion of high school in 2013 and beyond." What is important to note here is that she engages in a reflexive process as she remembers "working with people on what I thought was just a garden, and now I see this as a space in the community that brings people together . . . [W]e can talk about our differences as we figure out how to make sure that people in this neighborhood have fruit and vegetables and just a place to come."

Figure 4.3 Working in the Garden

104 *Valerie Kinloch*

Figure 4.4 Community Garden

She ends with this: "We do care about our community and the people in it, as shown through our being involved in this. This is no longer just an assignment or project. It's a major part of who I've become. My life has been affected tremendously by my participation with others in this."

Chelsey's essay, her involvement in the community-engaged and service learning initiative, her willingness to partner with others, and her desire to understand the importance "of improving the school and community," point to how this project influenced her and how she influenced this project. In other words, the reciprocal nature of community-engaged activities is that such activities are only possible because people willingly work together in the face of differences and possible conflicts and in light of the vulnerabilities they may feel and the resistances they may encounter.

COMMUNITY ENGAGEMENT AND CRITICAL SERVICE LEARNING: REFRAMING THE NARRATIVE

What about the examples of critical service learning and community-engaged initiatives with young people at Truth High School and in the local community? What if we could do what donna Hicho asks us to do—see urban communities positively? To see them as "spiritual" and "familiar?" As places that are occupied by "close knit" relations? As "site[s] of resistance," to borrow a phrase from bell hooks (1981), that nurture and nourish as well as protect and love people from an unforgiving, racist world? What if we could see urban schools not as marginal, on the fringes, or underperforming, but as Rhonda Johnson sees them, as places that "focus on what's best for students and teachers?" As places that reject and work against deficit-oriented perspectives that want us to believe our students are not brilliant, competent intellectuals?

What if we all begin to see urban youth as critical thinkers, teachers, learners, activists, collaborators, ethnographers, and community-engaged partners? What if we see them as critically conscious human beings capable of contributing to the decision-making processes that impact their educational trajectories and their literacy lives? What if we actually ask urban youth how they see themselves and how they would like to be seen by us?

What if we see urban schools, communities, and the lives and literacies of urban youth in positive and loving ways? Would it impact how we teach? How we listen to and interact with young people? Would it change how we talk about and approach the work of teaching, learning, and even educational reform? To see differently, I believe, requires us to be ready and willing to rewrite the negative narratives that have been associated unfairly with many urban schools, communities, and youth in the U.S. When we rewrite these narratives, we open up possibilities for necessary, critical, and humanizing collaborative relationships with students, teachers, administrators, families, community groups, district leaders, and others (see also Kinloch, Nemeth, & Patterson, 2015; Roberts, Bell, & Murphy, 2008). We also open up multiple opportunities for young people to decide how they might create and participate in engaged activities and how they might critique the visible and invisible markers of inequity and inequality that daily circulate within the spaces of schools and local communities. For example, while Chelsey's participation in the garden project was important for how she learned to collaborate with other people, it was equally beneficial for how she came to understand that everyone has a responsibility to address social injustice. To restate her point, these issues "won't be solved if we don't come together, regardless of who we are."

Similarly, Jonathan's decision to enroll in an environmental class at Truth High School was influenced highly by his participation in Ms. Washington's English class and in the critical service learning and community-engaged initiative. As he shared, "I thought back to Ms. Washington's class and . . . not only the community, but also the environment. So, I figured I might as well work at this [science class], too." His sentiments point to an argument by Kinloch and Smagorinsky (2014) that a major role of these initiatives is to help students make connections between classroom instruction and community engagement and to support them as they learn to interact with other people. And that is exactly what Hailee was doing when she talked with teachers about the poster of the garden project and its name, "All It Takes Is One Hand." For Hailee, when we witness an injustice, when we see harm or danger being inflicted onto someone, or when we know that someone is in need of help, we have a responsibility to act and to respond, to "actually give help" and to "be generous."

So, what if? What if students had an opportunity to contribute to writing and/or responding to the bond issue and tax levy I referred to earlier—Issues

50 & 51? What if they were asked to conduct a study in the district on the adverse effects that obsolete technology plays on students' levels of academic achievement? What if they were invited to design a community-engaged and service learning project on safe and equitable learning spaces for students? What if they were asked to work with students, teachers, and community organizations in other districts to design school curricula that led to the creation of wheelchair accessible fruit and vegetable community gardens? What if they were encouraged to share their findings with school board members, superintendents, and community groups? What if these types of publicly engaged scholarship were a part of each and every student's schooling experiences? What if these engaged activities highlighted what we already know—that urban schools and communities are resourceful educative sites, that they provide opportunities for students to grapple with various social justice issues, and that they motivate students to partner with groups of people to solve problems, to attend to issues of representation and belonging, and to examine the politics of learning through reflexive lens? What if?

REFERENCES

Abravanel, S. A. (2003). *Building community through service-learning: The role of the community partner* [issue paper]. Denver, CO: Education Commission of the States.

Adejumo, C. O. (2010). Promoting artistic and cultural development through service-learning and critical pedagogy in a low-income community art program. *Visual Arts Research, 36*(1), 23–34.

Bartolomae, L. (1994). Beyond the methods fetish: Toward a humanizing pedagogy. *Harvard Educational Review, 62*(2), 173–194.

Battistoni, R. M. (1997). Service-learning in a democratic society: Essential practices for K-12 programs. In R. C. Wade (Ed.), *Community service-learning: A guide to including service in the public school curriculum* (pp. 131–141). Albany: State University of New York Press.

Calderón, J., & Cadena, G. R. (2007). Linking critical democratic pedagogy, multiculturalism, and service learning to a project-based approach. In J. Calderón (Ed.), *Race, poverty, and social justice: Multidisciplinary perspectives through service learning* (pp. 63–80). Sterling, VA: Stylus.

Campano, G. (2007). *Immigrant students and literacy: Reading, writing, and remembering.* New York, NY: Teachers College Press.

Cochran-Smith, M., & Lytle, S. L. (1993). *Inside/Outside: Teacher research and knowledge.* New York, NY: Teachers College Press.

Cochran-Smith, M., & Lytle, S. L. (1999). The teacher research movement: A decade later. *Educational Researcher, 28*(7), 15–25.

Freire, P., and Macedo, D. (1987). *Literacy: Reading the word and the world.* New York, NY: Bergin and Garvey.

Ginwright, S., & Cammarota, J. (2002). New terrain in youth development: The promise of a social justice approach. *Social Justice, 29,* 82–95.

hooks, b. (1981). Homeplace (a site of resistance). In *Yearning: Race, gender, and cultural politics* (pp. 41–49). Boston: South End Press.

Irizarry, J. G., & Brown, T. M. (2014). Humanizing research in dehumanizing spaces: The challenges and opportunities of conducting participatory action research with youth in schools. In D. Paris & M. T. Winn (Eds.), *Humanizing research: Decolonizing qualitative inquiry with youth and communities* (pp. 63–82). Los Angeles: Sage.

Israel, B. A., Schulz, A. J., Parker, E. A., & Becker, A. B. (1998). Review of community-based research: Assessing partnership approaches to improve public health. *Annual Review of Public Health, 19*, 173–202.

Kinloch, V. (2010). *Harlem on our minds: Place, race, and the literacies of urban youth.* New York, NY: Teachers College Press.

Kinloch, V. (2013). Difficult dialogues in literacy (urban) teacher education. In C. Kosnik, J. Rowsell, P. Williamson, R. Simon, & C. Beck (Eds.), *Literacy teacher educators: Preparing teachers for a changing world* (pp. 107–120). Rotterdam: Sense Publishers.

Kinloch, V. (2015). This issue: Critical service-learning initiatives. *Theory into Practice 54*(1), 1–4.

Kinloch, V., Nemeth, E., & Patterson, A. (2015). Reframing service-learning as learning and participation with urban youth. *Theory Into Practice 54*(1), 39–48.

Kinloch, V., & San Pedro, T. (2014). The space between listening and storying: Foundations for Projects in Humanization. In D. Paris & M. T. Winn (Eds.), *Humanizing research: Decolonizing qualitative inquiry with youth and communities* (pp. 21–42). Los Angeles, CA: Sage.

Kinloch, V., & Smagorinsky, P. (Eds.). (2014). *Service-learning in literacy education. Possibilities of teaching and learning.* Charlotte, NC: Information Age Publishing.

Koné, A., Sullivan, M., Senturia, K. D., Chrisman, N. J., Ciske, S. J., & Krieger, J. W. (2000). Improving collaboration between researchers and communities. *Public Health Reports, 115*(2–3): 243–248.

Maybach, C. W. (1996). Investigating urban community needs: Service learning from a social justice perspective. *Education and Urban Society, 28*(2), 224–236.

Michener, L., Cook, J., Ahmed, S. M., Yonas, M. A., Coyne-Bealey, R., & Aguilar-Gaxiola, S. (2012). Aligning the goals of community-engaged research: Why and how academic health centers can successfully engage with communities to improve health. *Academic Medicine, 87*(3), 285–291.

Mitchell, T. D. (2008). Traditional vs. critical service-learning: engaging the literature to differentiate 2 models. *Michigan Journal of Community Service Learning, 14*, 50–65.

Mitchell, T. D. (2015). Using a critical service-learning approach to facilitate civic identity development. *Theory Into Practice, 54*(1), 20–28.

Mulligan, M., & Nadarajah, Y. (2008). Working on the sustainability of local communities with a "community-engaged" research methodology. *Local Environment, 13*(2), 81–94.

Nemeth, E., Butler, T., Kinloch, V., Washington, T., & Reed, P. (2014). Transformative service-learning in urban schools and communities: Learning from challenges. In V. Kinloch & P. Smagorinsky (Eds.), *Service-learning in literacy education: Possibilities of teaching and learning* (pp. 3–26). Charlotte, NC: Information Age Publishing.

New England Resource Center for Higher Education. (n.d.). Carnegie Foundation community Engagement Classification. Boston: University of Massachusetts. Retrieved from www.nerche.org/index.php?option=com_content&view=article&id=341&Itemid=92#CE%20def

Paris, D. (2010). "A friend who understand fully": Notes on humanizing research in a multiethnic youth community. *International Journal of Qualitative Studies in Education, 24*(2), 1–13.

Richardson, L., & St. Pierre, E. A. (2000). Writing: A method of inquiry. In N. K. Denzin & Y. S. Lincoln (Eds.), *The Sage handbook of qualitative research* (3rd ed., pp. 959–978). Thousand Oaks, CA: Sage.

Roberts, R. A., Bell, L. A., & Murphy, B. (2008). Flipping the script: Analyzing youth talk about race and racism. *Anthropology & Education Quarterly, 39*(3), 334–354.

Smagorinsky, P., & Kinloch, V. (2014). Introduction. In V. Kinloch & P. Smagorinsky (Eds.), *Service-learning in literacy education: Possibilities of teaching and learning* (pp. ix–xxiii). Charlotte, NC: Information Age Publishing.

Wade, R. C. (2008). Service-learning for social justice in the elementary classroom: Can we get there from here? In D. W. Butin (Ed.), *Service learning and social justice education: Strengthening justice-oriented community based models of teaching and learning* (pp. 56–65). New York, NY: Routledge.

Willis, A. I., Montavon, M., Hall, H., Hunter, C., Burke, L., & Herrera, A. (2008). *On critically conscious research: Approaches to language and literacy research.* New York, NY: Teachers College Press.

Part II
Creating Safe, Creative Spaces for Youth Through Community Partnerships

5 "We Want This to Be Owned by You"
The Promise and Perils of Youth Participatory Action Research

Lawrence Torry Winn and Maisha T. Winn

As we ponder over the "loving critique" (Paris & Alim, 2014) of our experiences with YPAR, we do so with a "humanizing research" framework or a methodology that seeks to reposition the researcher-participant relationship as an act of reciprocity and mutual engagement (Paris & Winn, 2013). In a letter to communities, Tuck (2009) urges scholars to resist conducting "damage-centered" research in indigenous communities and other groups that have experienced marginalization and oppression, while Cruz and Sonn (2011) encourage researchers to "decolonize" their cultural perspectives that influence their investigations and interactions with historically oppressed communities of color. Similarly, Paris and Winn (2013) call for a "humanizing research" in which scholars become "worthy witnesses" in their sites by earning the respect and trust of participants and continuing to be reflective and critical of one's methods and stances.

YPAR is one methodological lens that takes into account the importance of research and the need to work with community members to humanize and honor their stories, knowledge, skills, and contributions. Youth participate and engage in systematic research and advocate for social change through action (Cammarota & Fine, 2007; Morrell, 2006). Grounded in an epistemology of solidarity (youth working with their elders, university-trained researchers collaborating with local youth experts, and economically privileged researching with members of the poor and working class), YPAR has a history of seeking justice for others and "represent[ing] and humaniz[ing] communities under siege . . . connect[ing] 'us' and 'them' and cultivating research as a tool for social justice" (Fine, 2012, p. 434). YPAR provides opportunities for youth, as well as their "adult allies" (Green, 2013), to reflect on their lived experiences, identify barriers and opportunities, learn about resources to assist with their most pressing issues, and find solutions to overcome obstacles.

While there are numerous examples of studies illustrating the value of YPAR (Fine, 2012; Morrell, 2006; Ozer & Wright, 2012; Stoudt, Fox, & Fine, 2012) and many important action-oriented works emerging from YPAR, there are also the challenges that come along with the work. After participating in two YPAR projects, we, like many social justice and value-centered scholars, grapple with the complexities and tensions of conducting YPAR with youth who are exposed routinely to a standardized curriculum with few opportunities to think, write, engage, challenge, and discuss critically socially and culturally relevant issues that impact their daily lives.

In this chapter, we conceptualize what it means to be equity-oriented scholars (Gutiérrez & Vossoughi, 2009) working with and for youth in a variety of settings. In the first YPAR project we discuss, African American youth in a public high school in the urban Southeast were invited to create a curriculum for a working group charged with engaging school policies on discipline and punishment and situating school policies in a statewide and national dialogue. This working group included two student representatives from each grade level (9th–12th), a member from the school security team, four classroom teachers (math, science, social studies, and English), the principal, and Maisha, who served as an instructional coach during the school's transition from a comprehensive high school to a small learning community. This collective of 9th through 12th grade students, the Change Agents, selected a team of adult allies to support their work. Their ultimate goal was to transform their school community from punitive to restorative. However, there were tensions in the process when it seemingly took too long to envision their work together without an adult leading, facilitating, or dictating the project.

In the second YPAR project, a community of African American boys, between the ages of 14 and 18, from working-class backgrounds, and coming of age in an affluent, White, progressive Midwestern college town, read, interpreted, and interrogated reports and data that impacted their lives and the lives of their families. This working group, the Alliance, met weekly in the evenings at their housing complex community space to discuss, debate, and learn more about topics that they considered important in their lives. For more than a year, Lawrence volunteered and led workshops with two other adult allies, Monica and Lance. After sharing local and national policy reports about racial disparities and inequities across the domains of education, workforce, criminal justice, and access to health care within the group, several of the teens became interested in learning more about the causes of inequities and finding solutions to implement in their communities. The youth decided that the upcoming topics and workshops would focus on racial disparities and inequities. Similar to the Change Agents, the Alliance identified elements of the school-to-prison pipeline as the main barriers to the aspirations of Black youth to succeed both in and out of school (Meiners & Winn, 2010; Winn, 2011).

In this chapter, we raise questions about how educators can use policy reports and data sets that count urban youth while potentially discounting their stories and lived experiences. We share our experiences with YPAR projects and a purposeful reflection of this work, hoping to build capacity for adult allies of youth.

BECOMING AN ADULT ALLY: WHEN AND WHERE DO WE ENTER AS RESEARCHERS

Youth residing in systematically oppressed communities often resist outsiders entering into their spaces without proving their authenticity and genuine commitment to getting to know, understand, and believe in them (Fisher, 2007; Winn & Ubiles, 2011). Far too often, youth workers, initiatives, and funding come and go, leaving the youth and their community feeling abandoned and distrustful toward any future programs. Although participatory action research seeks social justice and encourages collaboration with stakeholders, it's still research, which has the potential to dehumanize, colonize, misrepresent, and harm. Introducing research to communities of color is a process that takes time, commitment, and trust.

We learned from our work with youth over the past decade that gaining their trust has proved to be essential to becoming adult allies. Once trust is earned from the researchers, youth are more willing to invite them into their space and their community. For example, in January of 2013, several mothers invited Lawrence to participate and lead a workshop about academic success and career options for their sons and other youth who belonged to the Alliance. During his first few visits, he observed and listened to the group. Through blank stares and side comments, some of the members initially pushed back against Lawrence being there and insisted to Monica, the lead adult ally, that he "get to know [them]," and "know what this is about" before he officially joined the group. At one session, Lawrence brought his three-year-old son to the group. Several of the participants were drawn to his son and started asking questions:

> CHAPPELLE: What is his name?
> LAWRENCE: Ask him. He will tell you.
> CHAPPELLE: Yo, man, what's your name?
> LAWRENCE: He is being shy. He has to get to know you first. His name is Kamal.
> PRYOR [LAUGHS]: Is that an African name? Why did you name him that?
> LAWRENCE: Because your name tells a lot about who you are.
> PRYOR [TO KAMAL]: Man, you are my dude.

It was only after three months of observing that the youth started transitioning from whispering and laughing to offering handshakes and "hellos" to Lawrence. For several weeks they inquired about Kamal and wanted to know when he would return. There was an unexpected space that opened between Lawrence and the youth when he brought his son. It gave the youth and Lawrence a new way of seeing each other.

Several months later, Lawrence witnessed the difficulties that an adult who was interested in working with the group experienced when he visited session. The adult proposed that he lead several workshops on police and community relationships. Upon hearing the words "police," the youth became disengaged. The adult visitor left distraught because the session did not go as he had planned. After the session ended, the adult allies discussed the group's actions:

MONICA: You know what this about? It's not that the boys don't like him, but they have been let down before in the past. When we first started group, an older brotha helped lead the group, but he disappeared after several sessions. They are only acting up to see how he reacts. They also don't want to hear about the police.

LAWRENCE: I understand. They (the boys) did the same thing to me. Every now and then they still test me. This is their space that they created, and I respect that.

MONICA: Yes, they come faithfully and want to make sure that they don't get disappointed by someone else. Too many people have said they will help but come and go. All they have are each other.

LANCE: It took me close to a year to build trust with the guys. Before, they did not care for me and had no reason to trust me. I had to prove to them that I cared about them. It has finally paid off. Every now and then they push back. But I keep coming.

Lawrence and the youth building a mutual trusting relationship is the third principle of what Winn and Ubiles (2011) calls "worthy witnessing." The four principles include the following:

(1) Admission: How do researchers enter, and who grants them admission?
(2) Declaration: How do researchers introduce themselves (including political stances and worldviews that inform the work)?
(3) Revelation: How can researchers and participants achieve "equilibrium" in their trust for each other?
(4) Confidentiality: How can researchers make responsible decisions about what remains at the table versus what is written up and disseminated in scholarly writing?

In addition to "achieving equilibrium in their trust," understanding the participants' community is critical to establishing a relationship to conduct participatory action research.

Wallerstein and Duran (2008) define community as a socially constructed dimension of identity, created and re-created through social interactions (p. 47). Cruz and Sonn (2011) contend that researchers "decolonize" the way researchers perceive and interact with communities of color—especially the marginalized and oppressed. This requires that scholars refrain from applying researcher jargon, theoretical assumptions, and cultural biases to communities.

Instead, researchers should spend time learning about the strengths, attributes, history, experiences, challenges, and culture of the community because each community is unique. For example, Lawrence spent three years working with incarcerated youth in Newark, New Jersey, and three years teaching and mentoring college-bound high school students in Sacramento, California. Many of the youth from all three cities listened to similar music, watched and played basketball, and lived in under-resourced neighborhoods. Yet each group has experiences and histories that were uniquely situated.

Over a course of a year and a half of observing, sharing, and learning, Lawrence became familiar with the stories and aspirations of the members of the Alliance. He learned that many of their families recently relocated from big cities like Chicago, Detroit, and Milwaukee to this predominately White, affluent, and progressive college town because their parents believed (as advertised and celebrated in many magazines) that the new community had better schools, employment opportunities, and safe neighborhoods (Winn & Winn, 2015). Their recent migrant experience created a community context that was much different from the youth he worked with in Newark and Sacramento. It took Lawrence more time to learn the Alliance community and become a "worthy witness" than in other cities.

Maisha attempted to become a "worthy witness" with both students and staff at Du Bois High School. Initially her work focused on supporting the principal and leadership team; however, the leadership team could see that any progress they tried to make was being undermined by classroom and school climate. Maisha described this phenomenon as "small schools . . . big punishment" because the school-wide approach to discipline and safety remained the same in spite of the fact the school only had a quarter of its initial population. Du Bois was a small learning community that was once part of a large, comprehensive high school with most of its students being African American. However, in 2011 Maisha and a team of students and teachers engaged in a YPAR project seeking to change discipline policies that were hurting relationships between students and staff. While her role in Du Bois was to facilitate academic engagement and literacy across content areas, Maisha learned that the school community was lacking a basic understanding of how members defined "community" and what values could be agreed upon by students and staff alike. At the beginning of the group's first meeting, Maisha wrote the prompt "What is community?" on the board. Students, teachers, and staff read out their definitions:

> JAY (STUDENT): An area with people who have some type of characteristics: can be language, clothes, hairstyles, and sometimes around the same income.
> INDIA (STUDENT): A community is a group of people coming together as one to accomplish a goal.
> ADAM (STUDENT): Joining together as one where you can depend and rely on each other.

SHANTI (STUDENT): Community is a place where parents, authority, and children unite together as one.

RYAN (STUDENT): I think community is the society that you live in or are mostly around. It is also when you have family, friends, or close people that are helping you or guiding you in the right direction.

Common themes included "coming/joining together," "as one," "family," "friends," and "help." When the session ended, Maisha charged the group with putting theses definitions to work for the day by stating, "Community begins here so let's look out for each other." Later in the day, she saw Adam, a student participating in the Change Agents, and he went out of his way in a crowded hallway to speak. They both laughed and agreed it was a start.

Participatory action research engages community participants to identify problems, analyze the issue, and then advocate for social change. Scholars describe YPAR as youth-led research projects in which students exert power over key aspects of the research and action process (Cammarota & Fine, 2007; Morrell, 2006). Students select the topics, research methods, data analysis, and action steps with adults in a supportive role. YPAR projects "explicitly focuse[s] on the integration of systematic research implemented by young people, with guidance from adult facilitators. Thus, students' recommendations and actions for change are based in data as well as in their own life experiences" (Ozer & Wright, 2012, p. 268). YPAR is dependent on youth being invested and interested in the success of the project. The opportunity afforded to youth to decide on the issue and methodology to analyze and solve distinguishes YPAR from other methods.

We had several enduring questions throughout this work: How do we get the youth engaged and get them to lead the process? What are the roles of the adults and the roles of the youth? What happens if the youth stop participating? These are some of issues that we both experienced conducting our projects. In the next section, we provide "pedagogical portraits" (Winn & Johnson, 2011) that we hope can serve as sites of engagement for youth researchers and their adult allies.

GETTING YOUTH INTERESTED AND INVESTED IN ACTION RESEARCH

In the case of the Alliance, Lawrence introduced the concept of a YPAR project after the group spent time learning about each other, building trust, discussing politics, bonding over common values and aspirations, arguing about sports, and laughing at each other's jokes. In the summer of 2014, Lawrence presented the findings of a local racial disparity report on education to Alliance members to disrupt the tradition of presenting this work solely to those who are not directly impacted. According to the popular report, during the 2010–2011 academic year, only 50 percent of Black high school students in the region graduated on time; 21 percent of Black students were suspended from school compared to 2.3 percent of the region's White students; and Black juveniles (ages 10–17) were arrested at a rate of six times that of White juveniles (Wisconsin Council on Children and Families, 2013). Members of the Alliance and Lawrence discovered they shared the same concerns about the policing and schooling of Black youth. At the conclusion of his presentation, he asked the group if they have heard of the school-to-prison pipeline:

> LAWRENCE: Has anyone heard of the school-to-prison pipeline?
> CHAPPELLE: That's something that is about jails in our schools.
> LAWRENCE: I like that. Is there anything else?
> MALCOLM: It's about the system not caring about Black kids.
> LAWRENCE: Jails in schools, the system.
> PRYOR: I don't know.
> LAWRENCE: Well, it is important that you know about it because all the meetings I go to people are talking about the school-to-prison pipeline. And when they talk about it, they are talking about you. So you better know what folks are saying about you.

Their discussion about the school-to-prison pipeline prompted Lawrence to ask the youth if they were interested in learning more about racial inequities and disparities and if they would consider becoming part of the solution.

Without any pushback or hesitation, all 14 youth agreed to engage the project. In early September 2014, the youth discussed the inequities they were expereincing in their communities and schools. They drafted five possible research questions as seen in Table 5.1. In December of 2014, the group worked together to narrow their questions down to one. Seven participants wanted to research the policing of Black youth, and seven wanted to learn about why there were only a few Black teachers in the public schools. The question about policing created a dilemma because many of the participants had a tenuous relationship with the local police officers, especially after the murders of Trayvon Martin, Oscar Grant, and Michael Brown by police officers. They also demonstrated their disappointment of the police at an October 2013 presentation about police and community relationships. After back-and-forth dialogue between the police and members of the Alliance, eight youth walked out in unison as an act of protest because they believed the police continued to give scripted answers and were being dishonest. They expressed to the adult allies that meeting with the police was a waste of their time and would not lead to change. The police later suggested that the youth walking out was disrespectful and vowed not come back to the group again. Because of this incident, the adult allies pressed the youth

Table 5.1 Alliance Research Questions

Questions	Reasons
#1 Why do the police target Black youth?	The police stay on us! We are targets not only here but in Ferguson, Chicago, everywhere.
#2 Why aren't there any after-school programs in our community?	The club kicked us out.
#3 Why are they closing the only Walgreens in our community?	That is the only place around that our families can get groceries from. My mom gets her medication from there. The local grocery store is way too far.
#4 Why don't the schools teach us African American history?	We only get two days in February to talk about the same three people Dr. King, Rosa Parks, and Douglass. White people get the whole year. Why don't we have any Black teachers? We only have wWite teachers here.
#5 Why are there so many Black kids in the criminal system?	We get into trouble, but there is a double standard when White kids get into trouble.

to ensure that examining the policing of Black youth was something that they wanted to pursue:

> LAWRENCE: I thought you guys said that you don't like being around the police.
> PRYOR: We don't!
> LAWRENCE: Part of your research includes asking questions.
> MONICA: So are you all OK with asking the police questions?
> CHAPPELLE: Hell naw. I ain't snitching. They just want us to talk.
> LAWRENCE: No, you get to come up with the questions.
> PRYOR: So we get to ask them anything? Like, anything?
> LAWRENCE: That's your call.
> CHAPPELLE: I don't know, man, about this.

After going back-and-forth, seven of the members agreed to interview the police and others in the community about their experiences with the police, while the seven others chose to research Black teachers. Surprisingly, after stating his dislike for the police, Chappelle joined the team of researchers examining policing. Lawrence then invited the guys to think critically about the process:

> LAWRENCE: This is your project. So why to do you want to research the police and lack of Black teachers?

MALCOLM: We get to ask the police questions.
THOMAS: Break the cycle of youth living in poverty.
PRYOR: Find solutions to problems that have not been solved.
MALCOLM: Make it better for the next generation.
LAWRENCE: Is there anything else?
THOMAS: It's our chance to tell teachers and police how we feel and what we experience.
MALCOLM: Learn how to communicate and work together.
LAWRENCE: OK. You guys are on it. Again, this is your project, and Monica, Lance, and I are here to help you. You all come up with questions, interview (protocols), observe, meet with people, learn about the issues, and come up with solutions or recommendations. And y'all have to present at the end.
PRYOR: We got it. We got it.
LAWRENCE: I mean you have to stand up in front of people and talk about your project.

Youth participants in the Alliance's YPAR project accepted the responsibility to take the lead on their research. For example, after they narrowed down the questions to "Why do the police target Black youth?" and "Why are there only a few Black teachers in our public schools?" they, with the assistance of their adult allies, presented to the City Council Finance Committee to advocate for funding to help implement the project. The group unanimously chose Marcus as the speaker. They worked together to draft a script for Marcus and insisted that he practice. Marcus paraded his confidence, telling the group that he presents all the time: "This is nothing. I'm good." At the City Council Finance Committee meeting, Marcus spoke for five minutes about the benefits and importance of youth conducting research. Marcus's presentation surprised several members in the audience; one observer said, "He is really good. He is the next King, Jr." When he returned to his seat, Marcus was greeted by "good job(s)" and "Keep up the good work." Impressed with the project's purpose and the youth participation in the research, the committee awarded the Alliance a small grant to research, analyze, and publish a report about racial disparities and how to reduce social inequities. This grant gave the youth confidence about their work and confirmed the importance of YPAR and the impact that it could have on the larger community

Youth participants having an authentic role consists of speaking to the public about the issues, leading workshops, coming up with research topics and questions, writing reports, interviewing, analyzing data, and observing meetings. Maisha also discovered that when youth take the lead in naming the YPAR project and articulating its purpose, they become invested in the process. At Du Bois High School, the YPAR team and Maisha met to discuss school culture. Maisha volunteered to coordinate the group because she had more time than the staff; however, the principal, Ms. Toure, was active and engaged, offering support by way of time, space, and presence. Ms. Toure selected students who experienced harsh discipline policies as well as students who seemed to be slipping "under the radar" of the staff. Maisha shared the idea with the staff, and teachers volunteered. Maisha personally asked the school safety team, and one member volunteered who was an alumni of the school and familiar with the community. Unnamed at the time, the group agreed on the mission to address school climate issues and build community. Meetings were held in the principal's conference room, where students were seldom invited unless they were in trouble. One by one, students trickled in and smiled. When Jay, an 11th grader, walked in the room and looked around to find a place to sit, Maisha pointed to one of the chairs at the head of the table. Jay responded, "Oh for real," surprised and delighted that he could actually sit there. Shanti sat next to Maisha, while Monty, a well-spoken and outgoing freshman, sat next to Shanti. TiTi and Lex, the senior representatives, sat in chairs lining the walls. Ms. Toure summoned them to the table, "Please sit at the table. We want this to be owned by you—this is why we ask you to be at the table. This is yours." The students and the adult allies had a hard time coming up with a name for the group. After weeks of meeting, Jay made a suggestion:

> JAY: I think she (referring to Ms. Toure) said our name—"Change Agents." That should be our name. That made me feel important when she called us that!

Several weeks later, Maisha observed that participants arrived on time and felt comfortable coming into the conference room. However, it was obvious that Jay was missing. Maisha learned later he was involved in an off-campus altercation that would result potentially in him transferring to another school. One student, Adam, noticed Jay was not there to claim the seat at the head of the table:

> ADAM: Can I sit at the head of the table?
> MAISHA: This is your table, so sit where you like.
> ADAM: I have a friend who wants to join the group.
> MAISHA: That sounds great.... [W]hy don't you mention it to the group.

Maisha began where Jay left off and offered the question: *What or who is a "change agent"?* In an interesting turn of events, the adults in the group were eager to respond to this question when they had been more passive in the last session:

> MRS. SHIELDS
> (ENGLISH TEACHER): A change agent can work covertly/overtly.
> ADAM: It depends on the influence you have someone's life because sometimes you don't know if you are being a change agent or not because you don't know if a person is watching you.

MS. TOURE
(PRINCIPAL): People who change others must work on one's self first. If you want to change, you have to work on yourself.
MAISHA: So one of the questions I have for us and for myself is whether or not one has to be deliberate to be a change agent. Before we had this discussion, I really thought the course of action had to be mapped out, but I am really influenced by Adam and others around the table that it can also just happen.
MS. FOWLES
(SOCIAL STUDIES
TEACHER): I believe when you are deliberate, the rest will follow.
MS. SHIELDS
(ENGLISH
TEACHER): The common word in all of our responses is action.
MS. TOURE
(PRINCIPAL): There has to be a principle that drives us. We have to have something at the core. It is not us who determines we are change agents; it's others. We have to change ourselves.
SHANTI: I wanted to change myself, and my job had an opportunity to go to the King Center for this program. When my boss asked, none of my peers raised their hands, but I did not let that stop me. That was my first change.
MS. FOWLES
(SOCIAL STUDIES
TEACHER): I think the King Center has a "Wall of Tolerance," and it would be great for us to go visit. I am going to get some more information about that, so we can go.
MS. TOURE
(PRINCIPAL): I think we have to be leaders, and part of that is managing impulsivity. Being a leader is different, so we have to learn how to manage ourselves.

The teacher's and students' definitions of "change agent" were much different from Maisha's definition. She defined a change agent as "a catalyst for organizing, mobilizing, and acting on a principle or set of principles that stand for something." However, many of the participants' definitions were based on their lived experiences.

It was becoming clear that both the youth and the adult allies were becoming invested in the project. For example, youth participants took the lead in naming their group and defining their purpose. In the following weeks, students asked that they facilitate class activities. One such student, Shanti, was eager to share with the class her nonviolence training:

SHANTI: I participated in the Martin Luther King Nonviolence certification. I want to share this with you, even though I don't think anyone here is violent. I am certified to teach this. We had this activity where we interviewed someone and then we had to talk like we were them, like walking in their shoes.

The next week Shanti led the group with an icebreaker and community-building activity that she learned at the King Center. Everyone was encouraged to find a partner who they hadn't spoken with for any great length of time and interview him or her. The focal question was this: "If money were not an issue, where would you travel and why?" The groups exchanged their answers with each other, sparking an interesting conversation. Shanti shared her feedback and guided the discussion.

Shanti's out-of-school experience provided an authentic opportunity for youth participants to lead and to take ownership of the YPAR process. On the one hand, when youth are invested in the process, they become ambassadors recruiting other students to participate. On the other hand, some participants will fail to show up, others will become disengaged, and a few will encounter conflict. For example, shortly after leading a session on non-violence, Shanti was involved in an on-campus conflict on her way to a Change Agents meeting. Ms. Toure called parents, guardians, and students who caused and experienced harm and invited Maisha to be part of the dialogue. Because of Shanti's involvement in the Change Agents, Ms. Toure was able to begin her inquiry about the incident from the perspective that she saw Shanti's potential as a change agent and peacemaker.

RECOUNTING AND HUMANIZING YOUTH'S LIVED EXPERIENCES

With increased interest in racial disparities, police brutalities, incarceration rates, and educational inequities, the lives of youth of color sit at the front and center of news stories, scholarly articles, and table conversations. Some scholars and journalists use infographics and quantitative data to illustrate the vast differences between Whites and Black or Brown people. However, these data fail to illustrate the full picture and provide an explanation for the historical causes of racial disparities and inequities. These data neglect to address the effects of racism and socioeconomic oppression. Furthermore, a select group of individuals often have access to policy briefs and reports. When we began our YPAR projects, we wanted to introduce the Change Agents and the Alliance to reports such as Children's Defense Fund's (CDF) *The State of Black Children and Families: Black Perspectives on What Black Children Face and What the Future Holds* (2011) and the *Race to Equity Report* (2013), which statistically projected their educational, career, and life trajectories. Our goal was to familiarize the youth with issues that policy makers identify as the most important and to engage the youth to think about how their experiences relate to the data.

In the Change Agents' third meeting, Maisha passed out CDF policy reports to the group. After feeling self-conscious that students still seemed to be looking for her to lead, she asked students what they thought CDF did:

> SHANTI: They raise money to help children. They help defend children—like poor children.
>
> MAISHA: All of these are solid contributions. The Children's Defense Fund is committed to advocating for children, especially children from vulnerable populations. Let's look at the cover page for their report on the state of Black children. What stands out on this title page?
>
> JAY: It says Black perspectives on what Black children face and what the future holds.
>
> MAISHA: Why is that important to you?
>
> JAY: 'Cause it's better that Black people were asked because they are closer to the situation and probably care more.
>
> MAISHA: OK, what else?
>
> LEANNA: They used qualitative and quantitative research.
>
> MAISHA: Is everyone familiar with qualitative and quantitative research?
>
> [A few nods]
>
> MAISHA: Tell me about it.
>
> ADAM: Quantitative research involves numbers and statistics, and qualitative is more—I don't know—quality I guess.
>
> MAISHA: OK, so quantitative research may include statistical analysis. Say you collect survey data from everyone in the school and then analyze the data, right? But if you interview every student and then transcribe the interviews and code them for emergent themes, then you would be doing qualitative research. Both are equally important, which is why they used mixed methods. Is there anything else?
>
> MS. ALANA (MATH TEACHER): I really like the children's art (the CDF logo). It personalizes the report.
>
> MAISHA: Everyone has a copy of the actual report as well as the PowerPoint presentation that was used to introduce the report. Why don't we work with partners or in small groups and discuss some of the findings, and then we will get back together.

Small groups provided a way for Maisha to decentralize her role and also make sure there was more dialogue. One of the school security staff members contributed for the first time in the small groups. The small groups listed the most serious problems that their communities faced.

The top issues varied from violence and guns to respect between men and women, to drugs.

> CHRISTIANA: I think the disrespect and mistreatment of women and girls are the most serious problem because boys think it's OK to dis women, and it can give women low self-esteem.
>
> RYAN: I think violence is the most serious problem because it can lead to prison.
>
> MR. FRANK (SCHOOL SECURITY): I agree because that's the biggest issue in schools and on the streets. It's all one big chain. It's hard to say what's the most serious because everything leads to another thing.
>
> LEANNA: We saw that too. Like drugs and prison are related, and I think unemployment is important, but that comes much later. I think adults and youth see these things differently because this is what adults say are the most serious problems in the community. Adults see the outcome, but we see the process. We are at the ground level, so things like teen pregnancy and violence are our main concerns because that's our every day.
>
> MS. TOURE: You know I was amazed to see "poorly performing schools" so low on the list of "serious problems" in the Black community. Black people did not see the schools as having an impact on Black children. When I look at this, I see the value of a Black man is high; our kings are being captured. Black people or we're saying we want to work; we are not blaming schools. This is so in line with our town hall meetings. You often have a conservative view that Blacks have choices, and it's up to them to do better.
>
> MAISHA: I agree. I thought education would be at the top of all these lists, and that could be because I'm an educator and, perhaps, education centered. I believe that mis-education is at the core of so many of Black peoples' issues.... I know we are running out of time. I'm wondering if you would like to look at the CDF "Cradle-to-Prison Pipeline" report next week?
>
> RYAN: Wait, are they saying that they already know which babies go to prison?
>
> ADAM: Prison growth is built on third and fourth grade reading performance.
>
> RYAN: What?
>
> SEVERAL STUDENTS: Yes, let's read that.

"We Want This to Be Owned by You" 125

This session seemed to galvanize the group. Ms. Toure's urging for change to begin within individuals resonated for everyone at the table—especially for Ryan. He, like Shanti, wanted to lead future sessions. Ryan also wanted to know what books and articles Maisha could access for them. Through a small grant, she purchased class sets of Noguera's *The Trouble With Black Boys, Sugar and Spice and No Longer Nice; Interview* (Student Press Initiative) and *Letters From Young Activists*. Ryan really liked the *Young Activists* book and would like for the Change Agents to use this book as a blueprint for the upcoming school year. Ryan also wanted summer reading assignments. It was in this moment that as the adult initiator—a term borrowed from poet and activist Gwendolyn Brooks (Fisher, 2009)—that Maisha realized that some youth may want and need more time to cultivate their ideas independently of the YPAR group. What Maisha needed and wanted was more time with youth participants, especially those seeking out more outside reading. Maisha and Ryan talked about spending time this summer reading the newspapers such as the *Atlanta Journal Constitution* and *New York Times* and listening to the National Public Radio (NPR) and Democracy Now. Ryan shared that he would work for his father this summer doing remodeling; his father has taught him how to lay tile:

> RYAN: My dad said you may not learn anything in school, but you will always be able to make some money when you can fix things. My dad and I did not used to talk that much, but now I see why. He works really hard. He turns red in the summer on top on the roof working. We talk more, and I understand him.
> MAISHA: Have you heard of Booker T. Washington?
> RYAN: Yes.
> MAISHA: Have you heard of W. E. B. Du Bois?
> RYAN: No, I have not.

They continued their conversation by discussing the value of physical labor, growing vegetables and livestock, and being self-sufficient by being able to build using the famous Booker T. Washington and W. E. B. Du Bois debates. After spending some time examining these arguments, Ryan asserted, "You need both." These transactions reminded Maisha of the documented "downtime" in her ethnography of a theater program for incarcerated and formerly incarcerated girls, *Girl Time*. "Downtime," or opportunities for teaching artists and student artists to have conversations over meals, during rides to field trips, or while working side by side, became essential for building relationships and pathways to learning (Winn, 2011).

Much like the Change Agents, members of the Alliance read policy reports and the *Race to Equity Report* in particular. The report reveals that only 50 percent of Black high school students in the region graduated on time (2001–11); 21 percent of Black students were suspended from school compared to 2.3 percent of the region's White students; and Black juveniles (ages 10–17) were arrested at a rate of six times that of White juveniles (Wisconsin Council on Children and Families, 2013). Many of the youth indicated that they knew about the numbers because they see it every day. When the group discussed the reasons for the disparities and inequities, Malcolm suggested slavery, and many of his friends laughed at him. Other youth suggested that system doesn't work for Blacks, and White people don't care about them. When the youth read and interrogated terms such as "high school graduate rate," "3rd grade reading proficiency," and "suspensions," they connected the challenges of Black students with the school's inability to relate and care for them:

> LAWRENCE: Why do you think only 50 percent of Black high school students in the region graduated on time?
> CHAPPELLE: Black students know that schools don't care about them. So some show up or don't show up.
> PRYOR: School is not interesting. They don't teach us nothing.

In previous conversation, Pryor was more forthcoming about his school experience and race. He believed that "White teachers don't care" about him and other Black students and "don't teach anything engaging or interesting" (Winn & Winn, 2015). He also stated that White teachers wanted Black students to "act like them." When Lawrence inquired if he had any Black teachers, Pryor responded that he did not have one Black teacher as a student and did not recall having any Black janitors at any of his schools.

In 2014 the school district reported that only 2 percent of the teaching force was Black.

Some of the youth expressed that the White teachers don't how who to connect and often teach "boring and bogus stuff." During one class session, we discussed why there were less than 80 African American teachers out 3,000 total. Their reasons included the following:

- They (White people) don't care about us.
- The system doesn't work for you if it was not built for you.
- Keep things for themselves (White people).
- We don't matter.

The students then brainstormed why it is important to have Black teachers (Winn & Winn, 2015):

- To engage us.
- Black teachers can relate to us.
- It's not all about academics but life skills.
- We can learn about our history and ourselves.

The youth had strong opinions about their experiences with White teachers and Black teachers. Their overall reaction to the report is that White people don't care about Black people. Pryor spoke candidly about the report:

> PRYOR: We know the numbers, but there is nothing we can do about it. Every year it's the same thing—people tell us that we are going to jail.
> LAWRENCE: Should we just give up?
> PRYOR: It is what it is. We've been talking about stuff like this for years. Nothing has changed.

Pryor made a valid point about inequities and social change. As Pryor indicated, "we live the numbers." Black youth are aware of the history of slavery, segregation, racism, failing schools, incarceration, high unemployment, and teen pregnancy. When they read and interrogate policy reports and data sets that "count" them, they also experience being "discounted." If there is no time to analyze and reflect, data potentially can cause more harm to youth. Pryor and the other youth want to be accurately represented in data and want data to do more than count them as numbers but count them as promises. To be "counted," youth must have forums in which their voices cannot only be heard but "exalted" if not amplified (Fisher, 2007). However, there has to be a step after this; those of us with privilege and access to forums where youth voices can, indeed, be amplified must open doors, set tables, pull up chairs, and use or positionality to support youth in creating the levers of change they want to see in their communities and schools.

FINAL THOUGHTS (FOR NOW)

When we started our projects, we imagined exchanging stories of how these two YPAR projects created large-scale change in their schools and communities that would be visible to others. We knew the research process would not be neat and tidy and welcomed tensions to optimize learning experiences. However, we came to value that this notion of change and transformation, much like the words of Ms. Toure, had to begin with the individual to get to the important work of the collective. We realized that self-reflection and individual transformation had to serve as the initial phases of the work as opposed to systemic changes in school policies. To address and change school climate meant that community members needed to explore their own dispositions toward the Du Bois learning community. For example, the Change Agents inspired an exercise for the Du Bois staff in which Ms. Toure asked teachers to describe their philosophy of discipline for one to two students. Maisha also conducted an exercise with teachers in which they defined "discipline" and did a community reading of Wayne

Yang's (2009) "Discipline or Punish? Some Suggestions for School Policy and Teacher Practice."

We also learned that for youth in these particular settings that their educational trajectories primarily consisted of teacher-focused and teacher-driven transactions. In the case of Du Bois, there was a policy change to transform a large, comprehensive high school into a small learning community that focused in inquiry-driven curriculum. This work was slow and tedious. To engage in YPAR projects, we had to design an infrastructure in which the youth we worked with understood that their questions, ideas, and solutions mattered. This was new for youth in the Alliance, who experienced "urban pedagogies" for most of their K–12 careers or an education that was focused more on the policing and management of their bodies and voices than promoting intellectual growth and development (Duncan, 2000). While Duncan found urban pedagogies to be consistent in schools that largely served Black and Latino students from working-class and working-poor backgrounds, Lawrence's work with the Alliance demonstrated that even in schools in affluent White communities, Black youth have similar experiences (Winn & Winn, 2015).

YPAR presents opportunities to represent accurately the lived experiences of youth from multiethnic and multilingual backgrounds in humanizing and collaborative ways that reject using deficit lenses and monolithic stories of young people. Collaborative efforts to identify problems, find solutions, and implement action are what makes YPAR especially compelling. Using this methodology allows us to move beyond stating the problems and providing more evidence about the inequalities we already understand are pervasive in communities and schools. However, we also experienced tensions in the process, including when and where to enter as well as exit. We struggled with how involved we should be in the process and felt conflicted when youth participants looked to us to guide them, set the agenda, ask the next question, and provide a new challenge. Although we understood YPAR as a process of becoming engaged civic actors for young people, we did not expect to be so central to the projects for so long as we hoped that the work would, indeed, be "owned" by youth. Tensions, of course, present learning opportunities for youth and adult initiators. In our efforts to decolonize research methods and practices, we lost sight of the fact that some youth might benefit from purposeful scaffolding such as "guided participation" in YPAR to get to the phase where youth take ownership of the process and, when relevant, the product(s). This is where we challenge ourselves to think about the ways in which we can support youth with their process and product goals in YPAR.

REFERENCES

Cammarota, J., & Fine, M. (Eds.). (2007). *Revolutionizing education: Youth participatory action research*. New York, NY: Routledge.

Cruz, M. R., & Sonn, C. C. (2011). (De) colonizing culture in community psychology: Reflections from critical social science. *American Journal of Community Psychology, 47*(1–2), 203–214.

Duncan, G. A. (2000). Urban pedagogies and the celling of adolescents of color. *Social Justice, 2*(3), 29–42.

Fine, M. (2012). Resuscitating critical psychology for "Revolting" times. *Journal of Social Issues, 68*(2), 416–438.

Fisher, M. T. (2007). *Writing in rhythm: Spoken word poetry in urban classrooms.* New York, NY: Teachers College Press.

Fisher, M. T. (2009). *Black literate lives: Historical and contemporary perspectives.* New York, NY: Routledge. Critical Social Thought Series.

Green, K. (2013). Doing double Dutch methodology: Playing with the practice of participant observer. In D. Paris & M. T. Winn (Eds.), *Humanizing research, decolonizing qualitative inquiry with youth and communities* (pp. 147–160). Thousand Oaks, CA: SAGE.

Gutiérrez, K. D., & Vossoughi, S. (2009). Lifting off the ground to return anew: Mediated praxis, transformative learning, and social design experiments. *Journal of Teacher Education, 61*(1–2), 100–117.

Meiners, E. R., & Winn, M. T. (2010). Resisting the school to prison pipeline: The practice to build abolition democracies. *Race Ethnicity and Education, 13*(3), 271–276.

Morrell, F. (2006). *Youth participatory action research as critical pedagogy: Lessons from practices.* Annual meeting of the American Educational Research Association conference presentation, San Francisco, CA.

Noguera, P. A. (2003). The trouble with Black boys: The role and influence of environmental and cultural factors on the academic performance of African American males. *Urban education, 38*(4), 431–459.

Ozer, E. J., & Wright, D. (2012). Beyond school spirit: The effects of youth-led participatory action research in two urban high schools. *Journal of Research on Adolescence, 22*(2), 267–283.

Paris, D., & Alim, H. S. (2014). What are we seeking to sustain through culturally sustaining pedagogy: A loving critique forward. *Harvard Educational Review, 84*(1), 85–100.

Paris, D., & Winn, M. T. (Eds.). (2013). *Humanizing research: Decolonizing qualitative inquiry with youth and communities.* Thousand Oaks, CA: SAGE.

Stoudt, B. G., Fox, M., & Fine, M. (2012). Contesting privilege with critical participatory action research. *Journal of Social Issues, 68*(1), 178–193.

Tuck, E. (2009). Suspending damage: A letter to communities. *Harvard Educational Review, 79*(3), 409–427.

Wallerstein, N., & Duran, B. (2008). The theoretical, historical and practice roots of CBPR. In M. Minkler & N. Wallerstein (Eds.), *Community based participatory research for health: From process to outcomes* (pp. 25–46). San Francisco, CA: Jossey-Bass.

Winn, M. T. (2011). *Girl Time: Literacy, justice, and the school-to-prison pipeline.* New York, NY: Teachers College Press. Teaching for Social Justice Series.

Winn, M. T., & Johnson, L. P. (2011). *Writing instruction in the culturally relevant classroom.* Urbana, IL: National Council of Teachers of English.

Winn, M. T., & Ubiles, J. R. (2011). Worthy witnessing: Collaborative research in urban classrooms. In A. Ball & C. Tyson (Eds.), *Studying diversity in teacher education* (pp. 295–308). New York, NY: Rowman & Littlefield.

Winn, L. T., & Winn, M. T. (2015). Expectations and realities: Education, the discipline gap, and the experiences of Black families migrating to small cities. *Race and Social Problems, 7,* 73–83.

Wisconsin Council on Children and Families. (2013). *Race to equity: A baseline report on racial disparities in Dane County.* Madison, WI: Author.

Yang, W. (2009). Discipline or punish? Some suggestions for school policy and teacher practice. *English Education, 87*(1), 49–61.

6 Writing Our Lives
The Power of Youth Literacies and Community Engagement

Marcelle M. Haddix and Alvina Mardhani-Bayne

"In school you kinda contradict yourself and you kinda like, you know, cover up some stuff, like you kind of hide yourself in school but when you're outside of school, it's like you open yourself up. You unfold everything." Brenda, one of the youth writers from the *Writing Our Lives* program, shared how she experienced writing that took place in school versus the kinds of writing practices she engaged with outside of school. (All student names are pseudonyms). Brenda was participating in a *Writing Our Lives* after-school creative writing workshop that took place in the library at her high school. The program was on a drop-in basis for youth writers looking for an outlet to compose creatively in various modes and to share their writing in a youth-inspired, youth-led collective. *Writing Our Lives*, a year-round program providing after-school and summer workshops and annual youth writing conferences, grew from the urging of young people like Eric, a budding screenwriter, who said, "For me, writing is like breathing. I need it to survive." Eric became involved with *Writing Our Lives* when he received an invitation from Marcelle, first author, who attended the staging of one of his plays at a high school showcase. Eric participated in a summer program that encouraged his interest in screenwriting and supported his application to college programs. Eric and Brenda represent two examples of the youth writers who sought opportunities and spaces that encouraged their writing ambitions and that offered the necessary resources for them to hone their crafts. In that way, *Writing Our Lives* emerged from a call by youth writers who clearly understood that the demands on writing curriculum and pedagogy in school did not readily connect to the kinds of writing that fostered creativity and authenticity as they developed writer identities.

What can I do to help change what is going on in my community, in my local schools, and in the lives of young people? This question was at the forefront of Marcelle's desire to support and help develop community spaces for literacy practices of youth writers like Brenda and Eric. After moving into a new community and attending local meetings where families and other community members lamented the educational experiences of their children, she decided that, as a parent of a school-age child too, she needed to find ways to leverage her skills and expertise as a literacy scholar and English educator to right the educational wrongs done to children who community members declared, "can't read or write! They don't know their own history." The community was angered by what they experienced as a failing of the school district—the system was not meeting their expectations or the academic or social needs of their children. Even more damaging was that the community's understanding of its youth's literacy practices was miscolored and overshadowed by district test score results and other academic measures.

During the summer in 2009, Marcelle began offering writing workshops at a local library throughout the week, and young people arrived each day ready to write, ready to talk about their writing, and ready to share their writing. The decision to offer these writing workshops resulted from her involvement in community forums and dialogues about the pervasiveness of educational failure in their school communities and the fact that Black children were being failed at alarming rates. Although school-sanctioned standards constructed these youths as nonreaders and writers, this community space—the library—allowed for the reseeing and re-knowing (Vasudevan, 2006) of the literacies of these young people. Listening to and learning from the youth who attended the workshops, the first author expanded the program beyond the library space to cultivate the spaces that encouraged and supported the literacy needs and interests of youth that extended past school walls—the spaces in libraries, in community centers, in churches, and even in the "other spaces" (Wissman, 2011) inside schools. *Writing Our Lives*, which is an extension of the library writing workshops initiated in 2009, now in its sixth year, is a youth writing project for youth Grades 6 through 12 in the greater Syracuse area to celebrate youth literacies and to make visible the kinds of spaces that support their literacy interests and needs.

In this chapter, we highlight the experiences of youth writers, teachers, parents, artists, and community members who partner together to cultivate spaces for authentic writing practices within this urban community through the *Writing Our Lives* youth writing project. This project has many components, including after-school writing programs, summer writing institutes, book clubs, digital composing programs, staged theatrical performances, and an annual youth writing conference. *Writing Our Lives* is an effort to provide youth writers with opportunities to write, create, produce, and perform their stories and experiences in authentic ways and forms. Like other programs the authors in this book describe, *Writing Our Lives* reflects a community-engaged model for supporting the everyday, authentic literacy practices of youth writers, particularly those from low-income urban communities and low-performing school districts. With the demands placed on low-performing schools to meet high stakes standards and various assessment benchmarks, there is little time for authentic writing that captures the interests and experiences of young people. Instead, more emphasis in writing instruction is placed on making sure that students are able to "pass the test" and graduate. These goals do not and should not be mutually exclusive.

Writing Our Lives is an example of a community-engaged approach with aims to address "the problem" of the achievement gap for urban youth. Importantly, the community—the youth, parents, and other members—has articulated what they see as "the problem." Learning to be literate is not merely a means to fulfill the goals of the school system but a means to ensure that youth acquire knowledge through authentic literacy practices that reflect the interests of youth and their families.

SITUATING THE WORK: FROM A DEFICIT FRAMING TO PRESUMED WRITING COMPETENCE

In this chapter, we share what and how we learn from listening to the voices of the youth writers who have participated in the *Writing Our Lives* project and discuss the implications of this community-engaged and collaborative work for students' lives and for teaching and learning within school communities. The examples we share emphasize how *Writing Our Lives* is designed first to validate the writing practices that young people engage in within their own lives and then to provide a space to support those practices. From our discussion of these learnings, we address and directly challenge the idea that "young people hate to write" and, more pointedly, that "urban, African American young people hate to write." We challenge deficit and oppressive framing of urban youth as disengaged learners and advocate strongly for seeing all youth as writers. For some students of color in urban environments, it is rare to be seen as competent writers and contributors to classroom learning. Instead, the dominant view of students of color in urban classrooms is one of presumed incompetence—students of color are seen as problems and are associated with a lack of ability and, ultimately, failure (Haddix, 2012). We argue that literacy is an everyday practice for youth. This is particularly evident when we begin to understand that youth from urban communities are already competent writers.

Like others (e.g., Camangian, 2010; Johnson & Vasudevan, 2012; Muhammad, 2012), we have seen that when adults are cautious and deliberate in their view of students as potentially competent writers, students may grow in terms of their confidence and abilities. Indeed, research demonstrates that youth writers of color also compose on their own in numerous sophisticated ways. Rather than being confined to school-based genres and materials, youth writers may use more variety and modes, such as writing on social networking sites, creating spontaneous poetic "scribbles," and creating songs (Alim, Baugh, & Bucholtz, 2011; Sarkar & Allen, 2007; Stewart, 2014; Yi, 2010). This writing is complex and requires the synthetic use of multiple skills that educators often fail to incorporate in schools. They do not value the multilingual, multi-literate, and multicultural assets of their students, and in turn, they do not acknowledge their assets as writers (Stewart, 2014).

These deficit-based views stem from a variety of sources, including sensationalized news reporting that positions these students as trouble and troubled and a growing disconnect between the relatively homogeneous teacher population and their heterogeneous student body. While the majority of American teachers are White, monolingual, and female, their classrooms are increasing in terms of ethnic and linguistic diversity (Haddix & Price-Dennis, 2013; Kelly, 2006). In general, the relatively homogeneous body of teachers does not value the multilingual, multi-literate, and multicultural assets of their students and in turn does not acknowledge their assets as writers (Stewart, 2014). Additionally, the kinds of writing privileged in schools are limited in genre and mode; writing that includes visual images, for example, does not "count" in the same way an essay does (Johnson & Vasudevan, 2012). Thus, rather than celebrating the abilities of students of color as writers, narrow definitions of literacy as monolingual and monomodal means that teachers may not acknowledge the full range of literacy practices their students exhibit and may instead see them as unskilled rather than celebrating the abilities of students of color.

When students of color are given the opportunity to write in adult-directed, out-of-school spaces, this discourse of inability may follow them. When adults create "classroom-like ensembles," in which the activities and cultural practices associated with classrooms are enacted in out-of-school spaces, problematic deficit-based perspectives may be recreated and reified (Leander, Phillips, & Headrick Taylor, 2010, p. 332). Wright and Mahiri (2012) discuss the case of a student who participated in a literacy program that used an asset-based, apprenticeship approach. Students in the program were required to reflect on their skills and list the resources and knowledge that they carried with them. Additionally, rather than experiencing a top-down teaching pedagogy, the use of an apprenticeship model disrupted the traditional teacher-student dichotomy and led to more equitable relationships between the students and their adult instructors. These departures from conventional classroom practices were associated with positive growth in literacy skills for the participants and demonstrate that students of color are not inherently deficient as writers.

For example, adolescents who participate in the Quebecois hip-hop scene as rappers incorporate multiple languages in their arrangements and in so doing embrace diversity while denying monolingual and monocultural representations of culture. Their lyrics also contain socially conscious messages, and they use their writing to protest issues such as racial inequality and oppression (Sarkar & Allen, 2007). Additionally, the use of social media to connect with family members in other countries means that youth writers are engaging in multimodal communication across several borders: linguistic, cultural, social, and geographic (Stewart, 2014). However, while composing practices such as these are sophisticated, youth tend not to see them as "real" writing but instead regard them as inconsequential or frivolous. Therefore, youth writers of color do not value their spontaneous and self-directed writing as such, which may contribute to their sense of inadequacy in classrooms (Yi, 2010). However, as Yi (2010) points out, self-guided writing done outside of schools can be reflected in writing that occurs in the classroom, which indicates that the existing in- versus out-of-school dichotomy need not remain dominant.

RETHINKING COMMUNITY ENGAGEMENT

Our work with *Writing Our Lives* begins by critically reflecting on what it means to be community engaged. Specifically, we ask a number of questions (Haddix, 2015) to instigate a process of critical self-interrogation about the underlying assumptions and ideologies that encourage an individual's resolve to want to give back to the community:

- What does it mean to be of service?
- How do you understand your role?
- How do you understand the position and role of people from this community?
- What do you bring to this community?
- What do you take from this community?
- How do you develop a community partnership that honors the "funds of knowledge" of the community members?
- How do you critically and purposefully engage in questioning who you are by addressing any assumptions you might have of people and communities that are different from you and from what you know (Haddix, 2015, p. 66)?

As we think about the work that we engage in with youth and communities, a first step for that engagement entails unpacking how we position ourselves in relationship to the work. The idea of community engagement has different meanings and understandings for individuals based on their social locations.

In our work, "community-engaged work" means that community members take time to establish relationships with and live and work together for the good of the community. It is not, for us, a form of service learning or volunteerism where those deemed more privileged help or "save" the less fortunate so that they, the privileged, might feel better about their privilege. As scholar and activist Lilla Watson said, "If you have come to help me, you are wasting your time. But if you have come because your liberation is bound up with mine, then let us work together." Our approach toward community engagement is grounded in a concept of unity within a community—*I am you; you are me; we are one*—an idea that we introduce and discuss in our *Writing Our Lives* programs. This requires that we enter into the project with the understanding that this is a reciprocal relationship.

Just as we might bring our skills and knowledges to the space, we are open to and welcome the opportunity to learn with youth and communities.

Writing Our Lives began because of an articulated need and observations within the community, an idea that emanated as a response to Marcelle's participation in community forums on the state of education for urban youth and conversations with other community members. It was a not a school-sanctioned or research-based intervention to improve the academic achievement of urban youth for working-class communities. Instead, youth, families, and other community members are the primary stakeholders in this project. The community-engaged project is led by their questions: What do the youth want? What do the youth need? And, what do they want and need to envision and enliven a positive sense of identity and well-being? What do they want and need to create and engineer productive and successful life outcomes? The goals and objectives of this project surpass a district's mandate to increase test scores. The project is very much about cultivating leaders within the community by providing the resources and spaces for their optimal growth as literate beings. Those future leaders will help realize community goals to improve the social conditions for all of its members.

COMMUNITY ENGAGEMENT WITH/IN YOUTH LITERACY SPACES

Although *Writing Our Lives* was first conceptualized out of the dialogue initiated by families and communities, listening to the youth and learning about their interests required another level of engagement, one that positioned the youth as knowledge producers and decision makers right alongside other members of the community. While parents and others were deeply concerned about the academic achievement of their youth, we had to be prepared for the disconnect that can occur when leveraging the voices of the youth. Their identity constructions as writers in other spaces were not defined by school measures. When beginning a workshop with youth, we first ask them to fill in the blank to the statement, "I am a [blank] writer." They can fill in the blank with whatever adjectives or descriptive words or phrases they choose, but in making this statement, they are indeed declaring that they are writers. This process of reclaiming their writer identities is important because if left to school measures, many of the students identify as nonwriters, or they do not understand the writing that is done in school to be "real writing." Instead, it involves writing for tests or other assignments. This is not the kind of authentic writing that young people are engaged in beyond school walls. In that way, *Writing Our Lives* cannot be about meeting school literacy demands—it is about meeting the demands of the youth writers who are writing their worlds and writing for their lives.

Over the years, many *Writing Our Lives* participants have commented on how writing is a deeply personal practice for them, and they see a significant difference in the expectations for writing in school from the kinds of writing they do outside of school, as articulated by Brenda at the beginning of this chapter. These other spaces are essential for youth writers to tell and share their stories and to have their lived experiences witnessed, affirmed, and validated. This is critical in an era when mainstream messages would have most Black and Brown youth believe that their lives do not matter. In the *Writing Our Lives* project, then, we work to support youth's sharing of the personal in a public space that acknowledges the importance of the individual voice and story in strengthening the collective community. The issues that are personal or individual in nature become catalysts for change when the individual stands up or shares his or her story in a public space.

In honoring the commitment to the personal by *Writing Our Lives* youth writers, past themes for our writing events and conferences have included "FREE Writing: Youth Writing for Change" and "Youth Lives Matter." Just as we interrogate what we mean by community engagement and how these understandings inform our articulation of the *Writing Our Lives* programs, it is just as essential that we dialogue with youth participants about what

Figure 6.1 Student Definition of Community Engagement

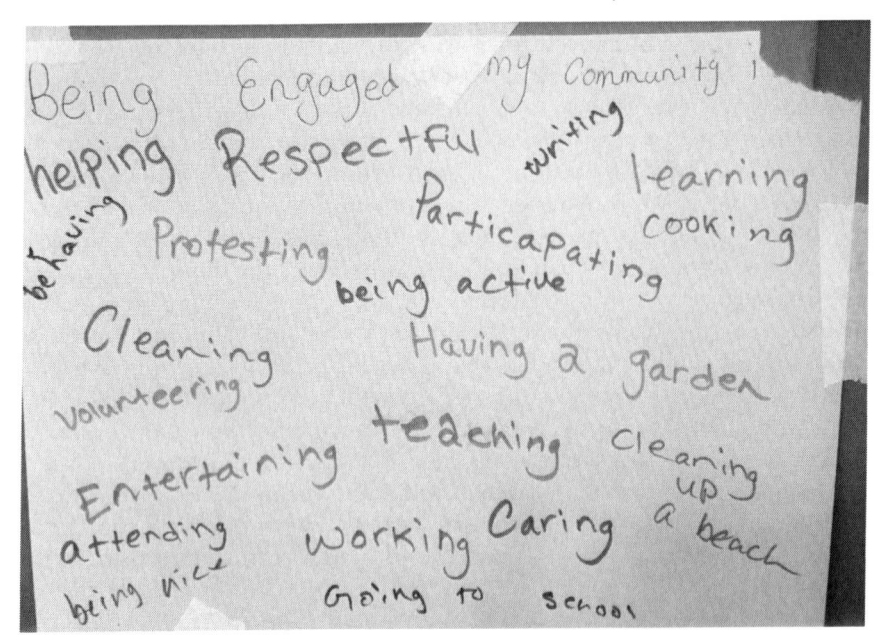

Figure 6.2 Student Word Collage of Community Engagement

community and community engagement means for them. One way we do this is to ask participants to draw a visual representation or a word collage illustrating their definitions of these ideas.

THE *WRITING OUR LIVES* PROJECT: LISTENING AND LEARNING FROM THE YOUTH

Conceptualized as an inviting space for writing and writers, and that also includes food and music, *Writing Our Lives* has involved an annual youth writing conference, themed Saturday writing events, after-school writing programs, and summer writing institutes. The programs were open to all youth writers, ages 11 through 18. Through the *Writing Our Lives* project, we focus on how urban youth writers define, understand, challenge, and use writing in and out of their secondary and postsecondary school lives. We consider the ways 21st-century tools and technologies can be used to promote the writing identity of urban youth writers. We encourage, celebrate, and support the writing of urban youth writers as critical ethnographers of their own writing lives. Ultimately, we aim to provide writing events for participants to be leaders of writing instruction for themselves, teachers, peers, and members of the community. The programs focus on encouraging youth writers to communicate in multiple genres, multiple literacies, and multiple modes and tools. Writing workshops and activities are facilitated by youth writers, community artists, poets, and performers, university professors and students, and teachers. We recognize that the tools for writing extend well beyond pen and paper; youth writers compose using digital tools and social media; with markers, paint, and clay; and through performance and dance.

While we recognize the importance of cultivating other spaces and communities of practice, we also realize and understand that this work is not without challenges. Finding those spaces and sustaining access to those spaces has been in flux. The program has run in several local schools, libraries, and community centers. However, the ability to use these spaces depends upon the relationships with school and community leaders. For example, we hold the annual writing conference on a Saturday in a local school because a school space is the most appropriate place to accommodate 150 to 200 participants including 15 to 20 facilitators. But, as schools are in a perpetual state of reform, school leaders change, and school initiatives change. After establishing a partnership with one school leader and hosting several writing programs as part of an after-school and Saturday program, the program ceased after the school leader was reassigned to another district position. Similarly, we hosted *Writing Our Lives* in a community center in the early stages of the project, but the community center closed because of funding challenges. The success of this project involves partnership with community and school leaders to locate and maintain spaces that are readily available and accessible to youth writers.

For the past year, from 2014 to 2015, we have worked with a community center to offer after-school and summer writing programs. As part of its mission, the center is a committed space for community youth. The center offers regular workshops and activities; it has computer labs and comfortable seating areas for lounging, reading, and socializing; and they provide regular meals and snacks. They have a regular group of young people who come to the center after school and throughout the summer. Unlike school, however, where consistent attendance is expected, young people come and go as they please at the center. In that way, one cannot be sure that a student will show up one day to the next. These were all issues that we needed to take into consideration as we planned six-week sessions of *Writing Our Lives* activities for any youth who wanted to participate. We advertised through the center and left flyers at local schools and libraries.

When planning the first six week session of *Writing Our Lives*, we focused a great deal on crafting what we believed was an authentic, engaging, socially conscious writing task. We wanted our participants to write about something they cared about, with purpose, and for an audience greater than what they might be limited to in schools. To that end, we decided to have each participant write a short article on a social justice-focused topic of their choosing. We arranged for the writers to be given space in a local, community-based newspaper, *The Stand*, and planned each 90-minute meeting of *Writing Our Lives* to build on the previous one, with youth researching, writing, and editing a short article on a topic that mattered to them. We also arranged for journalists from a local community newspaper to work with *Writing Our Lives* participants to augment the authenticity of the writing. At the end of the six weeks, we intended to have each adolescent's work published in the newspaper.

There were several implications and consequences of this approach that we did not foresee when we planned these sessions. The first was directly related to logistics: To have participants' work develop over six weeks, with our guidance, they needed to attend every session fully. Unfortunately, this did not happen. In reality, attendance was inconsistent, and when youth did attend the workshop, many did not stay for the entirety of each session but instead arrived late or left early.

Because we had foreseen, based on previous experience, that attendance might be erratic, we initially intended to include a short writing project at the end of each meeting. For example, in a 90-minute session, students might spend 60 minutes on their article and the remainder of the time writing a short poem. The rationale for this was to ensure that students still had publishable work even if their articles were incomplete. Unfortunately, because youth left the sessions early, or arrived late, we did not have the ability to engage in short writing projects because of the loss of work time. Instead, we would spend that time trying to catch latecomers up, or we would see participants leave before the shorter compositions could get underway. By the third week of our meetings, we decided that the shorter pieces were untenable and decided to instead focus on ensuring the articles were completed. However, as explained, our participants' attendance was very sporadic at this point, and by the end of the first session, none of the students published any writing in *The Stand*.

Compounding this issue is a more fundamental problem with the adult-directed nature of our focus. For example, while we intended the community newspaper assignment to be a personal and authentic task for our participants, it was still, ultimately, one that we devised. We did not ask students if they wished to contribute to a community newspaper, but instead we *told* them that it was taking place. Because we valued this kind of writing, we assumed that the adolescents in *Writing Our Lives* would as well. Additionally, we believed that having each participant choose a topic would generate motivation and interest in the writing of newspaper articles. However, many of them resisted article writing by avoiding the sessions, constantly changing their topics so that they would not have enough material with which to write, or refusing to write when given time to do so.

We realized that we needed to make changes to our model for it to be relevant for the youth participants. For the second six-week session, we chose the theme of "Your Story, Your Way." Rather than having each meeting focused on the completion of a long-term project, we designed each weekly session as a stand-alone interaction with a particular way of expressing one's self. We tried to incorporate a variety of modes of literate practice—audio, visual, and the like—and provided the adolescents with prompts and materials but allowed them quite a bit more freedom than in the previous

Writing Our Lives 141

iteration of the project. For example, one session centered around composing spoken-word poetry, while the next focused on creating collages that represented definitions of self. For the spoken-word poetry session, we let youth writers know that they could write about anything that was important to them, but we also gave them the prompt, "Who am I?" LaLa, the focal student for our example in the following section, used the prompt to compose the following poem:

> I'm small but tall in my own little ways.
> I'm fierce but never careless.
> I'm bold but never reckless.
> I'm shy but not so sneaky.
> I tried to be sneaky but it didn't work.
> I'm mean when I have to be.
> I'm fussy sometimes but never bossy.
> I'm self confident but never conceited.

Figure 6.3 A Student Self-Definition Collage

142 *Marcelle M. Haddix and Alvina Mardhani-Bayne*

I'm quiet when there's a problem and loud when I'm having fun.
I'm creative and wise, loving and shy. I am LaLa and no not the dance.
I am a girl who loves sports, money, family, and friends.
—from "Who I Am" poem by LaLa, age 15

In this piece, LaLa defines who she is while at the same time countering and challenging misrepresentations of herself. This is critical when considering the deficit framing of urban youth's lives and experiences. Her declaration of self can be viewed as a form of resistance toward dominant stereotyping of young Black girls.

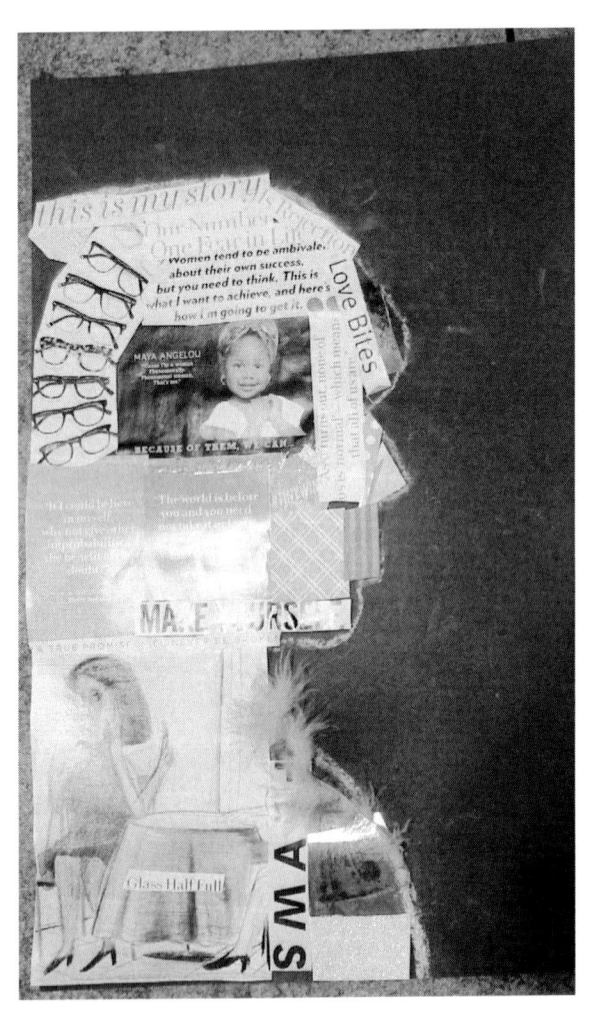

Figure 6.4 A Student Self-Definition Collage

In the same way, we facilitated a workshop where students created collages that represented their self-definitions. First, with chalk, we traced each student's silhouette on black poster paper. Then, students cut out words and images from magazines that they felt represented their identities and what they wanted to project out to the community and they positioned those images within their silhouettes. Their collages illustrated that they placed importance on education, love and relationships, style, and independence. This more youth-centered approach required a reframing and repurposing of the notion of community-engaged writing, which we explore in the case study of one student, which follows.

"YOUR STORY, YOUR WAY": WRITING THEIR STORIES

The second session of our new approach to *Writing Our Lives* focused on the use of the StoryJumper.com Web site as a means of composing stories. StoryJumper is a free-to-use Web site that allows students to design their own storybooks. StoryJumper provides users with access to a wide library of images, backgrounds, and fonts so that stories can be composed in a variety of ways. Some might create a story entirely of words, others might focus solely on pictures, and yet still others can use a combination. Part of our rationale for using StoryJumper was because of this flexibility; we wanted students to create their stories in a way that was authentic for them. We also chose StoryJumper in part because its library of images of people was diverse and included a range of ethnicities, which meant that our participants would be able to access images to represent themselves credibly.

Four female high school students of color attended the StoryJumper session, and three knew each other before the session began. After arriving at the after-school center, we gave each youth a computer, access to the Web site, and a list of prompts to which they could respond. After a short tutorial, each student was given time to construct her story, either with images, text, or both. They spent close to an hour composing and editing their stories, and then each participant shared with the larger group. Because we had a projector, we were able to show the stories to everyone in a large format, while the authors read them out loud.

One of our participants, LaLa, a female high school student, had an interesting approach to her story. She altered one of the prompts from "Write about the best thing that has happened to you recently" and chose to write about the worst thing that had happened her to her. She then proceeded to create a digital text that told the story of her recent relationship with a boy who had lied to her. We provide this example because LaLa's story and the way in which she shared it demonstrates the value in giving youth the freedom to define their community in their own way. When it came time to share the stories, this student was the first to tell her story to the others. Before beginning, she appeared nervous, clearing her throat and taking several deep breaths. When she read, however, her voice was strong.

> LALA: Alright. My story's called, "Worst Day Ever," by LaLa Brown. *(begins reading)* I dedicate my story to Cheddar Bomb. Thanks for this experience. I would have never had–
> NICOLE: *(whispers)* Who Cheddar Bomb?
> LALA: Never mind, you'll get it down later *(everyone laughs)*. I would have never had it and learned from my mistakes if it was not for yours. Thanks. *(advances the book forward on the computer and takes a brief pause)* OK. I really had a big crush on this boy–
> NICOLE: Oh-ho!
> LALA: But he did not know that. *(describing the picture)* And it says, "I like that boy, but look away quick." *(everyone laughs)*
> ALVINA: Are you the one with the blue hair?
> LALA: *(smiling)* No, that Shekaila.
> ALVINA: OK.
> LALA: She had to have blue hair. I couldn't have it. I said, One day, he started saying hi to me, then it progressed into hugs, then went into him complimenting me, saying how beautiful I am. He asked for my number, added me on Facebook. His nickname was Cheddar Bomb, because he looked like that boy that was off of 8 Mile. He had been inboxing me sweet nothings for quite some time. *(B laughs)* Cheddar made it seem like he liked me a lot when really it was all a lie. It really hurted me because it made me feel stupid. I felt that way because he would tell me these things, and I would fall for it. I would believe him and ended up getting hurt. I guess I learned my lesson. That was a lesson well learned. And that's the end of my story. So. *(everyone claps)*

After sharing her story, the other participants had questions for LaLa about the boy and their relationship, and she answered them all in a straightforward way. When asked about the time line of the story, LaLa explained that she had learned that same day that the boy had been lying to her, and the other participants offered support. Some of this support was sympathetic, with one participant exclaiming "Awwww!" when LaLa revealed the recent nature of the incident. Other support was an acknowledgement of the variety of feelings that LaLa might have in light of her male friend's falsehoods, as participants discussed how they would have been angry in LaLa's position. LaLa, however, explained that she had been angry earlier in the day but now had begun to realize that she had learned a valuable lesson from this experience.

For LaLa, the community for which she was writing was herself and the three other female students. She worked to share the lesson that she had learned from her relationship with her male friend and, from sharing it, received support from her peers in a variety of ways. The narrative that LaLa created could be seen as one that focuses on social justice. That is, LaLa is commenting on issues related to gender dynamics and inequities and offers advice to herself and her peers on how to avoid such injustice in the future. When writing for a community that was salient to her, LaLa was able to compose a social justice-focused text in an authentic way.

Unlike in the newspaper-centered writing sessions, the participants in the StoryJumper session were engaged with their writing and were interested in sharing it with others. Moreover, they were attentive when viewing and listening to the stories of their peers and responded in genuine ways. By giving youth the freedom to define the community for whom they were writing and express their stories in multiple ways, *Writing Our Lives* was able to create space for students to write texts with a focus on social justice that were authentic to them.

WRITING OUR LIVES EVEN IN SCRIPTED TIMES AND SPACES

In our work in the *Writing Our Lives* project, we witness the potential and promise present in young people's everyday literacy engagements, particularly those made invisible by mandated, scripted curricula and pedagogy. Yet, many of the *Writing Our Lives* participants will comment on how these are not the kinds of writing and literacy practices that they have the opportunity to participate in within school. And, in providing this description of the work, we are aware that we do not have to manage the many demands and expectations of K–12 teachers in school contexts today. This is a reasonable critique of our work with youth. Challenges do exist, but they are distinct from the tensions teachers often feel between their desire to provide authentic and purposeful literacy activities and at the same time have students perform well on standardized assessment measures. Yet, the youth literacies engaged with and within the *Writing Our Lives* project unintentionally align with Common Core Learning Standards for authentic writing for real purposes and audiences.

We are advocating for an alternative space that can facilitate positive learning outcomes for youth writers—one that hears the concerns of parents and community members, one that makes visible school and academic expectations, and one that validates the skills, abilities, interests, and needs of youth writers. One of the takeaways from engaging in *Writing Our Lives* work over the years is that we do not just want the writing that happens in our after-school programs or summer institutes to be confined to those other spaces. Instead, it is our hope that as students reclaim their identities as writers who have stories and experiences that matter, those identities are supported in school spaces. This can happen when, in schools, students are offered choice when selecting writing topics and modes of expressions. This can happen when students are provided with opportunities to compose, create, and produce using 21st-century digital tools. This can happen when students' processes of writing are assessed and not just the final product.

Just as teachers often feel pressure to stick to a script given curricular demands and standardized tests, *Writing Our Lives* easily can fall into a model of developing a workshop plan, following the script, and moving students toward a finished product. It is important that youth writers feel a sense of completion and accomplishment as they develop their writer identities. At the end of every *Writing Our Lives* session, there is an opportunity for the participants to share their work and to have their work on display for others to provide feedback and to admire. But, the power of youth literacies happens in those "unscripted spaces" (Gutiérrez, Rymes, & Larson, 1995), those moments that were not planned for but instead where the times when our roles as facilitators and participants were blurred. And in those moments, a community of writers grows together.

REFERENCES

Alim, H. S., Baugh, J., & Bucholtz, M. (2011). Global ill-literacies: Hip hop cultures, youth identities, and the politics of literacy. *Review of Research in Education*, 35, 120–146.

Camangian, P. (2010). Starting with self: Teaching autoethnography to foster critically caring literacies. *Research in the Teaching of English*, 45(2), 179–204.

Gutiérrez, K., Rymes, B., & Larson, J. (1995). Script, counterscript, and underlife in the classroom: James Brown versus *Brown v. Board of Education*. *Harvard Educational Review*, 65(3), 445–472.

Haddix, M. (2012). Reclaiming and rebuilding the writer identities of Black adolescent males. In D. E. Alvermann & K. A. Hinchman (Eds.), *Reconceptualizing the literacies in adolescents' lives: Bridging the everyday/academic divide* (3rd ed., pp. 112–131). New York, NY: Routledge.

Haddix, M. (2015). Preparing community-engaged teachers. *Theory Into Practice*, 54(1), 63–70.

Haddix, M., & Price-Dennis, D. (2013). Urban fiction and multicultural literature as transformative tools for preparing English teachers for diverse classrooms. *English Education*, 45(3), 247–283.

Johnson, E., & Vasudevan, L. (2012). Seeing and hearing students' lived and embodied critical literacy practices. *Theory Into Practice*, 51(1), 34–41.

Kelly, D. M. (2006). Frame work: Helping youth counter their misrepresentations in media. *Canadian Journal of Education/Revue Canadienne de L'éducation*, 29(1), 27–48.

Leander, K. M., Phillips, N. C., & Headrick Taylor, K. (2010). The changing social spaces of learning: Mapping new mobilities. *Review of Research in Education*, 34, 329–394.

Muhammad, G. E. (2012). Creating spaces for Black adolescent girls to "write it out!" *Journal of Adolescent & Adult Literacy*, 56(3), 203–211.

Sarkar, M., & Allen, D. (2007). Hybrid identities in Quebec hip-hop: Language, territory, and ethnicity in the mix. *Journal of Language, Identity, and Education*, 6(2), 117–130.

Stewart, M. A. (2014). Social networking, workplace, and entertainment literacies: The out-of-school literate lives of newcomer Latina/o adolescents. *Reading Research Quarterly, 49*(4), 365–369.

Vasudevan, L. M. (2006). Looking for angels: Knowing adolescents by engaging with their multimodal literacy practices. *Journal of Adolescent & Adult Literacy, 50*(4), 252–256.

Wissman, K. K. (2011). "Rise up!" Literacies, lived experiences, and identities within an in-school "other space." *Research in the Teaching of English, 45*(4), 405–438.

Wright, D. E., & Mahiri, J. (2012). Literacy learning within community action projects for social change. *Journal of Adolescent & Adult Literacy, 56*(2), 123–131.

Yi, Y. (2010). Adolescent multilingual writers' transitions across in-and out-of-school writing contexts. *Journal of Second Language Writing, 19*(1), 17–32.

7 "It Help[ed] Me Think Outside the Box"

Connecting Critical Pedagogy and Traditional Literacy in a Youth Mentoring Program[1]

Horace R. Hall and Beverly J. Trezek

> You guys [mentors and tutors] don't have to show up on Fridays and all that but you choose to and then you give us a chance to talk and I enjoyed it. And you know, I love the RTW program. . . . I love that they have energy and whatever and stuff like that 'cause sometimes you probably come down, sometimes sleepy or whatever. And they came in and like "Hey . . ." and all that (laughter). Yeah, kinda ups your spirit, gets you kinda happy and stuff like that and movin' with everything. "Oh, let's read." . . . I love seein' like the looks all on their faces, you know, there willing to help me. I enjoy their services."
>
> (Matthew, personal communication, May 5, 2012)

In this chapter, we describe how Matthew and other high school students experienced a youth-centered, school-based mentoring (SBM) program that positioned cultural knowledge and identity, academic skills, and social competence as central to its curriculum. This SBM program engaged adolescent youth in mentoring and tutoring sessions that were designed and implemented by professors and students in the College of Education from a local university. The program fostered collaborative relationships with high school mentees who had just as much to teach and contribute as their college-level mentors and tutors. The program's framework enabled mentees to develop a genuine sense of personal agency, confidence, and empowerment. The voices of mentees and their graduate student literacy tutors that emerged from interviews conducted by the authors offer rich accounts of participants' perceptions of the SBM program. Data from mentees and tutors revealed multiple factors that contributed to their regular program participation, and an analysis of data revealed information about the relationships formed and the synergy developed among and between mentees and tutors over the course of the program.

SITUATING THE WORK

Youth mentoring for elementary and secondary level students is one intervention that has been used widely for disrupting social and academic obstacles faced by African American youth (Boyd-Franklin & Franklin, 2000; Brooks, West-Olatunji, & Baker, 2005; Gordon, Iwamoto, Ward, Potts, & Boyd, 2009; Hall, 2006; Majors, 2001). Over the past 20 years, there has been substantial growth in national, state, and local programs that either emphasize youth mentoring as a primary focus or as one of numerous intervention methods (Barron-McKeagney, Woody, D., & D'Souza, 2002; DuBois & Karcher, 2005; Hall, 2006). Depending largely on the issues of their youth population, mentoring programs can concentrate on anything from literacy enhancement and social skill development to child-rearing preparation, vocational or occupational training, or physical education (Anderson & Blackwood, 2000; DuBois & Karcher, 2005; Foster, 2000; Irving, Moore, & Hamilton, 2003; Lee & Crammond, 1999; Sipe, 2002). Regardless of programmatic variance, youth mentoring generally is considered a vertically structured practice whereby a reliable, pro-social adult provides learning experiences to a youngster "lacking" personal guidance and support. However, more contemporary notions of youth mentoring are seen as reciprocal, cooperative, and youth centered.

In spite of generally recognized benefits associated with youth mentoring, SBM does bear its share of criticisms. This is particularly true of interventions that are deficit focused (Benson, 2003; Farmer, 2008; Hein, 2003; Liabo, Lucas, & Roberts., 2005). These are programs that have been designed based on the interpretation that the root causes of social dysfunction are located within the social deficiencies of young people and their families. Given this perspective, what tends to follow are culturally biased mediations largely based on what individuals are lacking rather than on the innate ability to change their lived circumstances as they see fit (Valencia, 1997). Concerning Black youth specifically, there is a dearth of evaluative studies that explore program design and effectiveness on students' internal agency and outlook on academic achievement (Brooks et al., 2005; Gordon et al., 2009). Without such inquiry, practitioners are repeatedly working without a blueprint—literally and metaphorically—when attempting to counter deficit-model interventions and to construct programmatic undertakings that assist Black students in reimagining their lives and taking ownership of their social and academic futures. Truly understanding the hindrances facing African American youth is not only essential in defying their negative societal and institutional experiences but also decisive in framing interventions that realistically assist this group in empowering their lives.

CONNECTING CRITICAL PEDAGOGY AND TRADITIONAL LITERACY

Strand 1: Critical Pedagogy

Developed by the first author in 2000, Reading Your World (RYW)[2] is a nonprofit, after-school SBM program that contracts its services to urban public high schools. These schools often are classified as Title I,[3] tend to be low performing with respect to state standards in reading and math, and generally house a majority of Black and/or Hispanic students from low-income families. Participation in RYW is voluntary for both mentees and mentors. Teachers and administrators who encourage students to join the program often describe potential participants as "low achieving," "underperforming," and/or "behavioral problems." As such, RYW is often expected to take a "missionary" stance to mentoring by converting young people into "model" students. Contrary to this assumption, the directors of RYW inform school leaders from the outset that the program is exclusively focused on addressing personal and institutional factors that lead students into such categories of deficit in the first place. Adult mentors are recruited from programs within the College of Education at a nearby university, and approximately two weeks prior to the program's launch, mentors are familiarized with the curriculum and trained to implement it.

RYW's curriculum draws on Freire's (1996) critical pedagogy and engages participants in reflecting on, questioning, and negotiating institutional processes of power and dominance that impact them directly or indirectly. Critical pedagogy compels students to become conscious of the world and one's experiences as historically created within specific power dynamics (Anderson & Irvine, 1993; McLaren, 1994). This pedagogical tool further assists students in understanding their cultural identities and developing oppositional discourses that redefine their lives from their own perspectives (Giroux, 2001). Through the use of critical pedagogical activities, mentors and mentees collectively engage in group dialogue of everyday texts that include analyses of media and how they convey information about cultural spaces and ethnic groups.

In the act of co-constructing knowledge, mentees and mentors expose institutional contradictions and seek to understand how dominant ideologies influence daily life choices (Freire, 1998; Shor & Freire, 1987). Mentoring infused with facets of critical pedagogy also holds the potential for producing balanced mentee-mentor relationships that enable participants to determine their own pursuits and to make their own choices (Freire, 1997). With an emphasis on seeing one's self and others as fully human and building collaborative mentee-mentor relationships, critical pedagogy becomes a necessary theoretical basis in challenging culturally deterministic frameworks and deficit-focused interventions. Even though RYW was designed primarily to assist adolescents in advancing self- and community awareness, when the program was implemented in one particular high school setting, an additional need became realized—the enhancement of necessary literacy skills for youth participants—specifically reading. Thus, a traditional literacy component was added to the existing curriculum for this group of mentees.

Strand 2: Traditional Literacy

For decades, researchers have documented gaps in reading-related skills that surface even before children begin school and in many cases expand thereafter (e.g., Hart & Risley, 1999). The fact that only one-third of eighth grade students in the U.S. are reading at a proficient level may be enough to give anyone pause, but for African American students the situation is even more distressing. According to the results of the National Assessment of Educational Progress (National Center for Education Statistics, 2009), only 16 percent of African American fourth graders and 14 percent of African American eighth graders performed at or above the proficient level in 2009. In viewing the results for African Americans specifically, these students performed, on average, six percentage points lower than females on reading assessments in fourth grade and nine points lower in eighth grade.

Examining the preliminary findings of the most recent National Assessment of Educational Progress assessment for the nation's 12th graders illustrates a similar pattern of performance. For example, these findings revealed a 30-point score gap on the 12th grade reading assessment between Black and White students. As with previous findings, there is also an achievement gap[4] when comparing the reading scores of Black male and female students, with females scoring approximately 10 points higher. When viewing 12th graders performing above the 75th percentile in reading, only 4 percent of these students were Black (National Center for Education Statistics, 2013).

In a recent meta-analytic review of interventions for adolescent struggling readers, Scammacca et al. (2007) indicate that adolescent learners continue to benefit from targeted literacy interventions at both the word and text level. Furthermore, the National Reading Panel (2000) reported that balanced, remedial literacy instruction should focus on developing skills in five core competencies: phonemic awareness, phonics, fluency, vocabulary, and comprehension. A curriculum that has been designed to provide intensified, accelerated, remedial reading instruction to students in third grade and higher is Corrective Reading-Decoding (Engelmann et al., 1999).

Through the use of carefully sequenced lessons and easy-to-follow teaching scripts within the curriculum, students are engaged in a variety of activities including those focused on: (1) applying phonetic decoding strategies to read words in isolation and in connected text, (2) reading with increased accuracy and rate, and (3) improving the ability to answer oral and written comprehension questions about selections read. Research findings reveal the overall effectiveness of the Corrective Reading-Decoding program in meeting the reading needs of remedial students in general (see Przychodzin-Havis et al., 2005 for review), and those enrolled in middle and high school specifically (Benner, Nelson, Stage, & Ralston, 2011; Lingo, Slaton, & Jolivette, 2006; Marchand Martella, Martella, Bettis, & Blakely, 2004; Marchand Martella, Martella, Orlob, & Ebey, 2000; Peterson, Marchand-Martella, & Martella, 2008).

Based on the results of screening assessments administered, mentees received small group or one-on-one instruction from the Corrective Reading-Decoding curriculum (Engelmann et al., 1999) or engaged in comprehension instruction related to a popular novel. Regardless of their literacy curricular placement, students also engaged in career and college readiness activities (e.g., completing career inventories, participating in campus tours, and observing college courses). A team of graduate and undergraduate students from the university's College of Education volunteered to serve as mentors for the critical pedagogy strand of the program or as literacy tutors for the traditional literacy strand of the program. In both cases, these college students received ongoing training and support from the program directors and authors—one a professor in educational policy studies and research and the other a professor in special education. A professor in counseling coordinated additional graduate student volunteers to provide career and college readiness sessions for the high school participants and their parents.

BUILDING BRIDGES—IMPLEMENTING A COMMUNITY-UNIVERSITY PARTNERSHIP

Over the course of two consecutive school years (2010–2012), RYW-Literacy (the revised name of the program that indicated the dual-strand curriculum) was implemented with approximately 20 high school students. The program involved students from a large, urban high school located in an economically stressed community. The student body was approximately 99 percent African American, reflecting the neighborhood's demographics. Teacher and staff composition was substantially more diverse at 45 percent White, 40 percent Black, and 8 percent Hispanic, with the remaining unspecified. Over the last several years, the high school struggled with poor student attendance and behavioral issues, combined with high suspension rates. During the course of the program's operation, the high school was on academic probation with below-average standardized test scores in reading and math.

The school's assistant principal and dean of curriculum recruited students for program participation based on their marginal school attendance and low-level reading achievement. The program operated out of two academic settings during the two-year period: the students' high school and a local university. Program sessions were held weekly for a total of three hours, with 90 minutes devoted to each curricular strand. In year one, a six-week pilot program was developed, and both critical and traditional literacy sessions were held Saturday mornings on the campus of the university. During the second year, the 90-minute critical literacy sessions occurred on Friday afternoons at the students' high school; however, the 90-minute traditional literacy sessions continued to be offered on Saturdays at the university campus. A total of 12 critical literacy and 9 traditional literacy sessions were offered during the second year of the program.

College students were offered the opportunity to participate in RYW-Literacy and serve as either mentors or tutors to fulfill the field experience requirements for their educational foundations or special education literacy courses. Each year, a culminating event also was held to offer mentors, mentees, program directors, and community members the opportunity to engage in dialogue regarding program experiences and to share viewpoints on student success and growth. While the program was not designed originally as a research study, the authors of this chapter initiated an inquiry that involved conducting in-depth, semi-structured, individual interviews with both high school student mentees and their literacy tutors. Essentially, we wanted to garner insights into participants' perspectives of and experiences with the RYW-Literacy program and evaluate program effectiveness.

Interviews with participants were conducted during the second year of the program. Mentees were invited to participate if they had attended at least 50 percent of the mentoring and literacy sessions conducted during that year. Only three high school mentees participated in the interviews. One had parental permission to participate in the study and provided assent. Because the remaining two participants were 18 years old, they were able to consent individually to be involved in the study. Literacy tutor volunteers also were recruited for the research investigation, and while a total of 13 provided consent to participate, due to scheduling and time constraints only seven interviews were conducted.

All individual interviews were audio recorded, and following interview sessions, verbatim transcripts were prepared by a graduate assistant to allow for data analysis. The authors then compared the resulting transcripts to the audio recordings to ensure accuracy and provided editing as needed. In reviewing the data, we were guided by two essential questions: (1) what factors contributed to participants' (i.e., mentees and tutors) consistent involvement in the program, and (2) what were participants' perceptions of the program? In addressing this query, we offer a dualistic programmatic that can support individuals in ascertaining what is advantageous or futile—in theory and practice—for designing well-defined program structures that mutually serve in outlining the literacy issues of African American youth while working with them to build personal agency and empowerment within their respective lives and communities.

MENTEE RESPONSES TO RYW-LITERACY

The authors were first interested in addressing the previously listed guiding questions from the perspective of mentees. The following interview passages from these youngsters speak to three significant aspects of RYW-Literacy that fundamentally emerged out of the intersection between curricular Strands 1 and 2: (1) critical pedagogy, (2) literacy development, and (3) mentor–mentee relationships.

Critical Pedagogy

In its application, critical pedagogy involves three main subsets that fall under the umbrella of what Freire termed "problem-posing education": dialogue, critique, and praxis (Freire, 1996). Dialogue entails students and educators voicing their social realities and examining lived experiences. This process is used to transcend traditional classroom settings where a culture of silence often permeates. Critique is the methodical analysis of both society and self with a focus on analyzing inequity, exploitation, and domination as related to the social constructs of race, class, and gender, for example. Praxis is the realization of how one's identity is attached to culture, political struggle, and human freedom coupled with reenvisioning one's self and community. David, a sophomore at the time, offered his impression of Strand 1:

> It gives you a better understanding of yourself, you know, to be real with you, if nobody else. And um, you know, it breaks downs the big things and make 'em seem simple. Um, like the Friday sessions that we have, you know, we talk about real stuff and that's what I like. . . . It um, help me think outside the box because last year I ain't really know what I wanted to be when I got older. Now I know. I know two things I'm considering about. Helping [our city] is one.
> (Personal communication, May 5, 2012)

In both programmatic runs, Strand 1 first involved establishing a culture of trust between mentees and mentors. Trust was viewed as a necessary component for building meaningful youth-adult partnerships, particularly as group discussions often veered toward sharing personal narratives. Trust building was something that began at the outset of the program and continually evolved throughout Strand 2. Trust was deemed vital as we understood that the classroom space needed to be one of freedom, autonomy, and humanism, where mentors and tutors were not superior beings with singular position, knowledge, or authority (Freire, 1997). On the contrary, program meetings involved mentors sharing their own personal stories of accomplishment, failure, and resilience. As mentors shared who they were, mentees started to open up and divulge their own lives. These forged relationships of mutual respect and care would later carry over into RYW-Literacy tutoring sessions.

With trust relatively established and growing, mentors and mentees then began assessing the roles that individuals, systems, and structures play in long-standing social inequities. Dialoguing about connections between lived experiences and the cultural world, mentors and mentees collectively interrogated unequal power relations and the existent status quo while visualizing possibilities for institutional and personal transformation—what David refers to as "talk about real stuff and that's what I like. . . . It um, help me think outside the box" (personal communication, May 5, 2012). For example, several program meetings during the second year were geared toward actively exploring the notion that schools are emblematic of the broader meta-culture. Within group sessions, participants drew comparisons between larger societal problems (i.e., poverty, high unemployment rates, and the overrepresentation of Black males in the penal system) and those within the smaller context of schooling (i.e., high suspension, expulsion, and dropout rates; inadequate school funding; and disproportionate referral and transfers into special education services). It is important to note that not only did mentees feel that they could openly voice their opinions within program meetings, but were quite adept at identifying organic links between schools and society. Matthew, a senior, commented:

> Well I come on Friday 'cause I enjoy the little conversations we have. Like we talk about what's going on with [the neighborhood] and about bettering ourselves and stuff like that. Like things we see everyday, you know. Things that people talk about but they never address the issue to anyone else they just talk amongs . . . you know, the situation among theirselves. And you know we kinda got an open insight on, you know, expressing our opinions. (Personal communication, May 5, 2012)

Larry, a senior, also affirmed:

> Y'all know how to talk to people. There's like teachers that try to put you out of class and whatever. Y'all know how to sit down, help a person out. (Personal communication, May 5, 2012)

In contrast to institutionalized silencing, or putting students "out of class" as Larry asserts (personal communication, May 5, 2012), Strand 1 functioned to construct a trusting learning environment where "open insight" (Matthew, personal communication May 5, 2012) enabled young people to build on their own innate capacity to be independent, critical thinkers who could openly externalize their ideas about the world and their nascent position within it.

Literacy Development

As previously noted, the academic divide between Black students and their White counterparts is a seriously persisting issue, distinctively with respect to reading proficiency. Educators, researchers, and policy makers have long pursued appropriate strategies and evidence-based research for assisting African American students with literacy skills. Given that mentees came into the program with a range of literacy needs, there had to be instruction to address this variation. As such, the Strand 2 curricula employed direct instruction in phonics, reading fluency, and reading comprehension skills as well as fostered the development of receptive and expressive language abilities. Initially, most of the mentees were unenthusiastic about this "scholastic" program component, particularly given that assistance in this area was not something they openly admitted to needing. Indeed, there were palpable feelings of shame or embarrassment among these high school students who were reading at an intermediate grade level or below. Despite this, the trust that was fostered in advance helped mentees shed their walls of resistance and engage the program's second strand. Mentors also expressed to mentees the essentialism of seeing and understanding intersections between deciphering the often abstract sociopolitical world and actually being able to read written words of the physical world.

While Strand 1 sessions prompted mentees to ponder the necessity of being well-developed readers of their environment, Strand 2 compelled them to be literate, interpretive learners who could reach beyond their high school academic experience.

David, who participated in the Corrective Reading-Decoding instruction, commented:

> I had my teacher, my 8th grade teacher, she sat down with me like after school every day.... You know, she sat down with me and she really helped me, you know, to catch me up. And I really appreciated that from her. So, that's the same thing here. And I know if you need help, why is you too proud to say it? You know because I'm not too proud to admit that I need help.... When I need help, I'm not scared to ask. You know, and that's something that we should take in [the neighborhood] and you know, spread around. If you need help, you shouldn't be scared to ask. But hows you's goin' to progress in life? And, you know, I mean you in college and you still reading at like freshman, you know, probably an 8th grade level, you know. So that's what I'm doin' this whole four years, if I can stay with the program, to see, you know, I want to be great, you know, great, excellent reader so I can look at going off to college with a full head. (Personal communication, May 5, 2012)

It was key for RYW-Literacy to create viable but enjoyable reading instruction for students who somehow entered high school without having foundational skills in reading. Therefore, the Corrective Reading-Decoding curriculum was used to allow mentees the time to practice and master individual skills before additional information and complexities were taught. Direct instruction techniques were used to help mentees convert print to sound and develop the phonologic processing pathways that they previously struggled to acquire when learning to read.

While a larger portion of the mentees were identified as struggling readers (about two-thirds), there was a smaller body of students who had adequate reading skills for their grade level and simply needed an extra push to engage and excel at reading. For these students, novel study was their group activity. Through this instruction, mentees were asked to analyze relatively short sections of text with multiple readings completed over several instructional lessons. These students read *The Hunger Games* (Collins,

2008), which was grade and ability appropriate. Matthew, who participated in novel study, shared his opinion of this instruction:

> I liked the novel study. Like the *Hunger Games*, I didn't really like know too much about the *Hunger Games* 'cause there was some book I was suggestin' but they're like, "No, let's read the *Hunger Games*, (laughter) let's read the *Hunger Games*.' So ahh . . . you know, we like on Chapter 8 or whatever in the book and it's been going pretty good. (Personal communication, May 5, 2012)

Through text-based questions and discussion, students were directed to examine and appreciate various aspects of the book. With tutor assistance, mentees highlighted key vocabulary terms that had their meanings shaped by different contexts. Tutors instructed mentees to pay attention to various aspects of the text including syntax, form, characterizations, descriptions, dialogue, and comprehension. The novel study supported this small group of independent readers by introducing them to a genre of literacy that allowed them to make connections from their own experience to the text while enhancing vocabulary and receptive and expressive language proficiencies.

MENTOR AND TUTOR RELATIONSHIPS

Educator enthusiasm is generally recognized as one of the most needed and indispensable qualities in effective instruction (Armbruster, Lehr, & Osborn, 2001; Pressley, 2003). By being energetic and vibrant, educators can generate learners' interest and eagerness to participate and explore classroom curriculum. In both RYW-Literacy programmatic strands, the authors understood "energy" as an essential tool for bringing about increased student performance and learning motivation as well as positive attitudes toward learning. David revealed his observation of tutor and mentor energy:

> They [tutors and mentors] are what keeps me going because they energy, the way they present theyself, you know, it's real nice. They got so much energy like when they reading, when um they ask me to read I be like y'all making me want to read now, y'all give me . . . um like they really want to help me like they my teacher, you know? So I'd be like if they can give me that much energy and they can try to help me, I should try to be, you know, as helpful to them as I can. You know, don't give them a hard time because they don't gotta do this, you know? (Personal communication, May 5, 2012)

The authors were well aware that students participating in RYW-Literacy were coming from a learning environment that was overwhelmed by emotional and behavioral issues. The secondary school these students attended had long witnessed high suspension rates with low student achievement outcomes. Thus, RYW-Literacy's programmatic efforts had to defy the strong probability that classroom learning for these students was one of boredom, alienation, and false competition. It was necessary for tutors and mentors to embody a powerful contagion of enthusiasm on student engagement by conveying passion and creating a positive collective of emotions. Whether or not tutor and mentor "energy" was a strong predictor of learners' extrinsic motivation, it proved impactful on a relative level based on the aforementioned mentee comments. Nevertheless, it is clear from program meetings, within both strands, that student learning was less about competition, performance, and rewards and more about a psychological investment in their own cognitive engagement and willingness to master literacy tasks. Matthew spoke to this explicitly in his interview:

> The first time that I came to the literacy program . . . there was a guy, Mr. Humphrey. He was saying something about a little job or something like that. Then uh . . . I was looking forward to like get some money and whatever. But then I really didn't know what the program was about, so you know, I wanted to participate in it. And then after awhile, being in like the RTW program, it was like way much more than that and stuff like that. Like I didn't really like care about the money too much and whatever. 'Cause I was like uhh . . . you know like wow you know whatever like to read aloud and like better my comprehension skills. And I've been getting better with reading with this program. You know, progresses. (Personal communication, May 5, 2012)

Here, Matthew is referring to the second year of RYW-Literacy's collaboration with the students' high school. The school's extracurricular program directors recognized that students often work after school and on weekends to provide much-needed supplementary income to their families' households. Yet, to keep them on academic track for graduation, school directors negotiated with students' parents the opportunity of earning a total of $250 for consistently attending all of the RYW-Literacy sessions.

In spite of studies that have shown how extrinsic motivations impair learners' interest and enjoyment in academics, the monetary arrangement between the school and students should be understood within this specific economic context. What the authors discovered, however, is that a majority of RYW youth participants, including Matthew, developed a curiosity and drive toward mastering their reading of text and the world equal to or beyond monetary compensation.

TUTOR RESPONSES TO RYW-LITERACY

Based on her experiences as a former high school special educator, remedial reading instructor, and instructor of special education literacy courses at the university level, the second author established several goals for the field experience opportunity offered to college-level graduate tutors. Based on Chall's (1996) interactive model, learning to read is viewed as a hierarchical, developmental process that involves the coordination of bottom-up, code-related skills associated with word identification (e.g., knowledge of letter-sound relationships) and top-down, language-based abilities related to comprehension (e.g., background knowledge, oral language, and vocabulary). While code-related skills typically are mastered by third grade, students who continue to struggle in this area often are identified as poor readers or those with reading disabilities (e.g., Stanovich, 1988; Wagner, Torgesen, & Rashotte, 1994; Wagner et al., 1997). Therefore, several goals were established for the field experience including: (1) to reinforce the philosophical orientation of the course, (2) to provide practical solutions for working with high school struggling readers, (3) to highlight tenets of diagnostic teaching, and (4) to demystify the high school teaching experience for university students seeking dual licensure in elementary and K–12 special education. The following excerpts from interviews with the tutors are used to explore goal attainment and gain insights into factors contributing to their participation.

GOAL ATTAINMENT

Specific comments from the tutors revealed that the philosophical approach to reading studied in their special education literacy course was reinforced by observations of and interactions with the high school student mentees. To illustrate her understanding of Chall's theory and need to address prerequisite abilities in the context of tutoring, Danielle commented:

> [T]hat just made me remember like from your class, like the ladder? I think about the ladder where the rungs like, as they're learning how like, the different phases of reading, um, the stages of reading. . . . Chall's reading stages of development, where like if one rung is missing, how it like really messes up your comprehension and everything else along the way. You have to backtrack and get, fix that rung, or nothing else is going to really stick along the way. And it's absolutely true. So like if you can't read in second grade, you're not going to be able to read. Just because you get older doesn't mean you suddenly get a skill like you never had. (Personal communication, May 5, 2012)

Further reinforcing key concepts discussed in class, tutors frequently expressed strong feelings regarding the reading challenges experienced by their high school mentees. They also commented on the lack of attention on the part of teachers to addresses these issues earlier, further reinforcing key concepts discussed in class. As Hailey stated,

> I would say they've just been passed through, passed through, passed through without, you know, cus' it's not like they're not capable, it's just

that, "Okay, go ahead, go ahead" and they just moved up grade levels without learning the basics. (Personal communication, May 5, 2012)

Mia offered a similar sentiment as she reflected on the possible limitations of the mentees' reading abilities:

> I think really the only thing that confounds me sometimes is just like how these kids have gotten to this point. And just meeting them, and talking with them, and engaging with them and knowing, you know, thinking of like three books off the top of my head that I know they would love and that would be great and that I think they would really relate to. Working with them and being like, I don't know when or if you would ever be able to read that. (Personal communication, May 5, 2012)

Comments offered by literacy tutors also revealed that they appreciated the opportunity to participate actively in their field experience and practice implementing strategies learned in class. As Carrie commented,

> I really felt like I was helping or making a difference with these students. Um, a lot of times when I go into schools for field experience, you're kind of like, pushed to the side, or you sit in the corner, you know you don't really get to interact with the kids. And in this case I was able to like work with them. (Personal communication, May 29, 2012)

Tutors also recognized that through the field experience, they were developing skills in diagnostic teaching that were applicable not only to the work being completed with their mentee but were transferable to other teaching situations. Jenna specifically reflected on this during her interview when stating,

> Well we got to apply exactly like what we learned. And I told you I'm actually kind of using it! I see myself, you know, I'm not even thinking about it, but we're doing a fifth grade book and I'm sitting there and I'm like, "OK, here's vocab. And here's this for this . . ." And, you know, "This could be good for imagery." And applying what I'm learning now and what we learned with you. (Personal communication, May 29, 2012)

Despite initial concerns about working with high school students, tutors saw that engaging in the RTW-Literacy field experience was valuable to their development as teachers. As Danielle indicated, "I've heard horror stories with high-schoolers, so I really wanted that experience" (personal communication, May 5, 2012). Mia echoed these feelings when stating that she was "apprehensive about working with the older kids" and "nervous about the older kids" but in the end commented, "[T]hey've been amazing" (personal communication, May 5, 2012). Tutors also commented that offering instructional sessions at the university might have impacted the high school students' attitudes toward instruction, thus providing a more positive experience for novice teachers.

> I wonder if this would be as successful if we went to their side, where they might already have a different kind of attitude or persona. Like, you're coming into MY classroom or MY school and you're going to help me? I feel like we might not get the same response if they didn't come to [the university] . . . that putting them in here puts them out of their element and kinda gives us a different side of them. (Denise, personal communication, May 29, 2014)

Related to the goal of demystifying the high school teaching experience, several tutors expressed that participating in the RTW-Literacy program caused them to reconsider teaching at the high school level in the future. As Carrie indicated:

> [E]xperiencing working with these umm like high school kids and wondering like how they made it this far without being able to read or with having like really minimal reading skills or literacy skills, like that makes me think of like—I guess—puts in perspective for what kind of teacher I want to be and has really opened up me to the idea of working with umm high school kids. (Personal communication, May 29, 2012)

Mia also spoke about a change in perspective and how her teaching interests evolved as a result of program participation:

> When I entered the program, my statement says that I want to do very young—early intervention, Pre-K, K, maybe first grade—and work primarily with students umm on the autism spectrum. Which I still love! That's, you know, that's definitely a passion of mine. But I have always had sort of, you know, maybe I should be teaching English, kind of thing. So, really engaging with kids and talking about literature has been a really interesting experience, and has really, umm, yeah, is perhaps you know, now I'm thinking maybe middle school, maybe the high school, you know um, reading resource something, so yeah, so we'll see. (Personal communication, May 5, 2012)

PROGRAM PARTICIPATION

While the majority of tutors indicated that they initially were interested in participating in the program to earn the required field experience hours for their literacy course, when specifically asked what factors contributed to their continued participation in the program, nearly all comments indicated that the high school students' commitment to the program strongly influenced their decisions to continue to participate. As Amelia stated:

> I noticed that the kids that I was working with came every week. So I didn't want to just stop coming cause I appreciated that they came every week. And I didn't want it to look like I didn't care, er like, I wasn't interested, because they showed good attendance. (Personal communication, May 24, 2012)

Carrie offered a similar comment when reflecting on her commitment and level of participation in the program:

> I really wanted to commit to the program because I felt like the kids were committing. Umm, they were coming on a Saturday morning I felt I should be able to come on a Saturday morning. So that was one of the reasons like I stayed with it. (Personal communication, May 29, 2012)

Interviews with several tutors also revealed that their own life experiences played a role in the decision to participate. As Danielle commented:

> I feel connected to the community. I'm not from that community, but I'm from like an impoverished neighborhood. From like, the local high school, you're not expected to kind of graduate from that high school.... And, the expectations were not that they would like amount to much. And sometimes when those expectations are out there, it's like a self-fulfilling prophecy. So, I really wanted to come on Saturday and kinda see what was actually going on and where these kids were at, and that's basically why I wanted to volunteer. (Personal communication, May 5, 2012)

Further reflecting on personal experiences, tutors also offered their perceptions on the experiences provided through the RYW-Literacy program and the potential impact of the information shared on their mentees. A comment from Denise best captures this insight:

> I know we had no part in this, but I thought the one Saturday where they saw presentations from other grad students about finding money for college and giving them different websites for college.... I really enjoyed that for them because it reminded me ... I was uh, I guess I was a sophomore in college, I was a McNair Scholar, so watching that presentation, being a McNair Scholar, it just, it didn't change, I guess, it did change my life. It just kind of put a little seed in my head of like, you can go get your Master's and you can even get your Ph.D. maybe.

And that's always in my head now. And I feel like, when I was watching those presentation, maybe they weren't listening to everything, maybe some things went over their head, but we were like, putting little seeds, little thoughts in their head. And I think that's what's really important in the whole RYW program. (Personal communication, May 29, 2012)

In sharing the mentees' comments regarding the level of "energy" the tutors brought to the program, Jenna indicated, "I felt like they [the mentees] brought energy here" (personal communication, May 29, 2012), whereas Denise provided a more specific example of the mentees' notion of energy:

I think that when they're referring to our energy, I think, I think of the times where we took attendance and we got our books and then we had a walk from here to the classroom. And I think that's what they are talking about because those walks weren't [high school] students and [university] tutors like walking and following. We were always as a group walking together. (Personal communication, May 29, 2012)

Overall, the comments offered by tutors during interview sessions clearly illustrated that the goals established for program participation were being met. Their statements revealed that providing literacy instruction through the Corrective Reading-Decoding program or novel study reinforced Chall's (1996) interactive model of reading development and offered them opportunities to explore curricular interventions that provide practical solutions for working with high school struggling readers. Furthermore, these experiences served to demystify the high school teaching experience and encouraged several tutors to reconsider working with this population of students in the future.

LESSONS REFRAMED: IMPLICATIONS FOR RESEARCH AND PRACTICE

In light of a dearth of research on well-designed youth interventions for moderating the range of social and academic challenges facing African American school-age youth, the contribution of the programmatic blueprint presented here rests in its ability to submit an anti-deficit mentoring model influenced by elements of critical pedagogy and traditional literacy within a specific cultural context. With an emphasis on seeing one's self and others as fully human, critical pedagogy and traditional literacy development become two vital, interconnected theoretical foundations for disrupting deficit-focused youth interventions and addressing the need for quality literacy education for underserved populations.

Despite a profusion of scholarly literature observing the debilitating socio-emotional issues confronting black students, RYW-Literacy mentees and tutors familiarized us with how these youth can and will react constructively when supported by youth-centered programmatic goals that focus on cultural identity, academic skills, and social competence of this ethnic group. Throughout the course of RYW-Literacy during both academic years, the authors observed mentees' developing sense of agency and confidence, realizing their voice and an awareness of their academic capacities that conceivably would not be inspired without an educational blueprint that provided sufficient time for these youth to render critical decisions and the ability to understand the different literacies that influence their lives.

Given a plethora of literature that underscores the social, political, and economic difficulties of African American youngsters, there need to be increased examinations of well-outlined mentoring models that authentically alleviate this group's circumstances. Youth workers, educators, and mentors should have an expansive array of effective evidence-based models they can utilize or modify depending on the needs and issues of the youngsters they are collaborating with. Such inquiries also may serve to offset stereotypical representations that these young people are intellectually indifferent and socially withdrawn. While this descriptive report seeks to fill the research gap on mentoring and tutoring pursuits conducive for African American adolescents, further inquiries might focus on mentoring across cultural communities and how critical pedagogy and literacy development as vehicles of voice and agency function in specific locations of marginalization and isolation.

The youngsters featured in this chapter exemplify a larger body of students that exist outside the boundaries of interventions that strive to understand how relation-based mediations can serve young people living through harsh circumstances. Fundamental to RYW-Literacy's programmatic efforts was the contemporary perception of youth mentoring as reciprocal and collaborative, with mentees having just as much to teach and to contribute as their mentors and tutors. Educators and youth workers must work to bring these realities to the head of their daily practices so that they and broader audiences can further develop blueprints that distinguish how African American adolescent youth, in the face of ostracism, use their experiences, abilities, and talents to navigate and endure both school and non-school settings.

Critical pedagogy combined with traditional literacy skill improvement plays an integral role in rethinking culturally deterministic frameworks and deficit-focused mediation practices. The programmatic blueprint outlined here evidences the empowering and transformative spirit of literacy and critical thinking and how, if applied authentically by students, educators, mentors, tutors, and other youth workers, it has the potential to afford youth from any background a breathing space to flourish and openly express their realities. From this, we can bear witness to students strengthening their intellectualism through the reading of their world and text, with the hope and ability of finding a space for them in our society as they see fit.

NOTES

1. Acknowledgement: We would like to thank the students, mentors, and tutors involved in the RYW-Literacy program and those who agreed to be participate in the interview sessions. We also would like to thank our collaborator, Dr. Erin Mason, for leading the counseling students in developing the career and college readiness activities used in the program.
2. Pseudonyms for the program and participants are used throughout this chapter. Actual names are not used to protect the identities of the participants. As such, references to identifiable information within participants' comments (e.g., name of school, neighborhood, or individual) have been blinded.
3. Title I, Part A of the 1965 Elementary and Secondary Education Act (ESEA) provides monetary support to states and school districts to meet the needs of academically at-risk students. The goal of Title I is to provide supplementary instructional activities and services that aid students identified as failing or most at risk of failing state performance standards in mathematics, reading, and writing. ESEA was reauthorized as the No Child Left Behind Act (NCLB) of 2001 under President George W. Bush.
4. Ladson-Billings (2006) refers to the achievement "gap" as a "one of the most pressing education-policy challenges that states currently face" and "a matter of race and class" (p. 3). The "gap" itself, according to Ladson-Billings, is often measured by standardized testing but must also include comparisons between African Americans and Latina/os with incomes comparable to those of Whites in areas of dropout rates, enrollment in honors classes, and college, graduate, and professional school admittance.

REFERENCES

Anderson, G. L., & Irvine, P. (1993). Informing critical literacy with ethnography. In C. Lankshear & P. L. McLaren (Eds.), *Critical literacy: Politics, praxis and the postmodern* (pp. 81–104). Albany: State University of New York Press.

Anderson, V., & Blackwood, J. (2000). M&M: A sweet deal for students and faculty. *Principal Leadership, 1*(2), 46–48.

Armbruster, B. B., Lehr, F., & Osborn, J. (2001). *Put reading first: The research building blocks for teaching children to read*. Washington, DC: U.S. Department of Education. Retrieved from https://lincs.ed.gov/publications/pdf/PRFbooklet.pdf

Barron-McKeagney, T., Woody, J. D., & D'Souza, H. J. (2002). Mentoring at-risk Latino children and their parents: Analysis of the parent child relationship and family strength. *Families in Society, 83*, 285–292. doi: 10.1606/1044-3894.19

Benner, G. J., Nelson, J. R., Stage, S. A., & Ralston, N. C. (2011). The influence of fidelity of implementation on the reading outcomes of middle school students experiencing reading difficulties. *Remedial and Special Education, 32*(1), 79–88. doi: 10.1177/0741932510361265

Benson, P. L. (2003). *Developmental assets and asset-building community: Conceptual and empirical foundations*. In R. M. Lerner & P. L. Benson (Eds.), Developmental assets and asset-building communities: Implications for research, policy, and practice (pp. 19–43). Norwell, MA: Kluwer Academic Publishers. doi: 10.1007/978-1-4615-0091-9

Boyd-Franklin, N. B., & Franklin, A. J. (2000). *Boys into men: Raising our African American teenage sons*. New York, NY: E. P. Dutton. doi: 10.2307/3211243

Brooks, M., West-Olatunji, C., & Baker, J. (2005). Use of rites of passage programs to foster resilience in African-American students. Missouri School Counselor Association: *The Counseling Interviewer, 37*(4), 54–59.

Chall, J. S. (1996). *Stages of reading development* (2nd ed.). New York, NY: McGraw-Hill. doi: 10.107/s0142716400005166

Collins, S. (2008). *The hunger games.* New York, NY: Scholastic Press.

DuBois, D. L., & Karcher, M. J. (Eds.). (2005). *Handbook of youth mentoring.* Thousand Oaks, CA: SAGE.

Engelmann, S., Meyer, L., Carnine, L., Becker, W., Eisele, J., & Johnson, G. (1999). *Corrective reading decoding level B: Decoding strategies.* Columbus, OH: Science Research Associates (SRA).

Farmer, E. (2008). From passive objects to active subjects: Young people, performance and possibility. *Journal of the Community Development Society, 39*(2), 1–15. doi: 10.1080/15575330809489731

Foster, B. L. (2000). Being there. *Washingtonian, 35*(12), 86–91.Freire, P. (1996). *Pedagogy of the oppressed* (2nd ed.). New York, NY: Continuum.

Freire, P. (1997). *Mentoring the mentor: A critical dialogue with Paulo Freire, 60.* New York, NY: Peter Lang.

Freire, P. (1998). *Pedagogy of freedom: Ethics, democracy, and civic discourse.* Lanham, MD: Rowman & Littlefield Publishers, Inc.

Giroux, H. A. (2001). *Theory and resistance in education: Towards a pedagogy for the opposition.* Westport, CT, & London: Bergin & Garvey.

Gordon, D. M., Iwamoto, D., Ward, N., Potts, R., & Boyd, E. (July 2009). Mentoring urban Black middle-school male students: Implications for academic achievement. *Journal of Negro Education, 78*(3), 277–228.

Hall, H. R. (2006). *Mentoring young men of color: Meeting the needs of African American and Latino students.* Lanham, MD: Rowman & Littlefield Publishing. doi: 10.5860/choice.44-3979

Hart, B., & Risley, T. R. (1999). *The social world of children learning to talk.* Baltimore, MD: Brookes Publishing.

Hein, K. (2003). Enhancing the assets for positive youth development: The vision values, and action agenda of the W.T. Grant Foundation. In R. M. Lerner & P. L. Benson (Eds.), *Developmental assets and asset-building communities: Implications for research, policy, and practice* (pp. 97–117). Norwell, MA: Kluwer Academic Publishers. doi: 10.1007/978-1-4615-0091-9_5

Irving, S. E., Moore, D. W., & Hamilton, R. J. (2003). Mentoring for high ability high school students. *Education & Training, 45,* 100–109. doi: 10.1108/00400910310464071

Ladson-Billings, G. (2006). From the achievement gap to the education debt: Understanding achievement in U.S. schools. *Educational Researcher, 35*(7), 3–12.

Lee, J., & Cramond, B. (1999). The positive effects of mentoring economically disadvantaged students. *Professional School Counseling, 2,* 172–178.

Liabo, K., Lucas, L., & Roberts, H. (2005). International: The U.K. and Europe. In D. L. DuBois & M. J. Karcher (Eds.). *Handbook of youth mentoring* (pp. 392–407). Thousand Oaks, CA: SAGE.

Lingo, A. S., Slaton, D. B., & Jolivette, K. (2006). Effects of Corrective Reading on the reading abilities and classroom behaviors of middle school students with reading deficits and challenging behavior. *Behavioral Disorders, 31*(3), 265–283.

Majors, R. G. (2001). *Educating our Black children: New directions and radical approaches*. London: Routlege Falmer.

Marchand-Martella, N., Martella, R. C., Bettis, D. F., & Blakely, M. (2004). Project Pals: A description of a high school-based tutorial program using Corrective Reading and peer-delivered instruction. *Reading and Writing Quarterly, 20*(2), 179–201. doi: 10.1080/10573560490264125

Marchand-Martella, N., Martella, R. C., Orlob, M., & Ebey, T. (2000). Conducting action research in a rural high school setting using peers as Corrective Reading instructors for students with disabilities. *Rural Special Education Quarterly, 19*(2), 20–30.

McLaren, P. (1994). *Life in schools: An introduction to critical pedagogy in the foundations of education* (2nd ed.). New York, NY: Longman. doi: 10.5860/choice.26-6389

National Center for Education Statistics. (2009). National Assessment of Educational Progress. Institute of Education Sciences, U.S. Department of Education, Washington, DC. Retrieved from http://nces.ed.gov/nationsreportcard/

National Center for Education Statistics. (2013). National Assessment of Educational Progress. Institute of Education Sciences, U.S. Department of Education, Washington, DC. Retrieved from http://nces.ed.gov/nationsreportcard/

National Reading Panel. (2000). *Report of the National Reading Panel: Teaching children to read–An evidence-based assessment of the scientific research literature on reading and its implications for reading instruction*. Jessup, MD: National Institute for Literacy at EDPubs.

Peterson, J. L., Marchand-Martella, N. E., & Martella, R. C. (2008). Assessing the effects of Corrective Reading Decoding B1 with a high school student with intellectual and developmental disabilities: A case study. *Journal of Direct Instruction, 8*(1), 41–52.

Pressley, M. (2003). A few things reading educators should know about instructional experiments. *The Reading Teacher, 57*(1), 64–71.

Przychodzin-Havis, A. M., Marchand-Martella, N. E., Martella, R. C., Miller, D. A., Warner, L., Leonard, B., & Chapman, S. (2005). An analysis of Corrective Reading research. *Journal of Direct Instruction, 5*(1), 37–65.

Scammacca, N., Roberts, G., Vaughn, S., Edmonds, M., Wexler, J., Reutebuch, C. K., & Torgesen, J. K. (2007). *Interventions for adolescent struggling readers: A meta-analysis with implications for practice*. Portsmouth, NH: RMC Research Corporation, Center on Instruction.

Shor, I., & Freire, P. (1987). *A pedagogy for liberation: Dialogues on transforming education*. Westport, CT: Bergin & Garvey.

Sipe, C. (2002). Mentoring programs for adolescents: A research summary. *Journal of Adolescent Health, 31*, 251–260. doi: 10.1016/s1054-139x(02)00498-6

Stanovich, K. E. (1988). The right and wrong places to look for the cognitive locus of reading disability. *Annals of Dyslexia, 38*, 154–157. doi: 10.1007/BF02648254

Valencia, R. R. (Ed.). (1997). *The evolution of deficit thinking: Educational thought and practice*. Washington, DC: Falmer Press.

Wagner, R. K., Torgesen, J. K., & Rashotte, C. A. (1994). Development of reading-related phonological processing abilities: New evidence of bidirectional causality from a latent variable longitudinal study. *Developmental Psychology, 30*, 73–87. doi: 10.1037//0012-1649.30.1.73

Wagner, R. K., Torgesen, J. K., Rashotte, C. A., Hecht, S. A., Barker, T. A., Burgess, S. R., . . . Garen, T. (1997). Changing relations between phonological processing abilities and word-level reading as children develop from beginning to skilled readers: A 5-year longitudinal study. *Developmental Psychology, 33*, 468–479. doi: 10.1037/0012-1649.33.3.468

8 Where Are They Now?
An Intergenerational Conversation on the Work of the Llano Grande Center for Research and Development

Francisco J. Guajardo, Miguel A. Guajardo, and Mark Cantú

HIGH SCHOOL STORIES

The Llano Grande Center for Research and Development was born in a classroom at Edcouch-Elsa High School (E-E HS) in rural South Texas as a college preparation program in response to chronically low levels of college attendance of local youth. The founders of the Llano Grande were themselves locals who had gone away to college, had traveled to different parts of the world, and returned with a new awareness of the possibilities for local youth in relation to higher education and community development. They nurtured a movement built on a curriculum focused on college preparation through the integration of community-based teaching and learning approaches intended to develop student academic skills, shape student personal and historical identities, and nurture a sense of hope for their future, the future of their families, and the future of their community. Within a generation, the organization gained acclaim from media outlets and attention from school districts and education nonprofits across the country because it had both reversed the endemic brain drain from this rural community and because it had re-culturalized the value system of teaching, learning, and college preparation. In short, Llano Grande reimagined the meaning of higher learning.

The systemic and chronically debilitating impact of the cultural incompatibilities (Cárdenas & Cárdenas, 1977) between children and the public schools in South Texas impelled the creation of the Llano Grande Center in the early 1990s. The authors of this article experienced this firsthand as they all claim to being treated as "individuals" when they first entered elementary school. "We were raised as an integral part of the family," said Miguel A. Guajardo. "But the school treats us, and all children, according to an ethos of the individual, consistent with the mythology of Americana, the extension of which is that you pull yourself up by the bootstraps," said Mark Cantú. The theory of incompatibility advanced by Cárdenas and Cárdenas in the 1970s suggested that a profound disconnect between Mexican American children and the schools they attended continues as status quo well into the 21st century. Llano Grande was born, in part, as an effort to rehabilitate that incompatibility. Llano Grande also was founded as a process through which children, families, and their community could find sources of strength through deep exploration of their stories and through examining their place in community and in history. The system of inquiry Llano Grande leads focused on whether the stories and experiences of our people are at the center of the culture of the school, of its curriculum, of its leadership development process, and of its day-to-day operation.

Llano Grande began as a college preparation program, where teachers helped position students from this rural and economically distressed community to gain admission into the most prestigious universities in the country. The organization did this by infusing place-based academic development such as community-based studies, oral histories, community asset mapping, and storytelling at the center of the college preparation program. It became clear from the beginning that the stories of our students were compelling, inspiring, and exciting, and the best schools in the country would be hard pressed to turn them down. After five years of this work, after placing several dozen Mexican American students in Ivy League universities, and after raising the college-going rate of local high school graduates from 28 to more than 60 percent, Llano Grande and the local high school got people's attention. Although the mainstream media framed the story as a feel-good American story, as a Horatio Alger-like "poor community overcomes the odds-type story," the Llano Grande leadership understood the story as a process of re-culturalizing our schools through a program focused on making the schools compatible with children, families, and the community. To us, this was, and continues to be, an issue of respect—cultural and historical respect and with an eye toward the future. This is the ethos of the Llano Grande Center.

The stories of José Luis, Carmen, and Mark in this chapter represent that reimagination. The three came into the Llano Grande work as students at E-E HS in the 1990s, each connecting as they took classes with E-E HS teachers who were part of the Llano Grande network. José Luis's first contact occurred through an 11th grade English class, Carmen's through a sophomore-level world history class, and Mark's through an 11th grade U.S. history course. While in high school, each engaged in meaningful community-based research initiatives as part of their course work and as part of their work with Llano Grande. José Luis led an asset mapping initiative where he learned how to identify the cultural and social assets of the community and then mentored younger high school students as they walked the streets of Edcouch and Elsa to collect data for the production of an asset map.

The economic landscape of this rural region is not dotted with industrial parks, shopping malls, or a thriving financial industry. Instead, the community asset map that José Luis and others constructed showed a different community reality. It reflected a range of cultural, social, and historical assets that do not quite fit the conventional framework of a community and economic development paradigm. Among the range of assets the students identified, two stood out most prominently. The first was story, which impressed the students as the modality through which most community elders engaged them. "They just wanted to tell stories," said José Luis. The second most important asset was the Spanish language. "And they mostly told stories in Spanish," said José Luis. On the strength of the asset identification research, Llano Grande set out to integrate the assets into the teaching, learning, youth leadership, and community development process. A few years later, Carmen and Mark would step into that work.

When Carmen was a junior in high school, she joined a group of students whose Spanish language proficiency was markedly advanced, and together they founded an economic enterprise that was a Spanish-language immersion institute. They developed a marketing plan, created a curriculum, and organized a cottage industry by building a network of monolingual Spanish-speaking families, mostly elderly couples, to serve as host homes for Spanish immersion students who would travel to South Texas from different parts of the country. Carmen's leadership in establishing the Spanish Institute would serve her well later in high school and in her career as an advocate for rural communities. Mark similarly stepped into the Llano Grande work when he took the idea of story from the community asset map and turned it into a story collection initiative through an oral history project focused on reconstructing the labor history of the community. By enlisting the networking skills of his grandmother, who had been a laborer in the community for many years, Mark and his classmates engaged in *pláticas* with several dozen elders and documented their stories. The oral history research validated the hard work of elders in the community, documented the long-standing tradition of hard work in this community, and celebrated the years of resiliency, hard work, and triumph in what had been mostly known as an impoverished community. The collective work José Luis, Carmen, and Mark engaged in as high school students contested the debilitating perception of their community as a place mired in poverty as it simultaneously began to craft a community narrative of strength and hope.

SITUATING THE WORK: STORY, METHOD, AND A THEORY OF CHANGE IN ACTION

The teaching and learning vision of Llano Grande inextricably links self, family, and community as core components of its college preparation program and guides a youth leadership that embraces a theory of change that identifies and develops the stories of students, their families, and the community as critical components. It views relationships as a pillar of their sociocultural and historical existence. It understands place as the centerpiece for learning, as place is defined by the community in which the students live, the place of origin of their family, or the place many students travel to as part of the migrant farm working experience of a good number of students in this community. The Llano Grande theory of change helps students understand relationships, assets, stories, self, and place through a politic grounded in respect for family and an ethic of behavior that respects the dignity and experiences of elders. The politic is driven by action, or a series of pedagogical practices that explore stories, celebrate the strengths of children, study the community in which students and their families live, and do all this as a central part of youth leadership development and college preparation. In this chapter, we use Freire's (1973) concept of praxis to respond to these two questions: Where are they now, and how did their engagement with Llano Grande shape their private and public voices? Through a series of *pláticas*, we examine their work as high school students, follow them through college, and look at how they approach work as young professionals. We are all research partners in this work.

The preponderance of data that informs this chapter spans an entire generation. It is based on the life stories of the past 20 plus years of Llano Grande alumni who came of age as youth community leaders through their work with the Llano Grande and emerged as young professionals who came back home. The stories we share can help readers understand their development as civically engaged young professionals as a way to add to the literature of youth and adult partnerships that strengthen the communities they serve. The stories and voices of the alumni, and the authors, constitute data interpreted through the use of grounded theory (Glaser & Strauss, 1967) and collaborative inquiry as a framework for data analysis. We use the stories as pedagogical tools to inform the practices of educational practitioners, community-building ventures, and organizing efforts. In sharing stories, we create a new reality that is not the story of others but our own. As such, we have the power to deconstruct, make sense of, and share (Guajardo & Guajardo, 2002, 2004; Lather, 1991; Scheurich, 1997). The stories inform a new consciousness shaped by lived experience and by the people we engage. The stories reveal blind spots, those ontological truths that are less than obvious and seldom realized in the absence of deep and perpetual reflection on one's journey (Maturana & Varela, 1987). The storytelling process honors how we first began to understand the world around us, by sitting at the coffee table with Mama and Papa Grande and/or with Grandma Socorro to listen to the stories they shared about life. The retelling of story in public creates a space for a new story to emerge, a space to make sense of the story, and a space to retell the story (Maturana & Varela, 1987).

We place ourselves in the middle of the stories as research partners and do not claim to be objective. These are our lived experiences. We intentionally engage in a reciprocal teaching and learning process and weave our experiences throughout the text. This research is as much about the authors as it is about the youth who grew up in the organization and the community. We share the space, the knowledge, and the power. We use critical constructivist epistemologies that challenge the notion of objectivity (Guajardo &

Guajardo, 2002, 2004; Hurtado, 2003; Lather, 1986; Trueba, 1999), a type of research that has gained traction in recent literature among Chicana/o methodological and epistemological research (Delgado Bernal, 1998; Guajardo & Guajardo, 2002; Pizarro, 1998; Pizarro & Montoya, 2002; Trueba, 1999; Villenas, 1996). These stories are informed by the history of our families and communities. Each story tells a truth that is not told to us but rather constructed by us with the understanding of self, family, and community. The reflections and stories create a new narrative informed through conscientization. We lean heavily on Freire's wisdom and awareness of human history, when he argued

> In truth, conscientization is a requirement of our human condition. It is one of the roads we have to follow if we are to deepen our awareness of our world, of facts, of events, of the demands of human consciousness to develop our capacity of epistemological curiosity. Far from being alien to our human condition, conscientization is natural to "unfinished" humanity that is aware of its unfinishedness. (Freire, 1998, p. 55)

Critical self-awareness as an exploratory pedagogy guided the work that José Luis, Carmen, and Mark experienced as high school students and continues to direct what they do as adults. One purpose of this chapter, then, is to bring the stories of these youth to the center because students such as they have not commonly seen themselves in the chronicle of the dominant society. The stories open a world of hope and possibilities for population groups and communities that historically have been mired by the forces of economic underdevelopment and historical marginalization. Invariably, the stories (research) will take on a range of meaning based on the interpretation of the reader. We invite the reader to interact with the stories, to be curious, to question, and to add to the stories through the reader's own imagination.

The invitation is not only an intellectual exercise because this cannot be separate from lived experience that is not isolated but is interconnected as are students, teachers, professors, and mentors. The invitation is an acknowledgement of the text as a construction of the authors. We learn through a collective process that is committed to both telling the story and to bearing witnesses to a story-making process that is in perpetual construction. With this frame, we invite the reader to consider the construction of the enclosed stories that begin when the storytellers were youth who have emerged as active public citizens. This interconnectedness is a dynamic process we engage in and share with the research community. The stories that follow are a combination of reflective *plática* of becoming public people. The *pláticas* interplay with a methodology that is not situated on the sidelines, as a traditional observer would; rather, the methodology is positioned front and center to help frame questions and to help make the familiar strange.

CIRCLE *PLÁTICAS*: REFLECTIONS ON GROWTH, DEVELOPMENT, AND HIGHER LEARNING

An important pedagogy Llano Grande has employed since its inception in the early 1990s is the practice of circle. We use circle to teach, to probe, to organize, to create, and to recreate. *Plática* is another pedagogy Llano Grande uses as a form of inquiry—to learn from each other and about ourselves. Through those practices, we share the following exchanges that are about 20 years in the making. It is a compilation of *pláticas* documented through the years that are reflective in nature and primarily gleaned from debriefing sessions that followed Llano Grande programming. One *plática*, for example, took place after Mark and his team conducted an oral history with an elder. We share part of that transcript here. Another *plática* is taken from a staff meeting, when Carmen and other high school students organized a Spanish Institute. And another exchange was captured when José Luis debriefed on his early experiences in college.

The *plática* methodology grew organically out of lived experience as Mexicanos and Mexican Americans. When our parents engaged us to teach a lesson, to deal with situations of raising children, or simply to imagine a better day, they tended to start with, "*vamos a platicar*," which translates to "let's talk" but in a family and culturally nuanced manner. This culturally expressive form helped us make sense of numerous childhood experiences, and *pláticas* had a particular way of helping us build deeper relationships with our parents and, by extension, with others who became part of our lives. The *plática* practice emerged as a staple of how we built Llano Grande: its pedagogies, its research methods, its system of inquiry, and its day-to-day operation. We run staff meeting through *pláticas*, we conduct oral histories through *pláticas*, and we organize folks in community through similar modalities. Even larger-scaled practices spawned from the work of Llano Grande, such as the Community Learning Exchange, a national movement that brings communities together to learn from each other, are guided through *pláticas*. In short, *plática* has shaped our social, cultural, organizational, and even academic DNA (Guajardo & Guajardo, 2013).

Context: circle *plática* #1 with Mark, October 2000, at the Llano Grande House in Elsa, Texas. Teachers Francisco and Miguel sat with a group of 10 students for a *plática* led by Mark, who was a 17-year-old lead researcher on an oral history project. Of the students, only Mark is excerpted; Miguel and Francisco were present around the circle and posed questions intermittently.

> MARK: As I facilitate this debriefing circle, I'd like to pose the question: What lesson do you take from the oral history we did today? I'd like to begin by saying that I thought I knew all of my grandmother's stories, because I've spent the past 17 years listening to her tell stories. Some stories I've heard

more than a dozen times. But today she shared things that I had never heard, and I may not have ever heard if we didn't create this opportunity where she could share, where she could just talk to a curious audience. I didn't know there was a chapel in the labor camp. I didn't know she knew so many people, and so many people knew her. I had no idea she had a vision for her family. She wanted her kids to get an education. She believed in school so much, even though she didn't go past just a few years of formal schooling herself. I've gained a new appreciation for my grandmother, especially for the struggles she had to endure, as a workingwoman who faced so many obstacles—racism, sexism, and so much more. But she was always so hopeful. She just became a bigger hero to me. I will treasure this moment forever and use her experience and wisdom to guide me.

MIGUEL: Mark, what do you believe the impact of this experience will be on your grandmother?

MARK: I know for sure she'll be calling her *comadres*, and there's a bunch of them, so it's almost guaranteed that my grandma will generate a buzz in the community. And she'll call her kids, other relatives, she'll tell all her neighbors. She'll tell them she helped her grandson with a school assignment. I think she'll also call some of the people she talked about in the oral history to ask if they remember certain things, because she may have questions about some of the things we talked about in the interview. I think she'll even tell friends she sees at the grocery store about what we did here today.

FRANCISCO: Was her storytelling today any different than the storytelling you've seen her perform through the years?

MARK: Yes, I think she was much more reflective today. She also appeared more proud to be telling her stories. The stories she usually tells are around family, and I think most of us just listen to her casually, but today was different. Today, we made her stories formal. She was the same grandma I've always known, but today she was like a teacher. I was happy to see her as a teacher to others today.

Context: circle *plática* #2, with Mark, April 2015, at the campus of Texas State University in San Marcos, where Mark is completing a PhD in educational administration. Francisco, Miguel, and Mark sat with a group of 12 participants after a Community Learning Exchange, a process innovated by the Llano Grande Center for the purposes of bringing communities together.

MARK: Though we've come a long way from the days when we were in high school exploring questions such as "why are we not in the textbooks," in many ways what we do today was shaped by the experiences we had as teenagers going through Llano Grande. My experience today, for example, is all about helping schools look at themselves critically so they can understand stories of students, teachers, and the community. My work as a school reform advocate is rooted in those values I learned by listening to my grandmother. My values were shaped by the love I gained for my hometown, for my school, and for my family. Those are core values that drive my work today.

MIGUEL: Can you go a little deeper into those core values? Talk more specifically about your current work? And where are you now?

MARK: I work for an educational service center in San Antonio, and through that work I'm responsible for helping rural schools continuously improve. I'm in a position where I can influence schools at a much larger capacity and through a much wider audience.

I create spaces for conversations rather than dictate state minimums. By learning in public, in safe and purposely planned spaces, I do my best to encourage school leaders to think beyond what they have been told are best instructional practices. I ask them to look internally at the systems in their schools that might minimize opportunities to engage learners as equal parts in the process. I highlight the differences between individuals and help maximize ways to not only reach them, but utilize the differences they uncover rather than suppress them. I look for informal ways of teaching and knowing, the way my Llano Grande experience encouraged us to look for what was not told. The process of self-discovery and asking people to stop and reflect on who they are is a method that creates deep learning opportunities, especially for those who do not see themselves in the textbooks or the examples used to portray everyday life. A deeper consciousness is created as a result of examination and reflection. It can spark imagination, creativity, and if well fostered, leads to courage and the freedom to explore and move districts beyond their current work. Unfortunately, this type of learning is hardly seen in traditional schools. We must highlight this type of learning and reinforce this type of knowing so that more students have the opportunity to grow as individuals and add to the collective knowledge. If this is to happen, the process needs to begin with allowing administrators, teachers, and people in leadership positions to do this for themselves.

In short, I don't believe I would be leading school reform efforts that are guided by the need for critical self-reflection and an understanding of community, if I had not been so profoundly shaped by the Llano Grande way. My vision is to continue to understand myself, so I can help others understand themselves, and their communities.

Context: circle *plática* #1 with Carmen, March 2001, at E-E HS, where a circle *plática* takes place in preparation for launching a Spanish Institute, a youth-driven program. Francisco, Miguel, Carmen, and four other high school students who organized the Spanish Institute speak.

> FRANCISCO: Carmen, please give us an overview of the planning on the Spanish Immersion Institute?
> CARMEN: This report will address recruitment, housing, and curriculum, but first I'd like to talk about the reason we're doing this. As you know, the Llano Grande way is to look at the assets in our community. We all believe in that. In fact, it's one of the big reasons we're here—the main reason is because we have mentors who help us get into college. But let's face it: We're Mexican, most of us know Spanish, many of us are biliterate, and so the idea of a Spanish language institute makes sense to us. We're also involved in asset building, so we welcome the opportunity to be a part of this, and most importantly, we're grateful to be employed through this work, because as you know, three of the four us students sitting around this table *no tenemos papeles* (we don't have legal residence), so we appreciate the opportunity to have a job.
> About the Spanish Institute: we have two nurses coming, one from Wisconsin and one from California. They saw our website and said they want to learn Spanish because more and more of their patients are Spanish-speaking people. We have several youth from across the country coming, a couple from the Boston area and several from across the Valley (South Texas) have registered. They all said they're looking at learning Spanish for both cultural and social reasons. We have a principal from Harlem, two teachers from the Valley, and there's interest from other educators and health care professionals from different parts of the country. In some cases, participants say they learned of the Spanish Institute from Miguel or Francisco through a presentation at a conference; in other cases, they say they have a relationship with someone from Llano Grande. And in every case, they say they prefer to stay in the country and be immersed in learning Spanish,

rather than to go through the hassles of travelling abroad to learn the language. So in terms of recruitment, it looks like we have reasons to build this program into the future.

Housing and curriculum: We've thus secured housing from six different local families, most of them elderly couples who speak only Spanish. They're very excited about doing this and are committed to taking their guest on weekly excursions during the weekend. They'll go to church, to *la pulga*, they'll go into Mexico, most likely to Reynosa or Las Flores, and they'll take their guest to family events. We're trying to figure the weekly stipend to each host family. Much of that depends on if we get the grant we've applied for program support. We feel good about housing and are hopeful we'll get grant support. As far as the curriculum, we're working with a retired Spanish teacher from the high school to build a curriculum. She's very experienced and is working carefully with the four of us to make sure this language learning experience has a lot of social and cultural interaction. We'll do a little bit of textbook learning, but mostly conversational learning.

MIGUEL: Carmen, what have you seen as the most significant impact of this work?

CARMEN: I think we've seen how we can actually create opportunities in our community, if we simply look at our natural assets. From a youth perspective, this just makes a lot of sense. It helps us understand our cultural strengths, and I think it will help us as we develop our leadership skills and as we apply to college. From the community perspective, we've seen how people are beginning to look at themselves differently. Especially the elders, they get it; they know this is a good thing, but it seems like they're thinking—what took us so long to see things this way. Overall, this is fun, exciting, and important work that we're all happy to be a part of. And like we said earlier, we need work, so we're grateful.

Context: circle *plática* #2 with Carmen, May 2015, at a Llano Grande Center board of directors meeting, where Carmen is a board member. A circle *plática* ensues between Miguel, Francisco, Carmen, and other Llano Grande board members.

MIGUEL: Carmen, please give us an update on the rural broadband work you're doing.

CARMEN: So as you know, I've been working with the Center for Rural Strategies, a national organization that advocates for rural communities, for the past five years. I first met the leadership of Rural Strategies when I was an undergraduate student and Francisco sent me to Louisiana with a video team from Rural Strategies to document the aftermath of Hurricanes Rita and Katrina. They were interested in interviewing Spanish-speaking people, so they needed someone like me, and I was happy to work. We helped them and then they hired me fulltime. I had no idea then that I would carve out a niche as a rural broadband activist, but that's what I've become. I've spent the better part of the last three years learning everything about Internet law and how it affects rural places across the country. You guys should know that this is a very sad story about how big money pretty much controls the industry, and it almost doesn't matter how much we know or how much we push the industry to do the right thing, rural communities will continue to get the short end of the stick. It's the large telecommunications companies that control all this, and they only care about the bottom line. Not even the Federal Communications Commission can do much about impacting broadband policy, because the federal government is controlled by the big corporate money.

But I do find solace in the work, however, because I approach everything through a principled perspective. As much as I've learned that everything is political, I also still carry the strong sense of idealism I learned from my work as a kid with Llano Grande. I learned policy activism, as everyone around this circle knows, from our work when we testified before the Texas Legislature in support of House Bill 1403, which would allow students like myself who were undocumented to be able to attend public university in Texas. I was only 17 when I traveled up to Austin with you guys. That was a life-shaping experience. It was an experience that prepared me well to work on the national level, as I'm doing now advocating for rural communities across the country. If I could testify for human rights as a teenager, I can certainly testify in front of a Congressional Committee, which I've done, to advocate for communities such as the one that raised me. I'm proud of the work I do, and this fall I'll begin law school, so I can place myself in a better position to help.

Context: circle *plática* #1 with José Luis, April 1998, in New York City, during a documentation trip intended to conduct interviews with E-E HS alumni who were enrolled in Ivy League universities. José Luis joined a team comprised of Miguel, Francisco, and two videography students.

MIGUEL: José Luis, would you begin this circle *plática* with a reflection on where you are in life?

JOSÉ LUIS: Well, I'm 18 and am completing my freshman year at Stanford. You guys flew me here to New York to be part of this interview process. I know you brought me because I've been very close to the college prep work back home in Edcouch-Elsa, and because many of my high school classmates are going to school here, at places like Columbia, Yale, and Brown. So you brought me here so I wouldn't be left out, and I appreciate that. But I also have to say that much of what you guys were talking about when I was in high school is beginning to make sense to me, particularly because of the kinds of cultural, social, and intellectual experiences I'm going through at Stanford. I find myself wanting to learn much more about myself, about my family, and about my community. I think I'm predisposed to this because of what I did when I was in high school, but I don't think I had the critical awareness until I left my community and became immersed in a university environment where self-discovery is really valued. I'm hungry to know now, much hungrier than a few years ago.

FRANCISCO: Tell us a little more about this critical awareness. Where are the sources at Stanford that are pushing this?

JOSÉ LUIS: Chicanos from California are really pushing me on this, and really just the environment that nurtures a lot of inquiry challenges my thinking. But I mention Chicanos because as you know, we don't use the word Chicano in South Texas. California Chicanos tend to be more political about their ethnic identity. We in South Texas tend to be more colonized, more subdued as political beings. I remember the story you told us, Francisco, about your first year as a teacher when you used the word Chicano with your students. You had just returned from UT Austin, where you had studied with people like Rolando Hinojosa Smith, Américo Paredes, and Ricardo Romo. You felt you teach Chicano history and Chicano literature at your alma mater, but were quickly disappointed that the adults weren't too keen on anything having to do with Chicanismo. The prevailing thinking was that anything Chicano was for radicals. You told us that it was met with widespread disapproval. That's exactly the environment I come from. But I also think the environment I come from allows for an organization like Llano Grande to exist, an organization that practices a certain Chicano ethos, but does so through coded initiatives that it calls community based research, oral histories, and place based studies. I'm realizing more and more the power of words, the importance of messaging, and the need to use a language that our community finds acceptable. So really, the sources that are pushing my thinking at Stanford are not only those who are there, but also those who are not. I'm being pushed by those invisible voices from back home, those who care about kids, care about schools, care about the community. I'm encouraged by those who haven't found the language to be public about those things. I'm being pushed by the need to find my own voice so that I can do good work. That's what's pushing me.

MIGUEL: Can you talk about some of your formative experiences at Llano Grande?

JOSÉ LUIS: Probably the most formative experience was the asset identification and asset building process. I was still young enough and wasn't fully conditioned in deficit thinking. But even though I was young when I came into this way of thinking, I still felt the negative perceptions that others had of our community. Gaining the language of assets, funds of knowledge, and cultural capital was important, because it equipped us with the vocabulary to help make sense of our reality. Thinking in terms of personal assets and community assets has helped me get through my first year at Stanford. Many people there are very wealthy, but I'm able to manufacture my own sense of wealth through the lessons I learned in high school. It's been important psychological and cultural wealth that has helped me adapt.

Context: circle *plática* #2 with José Luis, May 2015, in his faculty office at the University of Texas Pan American, accompanied by Francisco and Miguel.

MIGUEL: José Luis, would you reflect on the important lessons you've learned during the past 20 years, since you first made contact with the Llano Grande work?

JOSÉ LUIS: Well, it's given my life and my professional identities very clear meaning. When I completed my PhD from UT Austin, I wrote about my story, just like the two of you did. Being introspective about my story, my family story, and my community story is the most important scholarly work I've done. I believe that because I have a firm sense of self, I am able to help young people find their voice and their purpose in life. The work we do is about helping our youth, and adults, gain greater self-awareness. That's the greatest gift I take from Llano Grande, and the most important gift I try to give to others.

Context: Closing Circle *Plática*

MIGUEL: We've revisited almost 25 years of Llano Grande lived experience, which is about half our lives for Francisco and me. I ask that we close our *plática* through one final circle by sharing a meaningful accomplishment you've witnessed or lived. And I'd like to begin by attempting to situate our work in historical perspective. In some ways, we could say our work is social justice work, or critical race work, or even work that follows the spirit of Chicano scholarship. But I think the truth is that we don't fit into any one box; our work is mostly interdisciplinary, it's hybrid work that takes from the traditions of many of our intellectual and personal mentors who come from academia and from our communities. If there is a category we don't shy away from in terms of defining our work, it is that we are unabashedly proud of the Mexicano and Mexican American communities that have so fueled the work of Llano Grande. Our cultural and historical upbringing is what gives spirit to the work.

MARK: I feel the same way, Miguel, and for me I'd like to say that Llano Grande helped me find my unique voice. It has been a constant struggle to live in a normative society; coming into the Llano Grande experience has been a huge burden, yet a blessing. Living this experience has set me up to live life as a public educator like a fish swimming up stream. The Llano Grande experience gave me the taste of what good pedagogy looks like, what sharing power tastes like, and what identity formation is about. Knowing what good teaching, learning, and leading in an authentic way looks like has forced me to resist many bad practices, even in higher education. This has informed my work as a public educator, yet it has created much tension from an educational system that in its rush toward accountability, efficiency and choice, misses the mark on equity, excellence, and access. I've worked to correct this at every point in my educational career and hope to document this process in my upcoming dissertation.

Getting the sense of what relational power looks like in name, definition, and practice has been a very empowering process I have lived by since I became a teacher in my middle school back home. It also informed my work as a campus leader in Central Texas and is what I use to facilitate school improvement seminars in my present job as a school improvement facilitator at a state regional center.

As powerful as the learning has been, it was the opportunity and invitation to learn about myself where I became comfortable in my own skin as a Mexican American gay man. Very few spaces had provided this kind of safe space for me and other young people in this region to have conversations about becoming and exploring their identity when the outside world was not always safe. This has been the most radical discovery that I have come to appreciate.

CARMEN: Because of my work with Llano Grande, I feel like I've contributed to shaping what this country is about. I feel connected to history. I also have to say that the whole experience has been a fabulous ride. I would have never imagined that a little girl who came across the Rio Grande River in a tire tube with her mother in search of a better life could live a life of so much privilege. The privilege does not come in monetary or material things. It comes in being part of a community that cares and with people who give of their time and themselves so that children can have better lives. This is what my mother did for me as a young child and this is what the Llano Grande community gave me as a student in public schools. This community has catapulted me to dream and live life in a very public way. I have been the author of my story, I have been the researcher of my genealogy across two continents, and I am committed to using my agency to explore the next chapter as an agent for change for people who do not have access to the necessary levers of power. This is the right thing to do. It is what I've been trained to do, and it is the dignified thing to do for those who cannot do it for themselves.

JOSÉ LUIS: I know we've shied away from being boxed into an identity corner; we're not this, and we're not that. I think that's been a good thing, because our work is unique because we're from this one particular community, and we came along during this one particular time in history. So our work really can't be replicated. The principles and strategies of the work can be transferred, but not the conditions, the characters, and the place.

But because of my connection to Llano Grande I know my place in history. I come from a Mexican American family that has lived in this country for several generations. My family is assimilated to the virtues and values of the American Dream, but in a Mexican context and community. My high school days were spent playing American football, hanging out with the boys, and witnessing several of my relatives ascend in the professoriate. My greatest gift in participating with the Llano Grande work is the opportunity to go through an ethno-genesis at a young period in my life. The introduction to a pedagogy that was grounded in important work, was relevant to my family, and piqued my curiosity about issues of race, class, and culture catapulted me into a space of exploration and identity formation. This gave me the foundation to place the macro level Chicano experience in a context of my community while in college. It also gave me meaningful experience to share while many of my college peers had only read about these experiences in books. This work has guided my professional and intellectual career; and became the focus of my dissertation topic and methodology.

FRANCISCO: I know we've resisted being called social justice workers, because the neoliberal movement has really hijacked that agenda. But that's neither here nor there. Our truth is that we work in our community, and we work to build hope with kids, families, and the region, as we help folks build skills. It has been a real treat to see the evolution of young Mexican American minds in action. I remember all of you as high school students and love having you as colleagues in the struggle for creating healthy communities of learning. I came back home in the early 1990's to teach in my alma mater with the idea that we were changing this place we call home, but I think it is fair to say that it has been the people of this community that continue to change me. We have done good work during the past 25 years, but I believe our best work is yet to come.

MIGUEL: I continue to see this work from Central Texas. It has been moving to be present and witness the work during the past generation. It has kept me connected to home in a significant and substantive way. I've also had the privilege to witness the growth of young people and the good and important work you are doing. Sitting in Jorge's dissertation committee was an opportunity to reflect. While I sat in that conference room at the University of Texas at Austin, I could not help but to think back to that cold winter day we met in New York, when we explored the possibilities of continuing to build an organization that was about youth, education, and community change. I now look forward to chairing Mark's dissertation and to celebrate Carmen's law degree. This work gives me hope and satisfaction that young people can change their community and impact it for the public good.

REFERENCES

Cárdenas, J. A., & Cárdenas, B. (1977). *The theory of incompatibilities: A conceptual framework for responding to the educational needs of Mexican American children.* San Antonio, TX: Intercultural Development Research Association.

Delgado Bernal, D. (1998). Using a Chicana feminist epistemology in educational research. *Harvard Educational Review*, 68(4), 555–582.
Freire, P. (1973). *Pedagogy of the oppressed*. New York, NY: Seabury.
Freire, P. (1998). *Pedagogy of freedom: Ethics, democracy, and civic courage*. Lanham: Rowman & Littlefield.
Glaser, B. G., & Strauss, A. L. (1967). *The discovery of grounded theory*. Chicago: Aldine.
Guajardo, F., & Guajardo, M. (2013). The power of plática. *Reflections: A journal of public rhetoric, civic writing, and service learning*, 13(1), 159–164.
Guajardo, M., & Guajardo, J. (2002). Critical ethnography and community change. In H. Trueba & Y. Zou (Eds.), *Ethnography in schools: Qualitative approaches to the study of education* (pp. 281–302). Lanham, MD: Rowman & Littlefield.
Guajardo, M., & Guajardo, F. (2004). The impact of *Brown* on the brown of south Texas: A micropolitical perspective on the education of Mexican Americans in a south Texas community. *American Educational Research Journal*, 41(3), 501–526. Retrieved from http://www.jstor.org/stable/3699437
Hurtado, A. (2003). *Voicing Chicana feminisms: Young women speak out on sexuality and identity*. New York, NY: New York University Press.
Lather, P. A. (1986). Research as praxis. *Harvard Educational Review*, 56, 257–277.
Lather, P. A. (1991). *Getting smart: Feminist research and pedagogy with/in the postmodern*. New York, NY: Routledge.
Maturana, H., & Varela, F. (1987). *The tree of knowledge*. Boston, MA: Shambhala Publications.
Pizarro, M. (1998). Chicana/o Power! Epistemology and methodology for social justice and empowerment in Chicana/o communities. *International Journal of Qualitative Studies in Education*, 11(1), 57–80.
Pizarro, M., & Montoya, M. (2002). Seeking educational self-determination: Raza studies for revolution. *Equity & Excellence in Education*, 35(3), 276–292.
Scheurich, J. (1997). *Research method in the postmodern*. New York, NY: Falmer Press.
Trueba, E. (1999). *Latinos unidos: From cultural diversity to the politics of solidarity*. Lanham, MD: Rowman & Littlefield.
Villenas, S. (1996). The colonizer/colonized Chicana ethnographer: Identity, marginalization, and co-optation in the field. *Harvard Educational Review*, 66(4), 711–731.

Part III
Literacies as a Civil and Human Right

9 Black "Youth Speak Truth" to Power
Literacy for Freedom,[1] Community Radio, and Civic Engagement

Keisha L. Green

> It's time for the real to be revealed. It's time for Youth Voices, the show that speaks the truth about what's going on in the world from the perspective of those who are the future. We've heard the adults, now it's our turn to talk. Get ready for the youth to speak the truth about politics, our community, peer pressure and other issues.
> ~Youth Voices radio promotion

> P—O W E R . . . We got the power . . . 'cause we are the collective.
> P—O W E R . . . We got the power . . . 'cause we are the collective.
> ~Youth Voices chant created June, 2010

At least twice a week, Youth Voices members[2] filter inside a humble, two-story, wood-paneled building bordering an urban public high school. Before climbing the stairs to occupy their second-floor meeting space, the youth must walk through a freshly painted hallway adorned with maps of continental Africa and framed images of important Black freedom fighters, including Harriet Tubman, Frederick Douglass, Ella Baker, Amiri Baraka, and Sonia Sanchez. On occasion, an all-Black youth ensemble of actors, singers, and dancers who share the space can be heard practicing on the ground floor auditorium for an upcoming performance. On many days, the youth are greeted by local community members lining the hallway as they await services from the food pantry housed downstairs and operated by three Black women who are mothers, aunties, and sisters to the members of Youth Voices. This building, which houses an organization dedicated to the elimination of poverty and oppression, particularly for communities of color, is, according to Youth Voices member Aniya, "like a second family." Upstairs resides an institute that regularly hosts workshops on undoing racism as well as the nonprofit organization that sponsors Youth Voices.

This chapter about Black youth in the Southeast insisting to thrive is a love letter of hope and possibility written at a time when systemic and individual manifestations of racism and other "-isms" persist across the United States. I focus on Black young people who regularly contend with being perceived as other, deficient, a problem, a menace, or illegal. By sharing highlights from the Youth Voices project, I hope to demonstrate how some Black youth conceptualize citizenship, develop a sense of citizenship, and engage in the public sphere. Civic education in school and out of school should help young people acquire and learn to use the skills, knowledge, and attitudes that will prepare them to be competent and responsible citizens throughout their lives (Torney-Purta, Lehmann, Oswald, & Schulz, 2001; Torney-Purta, Schwille, & Amadeo, 1999). Such a definition helps us with an intellectual understanding of the concept of civic education; however, just what does civic engagement look like? What does it look like to be involved authentically in one's own community or one's own life, and how can we measure or evaluate such engagement?

At a time when full citizenship rights and access to quality public secondary and higher education opportunities for Black youth are in question, the youth participating in Youth Voices demonstrate the promise and complexities of youth civic identity and engagement among marginalized youth of color in out-of-school contexts. These youth articulate their own bill of rights and demand first-class citizenship. Specifically, I focus on the ways in which Youth Voices maximizes opportunities for youth civic engagement by utilizing a model of youth development that involves knowing history or heritage knowledge (Hilliard, 1995; King, 2006) through popular political education, representing and voicing youth perspectives through community-based youth radio and creating meaningful change through civic engagement or community activism.

A NOTE ON METHODS

I have drawn upon on a conceptualization of participant observation that I describe as Double Dutch methodology (Green, 2014) to document the authentic, meaningful, and instructive ways in which South Works provided opportunities for youth, particularly Youth Voices, to practice agency in their own lives. Such an approach serves to humanize the research process by acknowledging the nuanced and complicated ways researchers interact with youth coresearchers and research participants—specifically researchers of color conducting research with communities of color. For a full description of the Youth Voices activity, I used multiple data sources informed by ethnographic research methods. I examined the literacy events in the youth radio space as well as sought to understand the youth participants' perceptions and their activities situated in a particular cultural, social, and political context (LeCompte & Schensul, 1999). Additionally, I observed, interviewed, and analyzed data from the adult participants who facilitated the youth development program. The adult allies provided information about the pedagogical strategies, curricular choices, and programmatic goals of the sponsoring nonprofit. Including adult participants offered an opportunity to analyze the nature of relationships between adults and youth in the context of the study using the multiple perspectives of both types of participants.

BACKGROUND OF YOUTH VOICES

Part of a burgeoning international youth media scene and inspired by the pioneering work of California-based Youth Radio, Youth Voices is a southern-based youth radio collective and one of three youth development programs facilitated by a southeastern community-based organization (CBO) situated in the ninth-largest metropolitan city in the U.S. The organization has an international reputation for documenting and promoting the historical role of the South, particularly its Black radical tradition. The Youth Voices-sponsoring nonprofit is organized around the needs of the surrounding community, offering initiatives designed to develop youth leadership from within the community.

Youth Voices participants meet after school during the week to develop the content of the program. Adult participants, who facilitate the youth development program, provide in-studio coordination and general program supervision. The Youth Voices mission includes centering youth voice and aims to "incorporate a human rights framework and encourage youth to examine their own lives and communities, recognizing the various forms of oppression that limit us all; then get that message across the air to their peers and families" (Arnold & Weusi, 2004). Youth Voices activity is concentrated within two locations: (1) the facility of a community-based nonprofit organization and (2) a "community-oriented, educational, alternative" station that broadcasts progressive information. The first location, a grassroots, community-based nonprofit organization, serves as the central hub of operations out of which the facilitators for the program work and where the youth radio participants meet regularly to research potential show topics, write scripts, and engage in political education workshops. Reflecting the fire for change growing inside budding revolutionaries, the walls of the Youth Voices meeting space are painted a glossy, bright red. In black, a mural of freedom fighters Malcolm X, Che Guevara, and Rosa Parks against a sprawling tree and its substantial roots greets all youth, staff, and volunteers at the second-floor entrance. The images are a symbolic representation of the "literacy for liberation" philosophy that undergirds the Youth Voices activity. Most Youth Voices meetings and work take place inside the nonprofit's multipurpose room, which serves as the organization's library. Several bookshelves contain a substantial collection of texts on social movements, politics, culture, race, and histories of particular ethnic groups and their struggle for liberation. There is also a computer and printer station and a small canteen area.

The second location, a noncommercial, listener-funded FM radio station for progressive information, is housed in a community center at the heart of

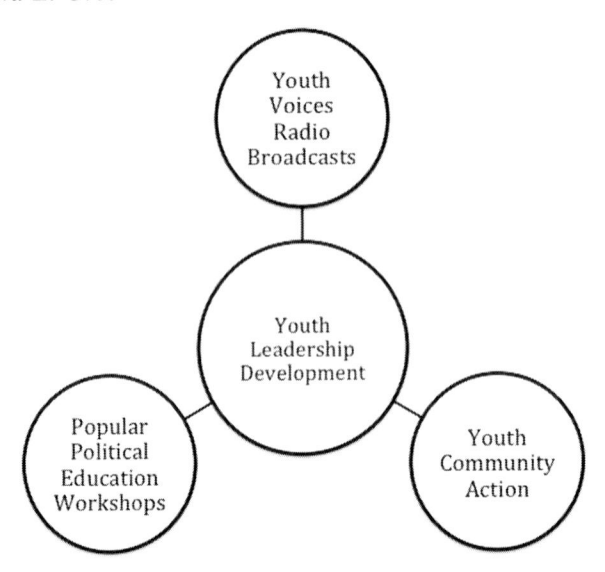

```
                    ┌─────────────┐
                    │   Youth     │
                    │   Voices    │
                    │   Radio     │
                    │ Broadcasts  │
                    └─────────────┘
                           │
                    ┌─────────────┐
                    │   Youth     │
                    │ Leadership  │
                    │ Development │
                    └─────────────┘
              ┌──────────┘ └──────────┐
       ┌─────────────┐         ┌─────────────┐
       │  Popular    │         │    Youth    │
       │  Political  │         │  Community  │
       │  Education  │         │   Action    │
       │  Workshops  │         │             │
       └─────────────┘         └─────────────┘
```

Figure 9.1 An Illustration of Youth Voices' Weekly Activities and Programmatic Goals

a culturally rich neighborhood known for its liberal atmosphere and walkable business district including an off-Broadway theater and playhouse. For more than 30 years, the station has provided a voice for those who traditionally have been denied access to the broadcast media. Until recently, youth were not a part of the station's historically marginalized groups represented on the airwaves. In an effort to address the absence of youth programming and to demonstrate the station's commitment to attracting a younger listening audience, two new youth programs were added to the station's program roster. Youth Voices is one of two youth programs broadcast on Friday evenings. To produce the broadcasts, the youth radio participants occupy the radio station's shared multipurpose meeting room. The figure illustrates the ongoing and bidirectional flow of the three components and overarching goal of the Youth Voices program.

LITERACY FOR FREEDOM

> I think education is really brought forth here but not so much in school.
>
> Aniya, 17, Youth Voices participant

The first and most fundamental way Youth Voices participants become involved authentically in their own communities and agents of change in their own lives is through popular and political education workshops that center on race, culture, and history, particularly of oppressed peoples in the U.S. South. Youth Voices facilitators, both veteran community activists, emerge as Freirian public intellectuals who believe in education for liberation. Facilitators, referred to as "adult allies" by the participants, are just as concerned with the youth's research, writing, and speaking skill development as they are with the youth's *conscientization* (Fisher, 2009; Freire, 1970). According to their proposal, "[Y]outh have played vital roles in various resistance movements and revolutions. Youth Voices will seek to foster and capture the spirit of youth activism inside and outside of the studio" (Arnold & Weusi, 2004). During the biweekly meetings, workshop facilitators used popular political education tools to engage participants. According to programmatic material obtained at the research site, popular education includes three tenets: "1) Valuing and using personal life experiences in educating each other; 2) Using multimedia and various techniques to create a framework for consciousness raising; and 3) Using our histories to build one future and take action" (South Works workshop material, 2008, unpublished). This kind of popular education includes active listening skills and is not education for education's sake. Instead, popular education is about reflection:

> Sharing experiences obstacles, victories, joys or struggle based on people's expressed needs; critical analysis of our collective practices and our understandings of their root case on society's structure. And new action new ways of looking at the world, engaging each other and acting for change. (South Works workshop material, 2008, unpublished)

This kind of popular education should be in schools, according to Miriam. She interprets popular education as "learning things through your perspective." During an interview about her experience in Youth Voices, Miriam goes on to describe popular education as "a space, an opportunity where youth can learn about different stuff that they are not going to tell you in school. That's what popular education is . . . [s]omething they're not going to tell you in school." Miriam's reflections echo Aniya's sentiment that education is "really" happening in the context of Youth Voices. The youth are learning about power and oppression, racism and liberation, as well as about community building all in a context that is inclusive of different experiences and dependent on broad participation.

LEARNING THROUGH PERSONAL EXPERIENCE

Standing in the upstairs hallway of a well-used CBO's office, 12 Black high school students are asked to consider a wall chart time line documenting historically significant events related to government programs and policies, major economic shifts, and social or popular movements occurring over the past 100 years in the U.S. The adult facilitators leading the youth participants through a political education workshop issue directives for navigating this particular literacy event—the goal of which is to "incorporate the [students'] lived experience with significant historical events." (Arnold & Weusi, 2004). The time line exercise exemplified the first tenet in popular education: valuing and using personal life experiences in educating each other.

Learning through multimedia. Beyond icebreakers such as the historical time line activity, Youth Voices participants are engaged through multimedia. Youth view YouTube clips, streaming video, or short documentaries that document social justice movements involving youth and adults across the country. The *Eyes on the Prize* video instruction and the idea of consciousness, vision, and strategy (CVS) analysis are examples of the second tenet in popular education: using multimedia and various techniques to create a framework for consciousness raising. Expanding the traditional notion of a literacy event, Morrell (2004) considers film and music as text. For example, the *Eyes on the Prize* (Hampton, 2010) documentary series on the Civil Rights Movement is a constant piece of the Youth Voices curriculum. Workshop participants view a section of the series once a week, and facilitators ask youth in their roles as "activists in training" to use the CVS process as an analytical tool and plan for action. To complete the consciousness part of the activity, adult allies ask youth to note what is taking place. Then, to construct the vision part of the activity, youth are asked to describe what they hope to see. Finally, for the strategy portion, youth and adults collaborate to develop ideas about how to move from consciousness to vision. Brainstorming yields ideas and concrete action steps to achieve what the youth hope to see happen in their communities, again a part of what Freire (1970) has referred to as "conscientization."

Learning from history. Another element of the Youth Voices curriculum includes the study of Black history, particularly in the U.S. Many of the Black youth participants attend public schools where Black history is either reduced to mere mentioning of prominent Black figures during Black History Month or not included at all. For instance, 16-year-old Miriam had no idea the events on Bloody Sunday March 7, 1965, in Selma, Alabama, propelled the Voting Rights Act of 1965 that President Johnson signed into law five months later. Reflecting on her experience traveling to Selma with Youth Voices, Miriam said, "I learned a lot about my history. I haven't heard [about Bloody Sunday] in my entire life at all. I learned a lot about what it was for and why it was significant for the south during Civil Rights." While in Selma, Miriam was able to record interviews with several elders of the Civil Rights Movement and interact with locals who participated in the march more than 40 years ago. Upon returning, Miriam was responsible for sharing what she learned with the Youth Voices group. By centering the voices, experiences, history, culture, and legacy of activism among African Americans in the U.S., particularly in the South, Youth Voices facilitators fulfill the third tenet of popular education: using multiple histories to build one future and take action.

YOUTH VOICES AND COMMUNITY RADIO

Sitting around rectangular tables in a room with dry-erase boards, Youth Voices participants are visited occasionally by station volunteers who freely move in and out of the space as the youth prepare for their broadcast. The station has two paid staffers who are usually on hand to greet the group and share updates about upcoming events or feedback about past broadcasts. Under the supervision of the volunteer facilitators, every other Friday night, with a red on-air sign aglow, the youth deliver their live broadcasts inside the main studio complete with the necessary broadcast equipment, including several microphones, mixers, and soundboard.

To describe the activity at work during radio broadcasts, I appropriated the term "air-shifting," an expression used by participants to refer to the technical and soundboard engineering at the radio station. In the context of this study, I use "air-shifting" to refer to the youth radio collective learning how to question, critique, and engage in social, political, and cultural discourse through community radio programming. In this way, youth radio production becomes a "pedagogy of disruption" by appropriating the access that they do have to media to become more than just consumers of popular culture; they are also producers and critics of culture (Giroux, 2006).

The youth participant's first act of air-shifting involved writing the script and selecting the music for the Youth Voices promotional piece to air on WKLG but not before hearing a history of the community-based radio station that would feature Youth Voices. Delivering this history and description of the current mission and programming policies of the radio station was Operations Director Ayinde Mfume. Mfume, a robust figure with salt-and-pepper dreadlocks, who discussed the ways in which community-sponsored radio differs from commercial radio and reviewed the station's mission to provide "free and open access to the broadcast media," particularly to those traditionally denied. Mfume spoke frankly about his high expectations of WKLG's newest and youngest cadre of program producers and explained that the youth were going to be more than just on air personalities. Indeed, Youth Voices was expected to carry out the mission of WKLG. With that admonition at the forefront, the following is the promotion created by the youth to advertise their new public affairs show:

[Background music plays: Lyrics by India Arie: "If young people would talk to old people, it would make us a better people all around." The music fades out as Youth Voices fade in.]

> Youth Voice 1 (Marcus): It's our time!
> Youth Voice 2 (Byron): Time for youth!
> Youth Voice 1: Time for truth!
> Youth Voice 2: 89.3
>
> The youth is you and me
> If you trace us to the motherland

You'll find our master plan
We're not from the same race
But we're from the same place
This is our time to talk about politics
How the world's gone crazy
How the government really is
So if you understand
The youth is here today
And if you do like this
We takin' compliments all day

Youth Voice 1: Tune in on Fridays at 7:30pm to hear youth speaking truth to power on your listener sponsored community radio station for progressive information WKLG 89.3 FM and at www.WKLG.org.
Youth Voice 2: Youth Voices!

[Background music plays: Lyrics by Goodie Mob's Cee-Lo: "You can't have no revolution without the women and you can't have no future without the children." Youth Voices fade out as music fades in.]

Creating the public service announcement, youth intentionally choose music that reflects the Youth Voices mission to "fight for change in [their] communities and communities beyond." The artist, India Arie, whose music provides the backdrop for the introduction, is well-known for her conscious lyrics and critique of sociocultural issues. Similarly, Cee-Lo is also a hip-hop artist who has experienced mainstream and pop success and is known for his political lyrics. Through the text of the promotion, Youth Voices display an awareness of their role as social change agents. Youth declare, "It's our time," implying an understanding of the sociopolitical and historical tensions around who has the right to speak. The value of radio as a means for sharing information has its source in a history of Black literate traditions that youth were indeed beginning to appreciate. According to historian V. P. Franklin (1984), "[E]ducation and literacy were greatly valued among Afro-Americans enslaved in the United States because knowledge and information helped one to survive in a hostile environment" in "their day-to-day experiences—from one generation to the next" (p. 161). The history of slavery and resistance in the U.S. has particular significance to this study situated in the Southeast.

According to the youth, "the world's gone crazy," and the government is not really what it seems to be—a democracy for the people and of the people. The Youth Voices radio promotion demonstrates that the activity of radio production in this context—one intentionally aimed at politicizing youth of color—serves as a bridge to cultivating critical literacy. As Camangian (2008) argues, "[C]ritical literacy in this sense poses an alternative discourse, one that stands against oppressive social conditions, ideologies and the institutions that marginalize the experiences and livelihoods of marginalized people" (p. 37). Like critical literacy, media literacy skills and access to media allow young people to change the tenor of mainstream broadcast media (Morrell, 2004). Corporate-owned media uphold a set of values, norms, and ways of being that support and reinforce interests of the dominant group (Dolby, 2003; McChesney, 1999; Morrell, 2004). To resist, reinterpret, or produce counter-narratives, Black and Brown youth, in particular, "need to understand the difference between reality and the media's various representations of reality and that media representations of themselves reflect ideologies and stances about the world" (Morrell, 2004, pp. 93–94).

COLLECTIVE YOUTH ACTION

> [Youth Voices] changed my life because it gave me a community awareness. I never really grasped the concept of community work until I was here at [Youth Voices] and now I feel like I have a responsibility to affect change in other people's lives not just my own.
>
> Aniya, 17, September 10, 2010

Civic engagement in the context of Youth Voices is about individual and collective community actions that serve the purpose of identifying and addressing public issues of concern (Sherrod, Torney-Purta, & Flanagan, 2010). It means promoting the quality of life in a community, through both political and nonpolitical processes. The building blocks of successful youth action included active group membership, community-based problem solving, and cultivating a political voice in the form of protest toward community action.

Active Group Membership

One indicator of civic engagement is active membership in a group or association. Youth participant involvement in Youth Voices is one of the more obvious observations of civic engagement. Youth Voices is a group of young people who consistently volunteer their time after school to attend multiple meetings or events each week. Letters to parents of Youth Voices participants double as application forms for each youth member. The forms list their requirements for membership and include a number of benefits as a result of participation. What follows is an abbreviated list of the program aspects that the youth can expect to experience from participating in the program:

- Getting leadership and organizing skills (public speaking, running meetings, strategizing, etc.)
- Being connected with youth leaders across the city, Southeast region, and nationally

- Gaining power and respect
- Access to a bimonthly youth radio show
- Running for leadership positions and signing up for committees
- Voting at meetings
- Membership card and free newsletters
- Invitations to all meetings, trainings, celebrations, and actions
- Opportunities for travel
- Support of Youth Voices on an individual level
- Responsibilities
- Attending popular political education meetings twice a week
- Participation in youth agreed-upon work
- Participation in one youth-led and facilitated fund-raising for the [Youth Voices] program
- Coming to organization-wide events
- Upholding Youth Voices agreed values
- Respecting yourself and others
- Taking responsibility for making positive change in yourself, your school, and community
- Continuing these changes across the region

The programmatic content and aims presented in the letter reveal opportunities for youth to be involved in broader civic activities after cultivating leadership skills within the Youth Voices operations. These opportunities include decision making, working collaboratively, and community organizing. For example, Miriam, in her description about her role in Youth Voices, mentions the kind of skills she is gaining through the experience.

> I'm an action team leader. It just means that we got a little bit more responsibility than the participants . . . which means that we interact with the staff. We are closer to the participants in age. We are the first line of defense and establish role modelship if you want to call it . . . and really just kind of set the rules. . . . I chose to participate in that role as a member of [Youth Voices] and it was a way for me to step up my leadership role and really practice facilitating and communicating with my peers on a level of positive leadership, positive role model and just a way to step up my game and really learn what it takes to you know be a responsible youth leader. (Interview, June 18, 2010)

Miriam's account of her role in Youth Voices illustrates the program's claim to provide youth with opportunities to develop the skills, knowledge, and attitudes needed for leadership. She is apprenticed into such a leadership role over time. Because of her active membership, she is invested in the overall success of the program and in her ability to forward the mission of Youth Voices as new youth join the organization.

Community Problem Solving

The concept of community within the context of Youth Voices refers to multiple social groups including, but not limited to, the youth program, youth in general, the local surrounding neighborhood, the broader city, as well as people of color. By joining Youth Voices and becoming an active member in the program, the youth participants essentially are signing up to engage in social change. Therefore, the young participants of Youth Voices encountered opportunities to engage in community problem solving. Before engaging in actual problem solving, the Youth Voices activities incorporated problem solving techniques and tools. The problem-solving skills gained and developed through the internal group work is preparation for tackling community problems at broader community levels.

One of the most important tools utilized by Youth Voices throughout their work with youth and adults is a set of guidelines. In the context of my work with youth, I found that the guidelines established a framework for how to conduct meetings and shape the environment of the meeting space. Youth members of a youth council collaborated with adults to create Guidelines for Youth Voices activities that existed in the nonprofit organization prior to Youth Voices. The guidelines are designed to circumvent problems that might occur within the youth space or youth meetings. Each guideline or ground rule is recited before meetings as a reminder for how to address potential problems that may arise among a group of teenage youth, including teasing, bullying, making controversial statements, extroverted youth speaking with more frequency than more introverted youth, and differing opinions and interests.

The guidelines may be well intentioned; however, two of the youth participants expressed concern with their effectiveness and authenticity. According to one youth participant, Shea, the youth were introduced to the guidelines because Youth Voices is more of a "collective organization and they [the adult allies] were enforcing the collectivism values." She went on to describe the utility of the guidelines as a necessary tool to make progress. In her words, "You gotta have rules to make things go. 'Cause if everybody had their way, we'd all be standing still." Shea did, however, express her concern for the time that it takes to allow for a collective process. According to Shea, "[I]t's a fair system," but "no one wants to be stuck in a situation because nothing's happening." In her view, being sure that everyone's opinion is heard may mean decisions or projects take longer to get done.

Also challenging the purpose of the guidelines, Sayisha claims they were created to "make people feel like they're not being controlled. It's less preachy. . . . [P]eople don't like that." However, she is not convinced that the Youth Voices program utilizes the guidelines as she describes. Instead, she feels like "sometimes it can be like overwhelming how much they [the adult allies] enforce it. Sometime they enforce it too much where it's kind of being contradicted." Continuing, Sayisha offers an example of how the "step up, step back" ground rule could be misleading or have unintended results. The principle is intended to be a reminder to be conscious of any one person dominating conversations in an effort to provide space for others to speak and act. According to Sayisha,

> Step up, step back. Like OK so sometimes we're told . . ."[P]eople who talk more step back and let people who don't talk as much or the people who they view as the underdogs speak." When you start to play that role you step back. Then all of a sudden they want you to step up because the people that normally don't step up, still don't step up. So you're stuck in a rock and a hard place. (Interview, May 19, 2009)

Sayisha's reflections highlight the challenge of creating an equitable and democratic space. The youth are learning inside Youth Voices how difficult it can be to generate consensus in spaces outside of Youth Voices. Through the "step up, step back" guideline, the youth are grappling with how particular voices, identities, and personalities could potentially and unintentionally silence others. Like the "step up, step back" principle, the "one mic" guideline is intended to ensure that a speaker is heard and not drowned out by multiple voices. By saying, "one mic," a youth or an adult ally may signal that one person has the floor and is speaking. As Shea and Sayisha note, the guidelines are not without flaws or points of contestation. Occasionally, youth help add new guidelines for particular workshops. Overall, these guidelines seem to help youth understand that to work together in a group, everyone needs to feel respected, heard, and valued. In this context, Youth Voices support solving problems in a way that requires broad participation and equity in representation among community members.

Another problem-solving technique used within the context of the Youth Voices community is reflection. After each educational workshop, activity, or radio broadcast, the youth participants evaluate what worked or what didn't work. Sometimes this process is referred to as the "+ or" or known as "plus" and "minus or change." Another version of the evaluation process that took place after radio broadcasts was "highlight" and "lowlight." Most often, though, the evaluation process is called, "yes, no, maybe next time." Either iteration of the evaluation process involves taking time as a group to reflect on the content, quality, and components of the experience in question. For example, after each radio broadcasts, the youth convene for about 30 additional minutes to critique the process and quality of the radio production. Even with inconsistency in applying reflective practice, the quality of the radio broadcasts have improved over time, and elements of sophistication are evident in the structural format of regular segments, including interviews, a Black radical tradition moment, and a group dialogue about the show topic to close the show.

Protesting as Political Voice

Protesting is another civic engagement feature of the Youth Voices program activities that is closely linked with community problem solving. One highly visible example occurred during the journey to the 2010 U.S. Social Forum in Detroit. Twenty-three youth boarded a bus with several representatives from a variety of CBOs who work in partnership with Youth Voices for social justice. Together, we traveled the road to Detroit, Michigan, retracing history along the way more than 40 years after the Freedom Riders tested the Supreme Court decision *Boynton v. Virginia*, desegregating interstate travel. Education on the bus included lectures about the Kentucky black coal miners and new sources of green energy as we passed the wind turbines.

Our journey to Detroit included being "schooled" by Nathan, a public intellectual and community organizer with the Youth Voices community. Stepping into the role of "teacher," Nathan helped us understand a theory of the African episteme. He explained his theory of an ecology of knowledge that recognizes the coexistence of other knowledges that allow for polyculturalism and recognize the limits of a single story, all-too-often from a dominant perspective. Youth Voices participants learned on their bus ride to the social forum about their roles as citizens. Not your typical school field trip, it was, according to an adult ally, "education on wheels." We connected with the historic migration of African Americans from the South to the North. The education grounded us for relating to the different communities with which we convened in Louisville, Kentucky, and Chicago, Illinois.

These two communities were in the midst of intense protest around environmental issues and housing rights, respectively. At each stop, the youth participants joined the protests, carrying their own signs and shouting chants in solidarity with both communities. Youth interviewed during the journey responded to their experiences in ways that connected their emerging sense of agency to the history they were learning about. According to Aaliyah,

> [The] spirits were so genuine, and the determination I felt from them, inspired me to want change even more and work hard for it. In Kentucky and Chicago I participated in protests, and the experience was very riveting, because I felt like one of my ancestors or someone that maybe I had seen before in a documentary, literally taking the steps forward to progression! (Interview, June 19, 2010)

Aaliyah's account of her experience protesting underscored the meaningfulness of civic action beyond local conditions. Stepping outside of the Youth Voices community, Aaliyah and her peers were able to see themselves connected to a larger social justice movement. Protesting was an act of working in solidarity with communities of color to make a better world. Similarly, Aniya described the kind of hands-on learning opportunities evident in their protest experiences. She recalled feeling "especially excited to have landed in Kentucky and witnessed the 'better air' protest because it really brought to life what environmental justice was. You could actually smell the pollution that was being admitted into the air from the factories that surrounded Louisville." Continuing, Aniya described how she felt being a part of a critical mass of demonstrators. She remembered being in "Chicago [where] a large protest was held. The police were on edge and were running around like chickens because they realized how powerful collective action was." These protest experiences served to shape the youth participants' attitudes about their own political efficacy and abilities to make change.

COMPLICATING CITIZENSHIP

When students were asked to compare their experiences of civic education in school with their experiences in Youth Voices programming, two themes emerged. According to the youth, civic education inside school focused primarily on the structural components of the U.S. government, including the three branches of government and cursory knowledge of the constitution. For instance, Sayisha, recalled, having "a civic law and government class." She went on to explain that in class, they "don't learn political rights. We learn about constitutional rights and social movements." Similarly, Miriam contends that her "civic class was on government and we're learning like how the government system works and stuff like that." According to Miriam, school-based curriculum taught her "the roles of the legislative branch and the president and stuff like that." Seemingly, the nature of civic education evident in the public school curriculum experienced by both Sayisha and Miriam was one dimensional, stopping short of the kind of critical civic education experienced by another youth participant, Naima, who recounted her experience as a student in an online home school run by her father. "We do learn about critically thinking about how to analyze what's going on politically. And we learn what it means as a person to be involved and [about] the power we have to be involved and the power at different levels." Naima's experience is more closely related to the type of civic education evident in the Youth Voices context.

My attempt to understand the kind of youth civic engagement apparent throughout the Youth Voices program uncovered youth perceptions of themselves as citizens. The term itself is an ill-defined concept, as Biko conveyed. An African American male and recent high school graduate, he admitted that "the word citizen throws me off a little bit." Pausing to collect his thoughts, Biko seemed resistant to internalizing an absolute or narrow idea of being a U.S. citizen. "I would call myself several different things." Biko elaborated,

> It may stir a little controversy. First and foremost I do identify myself as a Black male. And for my own sake and you know healing my woundedness I call myself an African. Just so not to lose touch from where

Black "Youth Speak Truth" to Power 203

I really come from. I guess as a citizen, I don't really feel [hesitates] . . . I guess like for one the incentives that come from being a citizen [he stops to reorganize his thoughts] . . . right, so truthfully, I can vote. I personally don't see where my vote really falls into place. So, I'm not sure how they can convince me that my voting has weight. I don't see how my voting has weight in the decision. Personally, I don't really see it . . . or really feel like my viewpoint, my world view, contributes to how this society operates. Especially as a youth, I feel like we do carry the torch of our ancestors and our elders. I don't really see [Southeastern city], the decision makers of [Southeastern city] really taking into account our voices or the work. . . . I don't see the mayor on this bus. I don't see the people who give citizenship to me . . . doing or making change for the better in our world, personally. (Interview, June 19, 2010)

Probing his thoughts about feeling disenfranchised or invisible to city decision makers, I asked Biko what, if anything, his participation in Youth Voices has taught him concerning his and other youth voices in relationship to power and influence. Essentially, I was asking Biko to tell me why he is participating as a youth action team leader if he believes that his "viewpoints" do not carry "weight." Biko expounded,

I do it for the people, for my people, for the people who struggle due to what's already set in place regarding how this society is run . . . people struggling because of that. We're all coming together . . . people who feel just like me about citizenship. The fact that we don't think that our voices are really heard or taken into consideration enough to really make the world what we want it to be. So, I feel like I'm a little ant in a big anthill of people who want to collectively move mountains. Just me being there . . . the energy that I give off. It's like one of them ants. I'm carrying my ten pounds. . . . I'm carrying double, triple however much they say an ant can carry times their weight. I believe everybody on this bus is as well. Each and every last one of us for one is the make up of everybody that existed in our blood before us. So, even that in and of itself is powerful. I feel like I'm comprised of all of my ancestors running through my blood. When necessary, I can call on them and react and respond and really be dynamic. I feel like everyone of us can. Especially at the social forum . . . when it comes to struggle and people who got fire inside of them . . . ain't nothing you can do but build or tear down, and tearing down ain't always a bad thing. (Interview, June 19, 2010)

The nature of civic engagement and attitudes about civic action in the context of Youth Voices was informed by a pan-Africanist sociopolitical worldview that involves struggling for the rights and liberation for all African people anywhere and everywhere, as evidenced by Biko's own perception of himself as a Black male African.

Sitting next to Biko, another youth leader in Youth Voices described her perception of a citizen: "I guess I see a citizen like being a person in your community, being there for a long time, knowing each other, communicating with people. Going to work in that community." According to Miriam, "[P]eople got like different perspectives" about citizenship. "People saying citizenship is like if you vote. . . . [I]t's all how you perceive it. It's like a label. . . . [Y]ou can label yourself as a girl. It's just a title. And some people like to be called citizen and some people don't." In describing who or what a citizen is, Miriam seemed to focus on the roles and responsibilities of a citizen rather than on any specific relationship to a particular geographic location, nation, or cultural group. She hinted at the idea that citizenship duties extend beyond voting to include an investment in "your" community.

Chiming in again, Biko adds to his previous thoughts: "I'm from America, from [city of study], I'm from [state of study]." Qualifying his statement, Biko continues, "Though I may have been born here, I wouldn't necessarily say I'm from here all the way . . . and how ever controversial that may seem . . . I think that for me it kind of helps me to reconnect with where I'm from. I didn't come over here . . ." His final words trail off as he alludes to the involuntary or forced migration of enslaved Africans to the Americas. Biko, like many of the Youth Voices participants, is influenced by the environment created by the sponsoring nonprofit organization. In this context, concepts about civic engagement and citizenship are informed by a prevailing Afrocentric worldview.

IMPLICATIONS

The Youth Voices program is designed to prepare Black youth, in particular, and youth of color generally, to be active in a society with policies and practices that often intentionally or unintentionally have a negative impact on their lives. The weekly political and popular education workshops, weekend retreats, technical training, radio broadcasts, field trips to partner organizations, and community action projects all are constructed to raise the consciousness of its participants. With each agenda item, current events discussion, or consideration of the youth program's guidelines, careful attention is given to creating spaces and opportunities for critical inquiry and dialogue, analysis of underlining or "hidden" messages, critique of ethnocentric forms of knowledge (in favor of indigenous ways of knowing), and reflection on possible civic actions. This type of democratic engagement and criticality often is missing from the public school context. In an interview, Aniya revealed what she perceived as a disconnect between the rhetoric and practice regarding her school's purported agenda to empower students:

> At my school we have something called the student government, but it's not a student government. It's just an exercise where we like put

up posters, but like after its over its still up to the principal [regarding] everything that goes on, so here [at Youth Voices] it's like the whole opposite of it. Like it's the people's choice, you get what I'm saying. They [the adult allies] suggest what to do, but they don't tell us. It's really our power. (Interview, June, 2010)

Aniya's reflection confronted the ways in which schools claim to give students choice and agency. In contrast, it is clear that Aniya perceives Youth Voices as a space for youth power.

A consistent thread evident in the diverse literacy practices of Youth Voices is a belief in the emancipatory power of and truth in African American culture and history. Refusing to accept the cultural deficit-laden rhetoric that shapes the current discourse around Black student achievement in the U.S., Youth Voices address the miseducation of youth of color (Hilliard, 1995; King, 2004; King & Hollins, 1997; Woodson, 1933) by making visible the significant contributions of communities of color and by connecting with the legacy of competency among the African American community, particularly as it relates to literacy and social action. Although diverse in class, gender, and degree of exposure to community activism, all of the youth share a common Afrocentric history and culture. According to Hilliard (1995),

> Groups that have a cultural identity draw upon it and replenish themselves not only through study, but through appropriate rituals and symbols. Rituals and symbols such as naming, rites of passage, holidays, distinctive dress, etc., help to formulate and to crystallize ideals, values, rules, which give meaning to life itself. This is the basis for group cohesion and solidarity that is a prerequisite to group power. (p. 69)

Youth Voices exemplify the ways in which Hilliard's theory of culture at the center of group cohesion and power manifests at the macro level among Blacks in America or people of the African diaspora. Such group cohesion and solidarity was evident in the Youth Voices literacy practices.

The race and culture of the participants in Youth Voices is not irrelevant to their learning and ways of engaging literacy. Instead, the ways in which the participants identify and acknowledge their cultural histories matter. For example, it mattered in their choices of radio broadcast content (e.g., opening song), and it was reflected in the ways the curriculum was forged from a Black radical tradition (King, 2006). Across all Youth Voices activities, literacy is embedded in the cultural practices of the youth participants. As Holt (1990) writes, within the African American community, knowledge is power, and literacy has been a cornerstone of accessing and leveraging that power. Similarly, Perry (2004) notes that historically literacy in the Black community is about liberation. In this way, the literacy goals in the context of Youth Voices are to educate, validate, and empower. They do so by utilizing curricular material including the *Black Radical Tradition Toolkit*, which includes narratives of the contributions of local Black leaders and community members. It includes attending to cultural history as evidenced in their use of the *Eyes on the Prize* documentary series and their field trips to places like Selma and Birmingham, Alabama, to retrace pivotal civil rights moments, all designed to enhance their knowledge, validate their cultural and racial experiences, and inspire their own legacies of liberation and change.

Such attention to race and culture reflects (or are indices of) what Lee (2005) and Lee and Ball (2005) frame as culturally responsive design. The curriculum and activities within the context of Youth Voices has been designed to make relevant the identities of the participants. In this space, it does matter that the youth all identify as Black (or African American, Caribbean, African, or of the Diaspora). Centering race and culture in the context of teaching and learning is significant because, as mentioned in the introduction, educators and researchers are seeking ways to improve the academic achievement of youth of color without severing them from their cultural roots. Literature suggests that such cultural competence is linked to growth in learning and literacy acquisition (King, 2004; Ladson-Billings, 1994). This kind of asset-based education, building on youth's cultural funds of knowledge is likely to be successful and has positive implications for student engagement and motivation.

Radio is one of the tools that the group uses to accomplish its overall mission to end oppression. The youth attempt to do so in an oppression-free space. Establishing such an inclusive and equitable space is not a static process as it presents daily challenges for the youth participants. This arena invites tensions that allow for growth and opportunity, which is in contrast to many public school environments that silence or limit the opportunity for youth to engage civically.

The stories from Youth Voices revealed that civic engagement among Black youth may be expressed differently from conventional indicators of youth civic engagement. Additionally, scholarship on citizenship and civic engagement among school-age youth reveals that the "civic education" gap between White students and students of color is expressed in poorly resourced schools where higher percentages of students of color are enrolled and opportunities for civic engagement are rare. Youth Voices provide insight into the circumstances in which students of color are likely to practice citizenship. Authentic opportunities that result in direct action or actualized change seem to engage the youth involved with Youth Voices. As such, civic engagement, in part, is achieved through youth media production.

One of the most salient themes to emerge from Youth Voices is the competence of the youth, including and in particular youth of color, to articulate what they need to succeed. As I suggested earlier, youth are absent from the proverbial table concerning public policy related to education reform in the U.S. Relegated to marginal (albeit critically important) spaces like youth centers or after-school programs, youth perspectives are rarely seriously taken up beyond novel and/or cursory nods. The examination of Youth Voices provides an instructive model for how to center youth voices and establish communities inside schools. The youth radio collective participants routinely attribute their connectedness to the content and goals of the program to the "family" atmosphere. If as educators we advocate for an authentic democracy, then teaching and learning literacy in an era of diversity and multiculturalism requires that members of viable communities need to feel ownership, agency, respected, valued, and empowered to thrive (Gilyard, 1996).

Youth Voices are an example of the capacity and agency of urban youth and emphasize the extent to which teacher education programs should include student voice. Students should be afforded opportunities to actively shape their education. Teachers through their curriculum and instruction have opportunities to incorporate civic engagement activities that promote lifelong civic participation. For example, teachers may integrate critical service learning (see National Service-Learning Conference Youth Series or United States Social Forum) or participatory action research (e.g., Camangian, 2008; Cammarota & Fine, 2008; Duncan-Andrade, 2006; Duncan-Andrade & Morrell, 2004; Morrell, 2004).

With access to programs or educational environments like Youth Voices, youth of color engaged in relevant learning experiences have the potential to develop high-order critical thinking skills, skills often rendered absent by the dominant role of static learning in schools, particularly for urban youth stigmatized via school-to-prison pipeline deficit beliefs about themselves and their communities. Instead educators should be versed in positive youth development theory that taps into the potential of youth as partners in designing and implementing curriculum. Youth Voices do not solve all ills or problems effecting youth of color but certainly offers innovative strategies and creative spaces for meaningful learning.

NOTES

1 A reference to Theresa Perry's (2004) chapter, "Freedom for Literacy and Literacy for Freedom" in the edited volume, *To Be Young, Gifted, and Black: Promoting High Achievement Among African American Students*.
2 All names of organizations, programs, and participants, both adult and youth, have been changed or altered.

REFERENCES

Arnold, J., & Weusi, L. (2004). *Youth Voices program proposal*, Unpublished.
Camangian, P. (2008). Untempered tongues: Teaching performance poetry for social justice. *English Teaching: Practice and Critique, 7*(2), 33–55.
Cammarota, J., & Fine, M. (Eds.). (2008). *Revolutionizing education: Youth participatory action research in motion*. New York, NY: Routledge.

Dolby, N. (2003). Popular culture and democratic practice. *Harvard Educational Review, 73*(3), 258–284.

Duncan-Andrade, J. (2006). Urban youth, media literacy, and increased critical civic participation. In S. Ginwright, P. Noguera, & J. Cammarota (Eds.), *Beyond resistance! Youth activism and community change: New democratic possibilities for practice and policy for America's youth* (pp. 149–169). New York, NY: Routledge.

Duncan-Andrade, J., & Morrell, E. (2004). What they do learn in school: Hip-Hop as a bridge to canonical poetry. In J. Mahiri (Ed.), *What they don't learn in school: Literacy in the lives of urban youth* (pp. 247–268). New York, NY: Peter Lang.

Fisher, M. T. (2009). *Black literate lives: Historical and contemporary perspectives.* New York: Routledge.

Franklin, V. P. (1984). *Black self-determination: A cultural history of the faith of the fathers.* Westport, CT: Lawrence Hill.

Freire, P. (1970). *Pedagogy of the oppressed.* New York, NY: Continuum.

Gilyard, K. (1996). *Let's flip the script: An African American discourse on language, literature, and learning.* Detroit, MI: Wayne State University Press.

Giroux, H. (2006). *America on the edge: Henry Giroux on politics, culture, and education.* New York, NY: Palgrave Macmillan

Green, K. (2014). Doing double Dutch methodology: Playing with the practice of participant observer. In D. Paris & M. Winn (Eds.), *Humanizing research, decolonizing qualitative inquiry with youth and communities* (pp. 147–160). Thousand Oaks, CA: SAGE.

Hampton, J. (Dir.). (2010). *Eyes on the prize: America's civil rights years 1954–1965.* United States: Blackside.

Hilliard, A. (1995). *The maroon within us: Selected essays on African American community socialization.* Baltimore, MD: Black Classic Press.

Holt, T. (1990). Knowledge is power: The Black struggle for literacy. In A. A. Lunsford, H. Moglen, & J. Slevin (Eds.), *The right to literacy* (pp. 91–102). New York, NY: Modern Language Association.

King, J. (2004). Culture-centered knowledge: Black studies, curriculum transformation, and social action. In J. A. Banks & C. A. McGee Banks (Eds.), *Handbook of research on multicultural education* (2nd ed., pp. 349–378). San Francisco: Jossey-Bass.

King, J. (2006). If justice is our objective: Diaspora literacy, heritage knowledge, and the praxis of critical studyin' for human freedom. In A. Ball (Ed.), *With more deliberate speed: Achieving equity and excellence in education—realizing the full potential of Brown V. Board of Education* (pp. 337–360). New York, NY: Wiley, John & Sons.

King, J., & Hollins, E. (1997). *Preparing teachers for cultural diversity.* New York, NY: Teachers College Press.

Ladson-Billings, G. (1994). *The dreamkeepers: Successful teachers of African American children.* San Francisco, CA: Jossey-Bass.

LeCompte, M., & Schensul, J. (1999). *Designing and conducting ethnographic research.* Walnut Creek, CA: Alta Mira Press.

Lee, C. D. (2005). Taking culture into account: Intervention research based on current views of cognition & learning. In J. King (Ed.), *Black education: A transformative research and action agenda for the new century* (pp. 73–114). Mahwah,

NJ: Lawrence Erlbaum (joint publication with the American Educational Research Association).

Lee, C. D., & Ball, A. (2005). All that glitters ain't gold: CHAT as a design and analytical tool in literacy research. In R. Beach, J. Green, T. Shannahan, & M. Kamil (Eds.), *Multidisciplinary perspectives on literacy research* (2nd ed., pp. 101–132). Cresskill, NH: Hampton Press (with the National Conference of Research in Language and Literacy).

McChesney, R. (1999). *Rich media, poor democracy: Communication politics in dubious times.* Champaign: University of Illinois Press.

Morrell, E. (2004). *Linking literacy and popular culture: Finding connections for lifelong learning.* Norwood, MA: Christopher-Gordon Publishers.

Perry, T. (2004). Freedom for literacy and literacy for freedom: The African-American philosophy of education. In T. Perry, C. Steele, & A. Hilliard (Eds.), *To be young, gifted, and black: Promoting high achievement among African American students* (pp. 11–51). Boston, MA: Beacon Press.

Sherrod, L. R., Torney-Purta, J., & Flanagan, C. A. (2010). *Handbook of research on civic engagement in youth.* Hoboken, NJ: Wiley.

Torney-Purta, J., Lehmann, R., Oswald, H., & Schulz, W. (2001). *Citizenship and education in twenty-eight countries: Civic knowledge and engagement at age fourteen.* Amsterdam, The Netherlands: International Association for the Evaluation of Educational Achievement.

Torney-Purta, J., Schwille, J., & Amadeo, J. (Eds.). (1999). *Civic education across countries: Twenty-four case studies from the IEA Civic Education Project.* Amsterdam, The Netherlands: International Association for the Evaluation of Educational Achievement.

Woodson, C. G. (1933). *The mis-education of the Negro.* Chicago: African American Images.

10 Bilingual Youth Voices in Middle School
Performance, Storytelling, and Photography

Ruth Harman, Lindy L. Johnson, and Edgar Escutia Chagoya

In May 2014 the third author of our chapter, Edgar Escutia Chagoya, stood up in his middle school media center and recounted the story of his journey from Mexico to the U.S. and his first months living in Athens, Georgia. A complete newcomer from Guanajuato when he joined our Rabbit Box Youth Voices (RBYV) project, 13-year-old Edgar thrived on preparing stories, photos, and poetry in Spanish and English for two public performances. Throughout this chapter, beginning with his comments, which follow, Edgar provides salient observations about what he and his fellow bilingual students need in school and why he became invested in the RBYV project. Ruth and Edgar met regularly when writing this chapter, and we have not edited his comments in any way in terms of content or grammar. Edgar also wanted to make sure that his comments were separate from our regular narrative so that readers could see read and interact with him directly. We indented and italicized Edgar's comments.

> *When coming to the States, students often can feel frustrated because they need to start school from scratch in English and the only reason they move to the States is for economic reasons. They are shocked when they go to school. In my case, I had to work in Mexico every morning with my parents and go to school in afternoon—so I was determined to study and do well in the States—but it is not easy for any of us.* (Edgar's comments)

In recent years, harsh immigration policies and discourses have created hostile environments for bilingual students and their communities in the U.S. and other immigrant-receiving nations (Allexsaht-Snider, Buxton, & Harman, 2013). Indeed, because of high-stakes testing fever and standard English-only mandates, instructional practices and curricula in most urban school districts in the U.S. fail to incorporate the cultural and linguistic interests of their diverse student populations (Gutiérrez, Asato, Santos, & Gotanda, 2002; Paris, 2012). In New Latino Diaspora states such as Georgia, the marginalization of emergent bilingual youth is heightened even more because Mexicans and El Salvadorans, for instance, do not fit into existent cultural models of minority students in the Southeast (Wortham, Murillo, & Hamann, 2002, p. 3).

Not coincidentally, the median annual earnings of Latinos more than 16 years old in Georgia is $18,300, with only 58 percent of Latinos graduating from high school and 41 percent of children under the age of 18 living in poverty (Pew Research, 2014). To compound these difficulties, new anti-immigration policies and practices in 2010 and 2011 further challenge our students. For example, a ban instituted by the Georgia University System Board of Regents in October 2010 was designed to prevent undocumented students from gaining admission to selective universities in the state regardless of high achievement records (University System of Georgia, 2010). In addition, although Georgia does not have an official English-only mandate, only rarely do Latino students enjoy the benefits of interacting in Spanish with bilingual educators or administrators (see Colomer & Harklau, 2009). The consequences of such policies and practices have been highly negative for the social and emotional well-being of adolescent bilingual learners and their mixed-status communities (Harman & Varga-Dobai, 2012; Stevenson & Beck, 2013).

Since I arrived in summer 2013 I have seen many cases where a student may get more and more depressed because he is in classes with English only speaking students who he can't even understand. The chances keep increasing every year that these students will drop out. (Edgar's comments)

Despite, or indeed because of, such daunting challenges and practices, critical educators and activists (e.g., the editors and authors of the individual chapters in this book) strive to implement resource pedagogies *with youth* that disrupt and replace the increasing teaching-to-the-test frenzy in public school contexts (see Ravitch, 2013). In a recent variation on this perspective, Paris (2012) proposed a model of culturally sustaining pedagogy that strives to incorporate the languages and cultures of students while also taking "a critical stance toward and critical action against unequal power relations" (p. 95). Inherent in such an approach is the belief that the linguistic, cultural, and literacy resources that students bring to school mediate disciplinary knowledge in multi-perspectival ways (e.g., Martínez-Roldán & Fránquiz, 2009; Moll, 2001). Knowledge, in other words, is not a product that can be transmitted to students but needs to be co-constructed through multiple cultural and linguistic lenses and modalities of classroom participants (see Freire, 1970; Gutiérrez, 2008).

Recent YPAR describes how emergent bilingual youth have created counter-narratives on their sociohistorical lives through collective arts processes such as drawing, film making, performance, and poetry writing (Chappell & Cahnmann-Taylor, 2013; Chappell & Faltis, 2013; Faltis, 2013; Ginwright, 2008). Medina and Campano (2006) reported how their critical use of performance supported students in reimagining and reinterpreting aspects of their personal, interpersonal, and institutional lives. Gutiérrez (2008) called for the creation of a resistant educational space that privileges and builds on students' culturally learned approaches to learning, including discourse, social practices, and political stances, arguing that the use of *teatro* (theater), critical theory, and discussion supported students in reframing every day and institutional literacies into "powerful literacies oriented toward critical social thought" (p. 149).

In this chapter, we describe how an arts-based project was developed at Coile Middle School (CMS) to engage youth and adult participants in storytelling, poetry writing, photography, and public presentations during the year 2013–2014. Ruth Harman is a university educator who has spent several years over the past decade working with teachers and students at CMS on genre-based pedagogies and arts-informed youth collaboration. Lindy L. Johnson is a university educator who has worked with teachers and students in Georgia and Virginia on incorporating critical digital literacies and multimodal composition into classrooms. Edgar is a soon-to-be eighth grader at CMS. The school is designated as a Title 1 institution with 95 percent of the school on a free lunch plan. It has a culturally diverse student body with 58 percent African Americans and 38 percent Latinos. The Latino population has increased exponentially in the past 10 years at CMS and indeed in most of the schools in our school district (see CMS Web site for more information, http://www.clarke.k12.ga.us/WRCoile.cfm.

The purpose of our chapter is to illustrate how participatory engagement in the arts affords bilingual and bidialectal youth with a range of social identities and voices to play and assume in the context of a trusting community of practice (see Greene, Burke, & McKenna, 2013). In our concluding section, we discuss the limitations of our work and the implications and challenges of carrying out such projects in the current climate of high-stakes accountability and lack of funding for the arts and public transportation in Georgia—and indeed nationwide.

CONTEXTUALIZING THE WORK: ROBUST COMMUNITIES OF PRACTICE AND SECOND LANGUAGE ACQUISITION

A critical sociocultural perspective on learning and teaching is adopted in a large range of recent studies related to second language acquisition of marginalized youth. Influenced primarily by Vygotskian theories of learning, the sociocultural perspective emphasizes the role of cultural tools and social interaction as key mediators in language and literacy development (Moll, 2001). Literacy is viewed as "a medium that constitutes and affirms the historical and existential moments of lived experience, not only the development of skills oriented to acquiring a dominant academic discourse" (Macedo, 2003, p. 13). Campano (2005), for example, developed a "second class" on the margins of official school space so that dialogic learning and teaching could occur by following the students' interests, desires, forms of cultural expression, and especially their stories. His focal participant, Carmen, began to relate her immigrant experiences through art and storytelling in ways she never had had the opportunity to share in the regular classroom.

From a Vygotskian perspective (e.g., Vygotsky, 1978), Carmen's learning and literacy development in Campano's second class was mediated by interaction with caring and invested participants who encouraged her to engage with a sociohistorical sense of past, present, and future. In this vein, Faltis and Coulter (2008) see bilingual language development as dependent on robust learning conditions such as full integration with classroom peers regardless of language or culture and involvement in a range of modalities and participation structures that strengthen and affirm cultural and social identities.

In a previous action research project, Ruth and colleagues (e.g., Harman & Varga-Dobai, 2012) found that a group of middle school Latina girls expanded their cultural and semiotic repertoires because they engaged actively in performance and storytelling and also because they needed to interact continuously with new participants and visitors who kept joining the community (cf. Medina & Campano, 2006). In an ever-increasing group of supporters and participants, the emergent bilingual learners frequently retold their experiences about their art making, producing a chain of literacy events that were connected to their original storytelling and performances (Bauman & Briggs, 1990). This process of taking a previous text informed by different modalities (e.g., theater games, storytelling, and body sculpting) and recontextualizing it in a stretch of oral or written discourse is a complex undertaking for emergent learners that promotes complex understandings of literacy as a social process (Gibbons, 2006; Harman & Smagorinsky, 2014). Indeed, bilingual students become truly agentive only when educators support them in producing visual, embodied, and verbal identity texts that they can choose to remix for communicative and aesthetic purposes (Cummins, 2001).

> *I feel that teachers and students need to work on changing school practices so that immigrant students are prepared to work in the United States. If not, the students cannot contribute to the national economy. Indeed I have learned most from my ESOL classes where the students and teacher listen and share with each other. The teachers need to give us time. I need time to understand and projects like RBYV give me chances to talk and write in different ways.* (Edgar's comments)

RABBIT BOX YOUTH VOICES PROJECT (RBYV): IT TAKES A VILLAGE

Through reflections and write-up of our recent RBYV project that lasted from October 2013 to May 2014, we realize that the collaborative environment at the middle school was crucial *to how* the youth members of our group responded to our call for active participation in a mostly after-school arts project. Adults and youth worked together through multiple modes (voices for storytelling, pens for writing, photography, etc.) to craft new spaces that enabled transformative learning to take place (Vasudevan, 2009). We begin with a description of the context of culture that promoted and fostered the dynamic participation of middle school Latino and African American students at Coile.

Coile Serves

Ruth Harman, first author of this paper, has been working with Kelli Bivins at CMS since 2009. In their first years working together, they developed a genre-based approach to teaching social studies in a sheltered English instruction context that supported students in performing, storytelling, and presenting their research at a national conference (see Harman et al., 2013). Kelli Bivins, a truly remarkable multicultural educator versed in Freire (e.g., 1970), already had begun a community endeavor called "Coile Serves" in 2007. Kelli used grant funds and a lot of community support from her family and friends over several years in setting up a collaborative partnership with mostly Latin@ and African American students and their communities. On her school Web site, her group describes the initiative in the following way:

> Students at W.R. Coile Middle School are committed to serving our community, making it a better place for all. In addition to service projects and working to become more academically prepared, we are proponents of shopping locally, creating art, and taking care of our environment and each other.
> (Coile Cougar Cares, 2015)

Some of the projects that the group spearheaded include participation in Peer Court in Athens, Parent Informational Sessions, Sustainability Environment Project, and poetry workshops. As they say on the Web site, the group is "committed and caring during the school day and as an after-school and weekend club."

Rabbit Box Storytelling

In our small college town of Athens, a group of artists and activists developed a storytelling project in 2012 very much informed by the national storytelling project, The Moth, which has shared thousands of stories worldwide that are a hybrid mix of documentary and drama (see http://themoth.org). On their Web site, the Athenian group describes how they hope that monthly storytelling will generate "a common understanding, a deeper

Bilingual Youth Voices in Middle School 215

sense of history, and a shared community" in our town (see Rabbit Box, 2015). In fall 2013 Matthew Epperson, one of its organizers, asked Kelli Bivins if she would be interested in organizing a youth night of storytelling with him. She, in turn, invited Ruth and other adult participants including the other ESOL teacher, Alicia Coughlan, to join the project. The key participants were 13 African American and Latino Coile students, one Latino high school student and a European American elementary school student who were all eager to write, perform, and share their life experiences. Over

Figure 10.1 Rabbit Box Poster for Coile Storytelling in Athens

time in our artist group of adults and youth, we added a professional storyteller, three professional photographers, a poet and several theater buffs, teachers, and graduate students

Story Telling and Performance (October 2013—January 2014)

Rabbit Box uses talented volunteers to support members of the Athens community in creating and performing stories for Rabbit Box events. Volunteer members help storytellers think about how to sequence their stories, how to tell a story in dramatic ways, and how to perform in front of a large audience. In mid-October, adult participants began to work alongside the student participants on building trust through theater and voice games and identifying themes that might be interesting for participants to develop into fully fleshed stories that would be performed at a special "Rabbit Box Jr." Most of the stories that student participants chose to share and perform were dramatic and often tragic moments in their lives, such as an uncle being electrocuted; learning how to kill a calf at the age of seven; arriving from Mexico to a new place and language; and being bullied. Over the course of two months, the group met weekly to workshop the stories and to think of how best to perform and sequence the stories.

> *I was already confident in Ms. Bivins' room because she always did different projects to make us feel confident. So I decided to join Rabbit Box Young. At first I was feeling very uncomfortable because most of the kids were older. When we started playing theater games and everyone was having fun, I felt much better. I was having problems at first to pick a good story but Ms. Coughlan helped me a lot and my Mom and Auntie. I decided to write about our move from Mexico to here because it was the making of a new life. I knew I was going to never go back—it was pretty hard to restart, mostly because of new culture and language. My Mom helped me remember several episodes of the journey. I knew nothing about the English at the beginning. I tried writing in English first but it was too hard and I knew I wasn't going to be ready in time to present so I switched to sharing it in Spanish.* (Edgar's comments)

Edgar's story was workshopped through theater and performance techniques each week. He wrote and narrated his trip from Mexico to Athens and the different ranges of emotions he experienced on the long journey, on his reunion with relatives in the U.S., and on his first days in his new school with almost no English. Importantly, in the narrative he identified his two ESOL teachers, Ms. Bivins and Ms. Coughlan, as being highly influential in making him feel more settled in the English environment (see Appendix 1 for Edgar's complete story in Spanish). On the night of the performance, our Rabbit Box gathered together nervously but also excitedly in a small green room waiting to appear on stage. Each of our student participants told their stories to a packed house of 170 family, friends, and Athens community members. They spoke with passion, commitment, and confidence.

All of us felt elated watching the young adolescent members shine under the lights of the famous Melting Point. For many of the youth participants, performing in front of a live audience was the highlight of the project and served as a touchstone experience that the students would revisit in their photography and poetry later on in the school year. Reflecting on his performance, Edgar shared immediately after the project, "I loved it. Being in front of everyone. I'm the center. Thank you for looking at me! And, the attention on me. I loved that." Similarly, Jesse Hernandez, another youth participant, said that the telling stories as part of Rabbit Box was challenging for him, but also the best part of the project, because, as he put it, "I love the attention." When talking with Edgar about this event, he remembered vividly preparing for the performance and standing up on stage. His comments follow.

> *I felt very nervous on the night of the performance but a friend came on stage with me and helped translate for me as I was speaking in Spanish. I tried to be strong and I followed my father's advice who said not to look at the audience but just to look at a point on the wall. I felt good because the people were understanding how difficult the trip to the United States was and also having to learn all in English (into new life). When they started clapping, I felt all my hard work I did to learn*

Figure 10.2 Edgar on Stage at Melting Point

the story and also to do well in school was worth it. I was able to let everything out, I felt pretty good. People don't understand what it is like (they have no idea of the feelings or anything), what is happening until they take the time. I felt I wasn't trapped by the story anymore but let the world know why I feel like I feel. (Edgar's comments)

As clearly stated by Edgar in his comments, he and his peers celebrated having a downtown, hip venue to make their stories known to a wider audience. Similarly, after reading a draft of this chapter, our Rabbit Box organizer Matt Epperson, volunteered the following comments about the process:

Rabbit Box Jr. was a special Rabbit Box evening in many ways. These were our youngest storytellers ever to take the Rabbit Box stage. Participating in the workshops, all of our students quickly learned from each other how they could form their life experiences into meaningful stories. Working with Jesse, he and I found out what fire really meant as a symbol to his family in the wake of an attack on his older sister. Their topics were not easy in many cases and the students relied on each other to have the courage to go on stage in front of 170 adults (see Rabbit box archive, 2015). The whole process was truly collaborative and made students and adults alike better storytellers for the experience. We have become a stronger community for doing Rabbit Box Jr., which is the mission statement of our organization. (E-mail communication, June 2015)

Reflecting on Rabbit Box Junior

When engaging with the youth participants of the project, it became clear to us that the act of storytelling was quite a complex activity that encouraged students to draw from a wide range of semiotic resources to share lived experiences that some had never written down or shared before. They also learned through the workshops and games how to play with shifts in prosody, intonation, and gesture to indicate and align with different characters and events when presenting stories (Bauman & Briggs, 1990). The collective storytelling in the group opened up a pathway for all of us to reach across boundaries of culture and language to understand each other's lived experiences in deeply meaningful ways (Roche & Sadowsky, 2003). Critical race theorists highlight how retelling of lived experiences of marginalized peoples are rarely shared in institutional contexts because the "truth" is shaped in such a way that the rights of the dominant community are guaranteed by silencing and distortion of these lived experiences (e.g., Delgado & Stephanic, 2012). In our after-school group, the interrelationships in the group along with time, space, and imagination were essential resources that afforded the tellers and the listeners with a collaborative space to extend and deepen their lived narratives and imaginary leaps into the future (Greene, 2001).

Taking Pictures That Tell Stories

Building on the positive momentum from the Melting Point event, Ruth invited three photographers and a poet to work with the students in the after-school program beginning in February 2014 (funded by small grant from Athfest Educates! See http://athfest.com/education). Ruth and the other adult members of RBYV saw the goal of the photography and poetry workshops as a way to continue to nurture the students' artistic abilities and sense of authorship by encouraging them to relay their narratives through visual forms. We conceptualized photography as a way viewers could literally "see" through the eyes of young people as they made decisions about what to photograph, how to frame their photographs, and how to make decisions about which photographs best conveyed the emotional impact they hoped to achieve in their stories.

The photography workshops, "Taking Pictures That Tell Stories," began with an exploration of basic composition rules such as the rule of thirds, filling the frame, creating depth, using leading lines and varying viewpoint. After learning some basic photography and composition skills, each of the three photographers led three to four students on a variety of on-location photo shoots in and around the town of Athens. Students were then given digital cameras to continue taking photos and documenting their stories in their own homes and neighborhoods and the small details of their lives. The students (literally) pictured their neighborhoods, schools, bedrooms, and other locales; they also pictured themselves as members of family systems and social communities. They came back to the bigger group with a mosaic of photos and oral descriptions that highlighted particular artistic insights and relationships to their community and home lives. Cleveland, for example, was especially proud of a photo he took of icicles on his mother's car because he said, "It was beautiful." Researchers, indeed, see visual imagery as a key element in social identity formation and for our youth members; the photos provided them with keener resources to articulate how they saw themselves at school or at home (Packard, Ellison, & Sequenzia, 2004, p. 3). Visual sociologist Doug Harper (2002) highlights the importance of the medium as "photos can jolt subjects into a new awareness of their social existence" (p. 21).

Because the focus in our RBYV project was on artistic representation, we encouraged participants to take photographs related to their story, not just in an illustrative manner but also in symbolic ways to get at the emotional aspects of their stories. Similar to the work of Curwood and Cowell (2011), we asked students to explore multiple interpretations of their personal narratives. For example, during one of the workshops, we asked students to

220 *Ruth Harman, Lindy L. Johnson, and Edgar Escutia Chagoya*

consider the key question: How can I compose images that complement the story that I want to tell? The photographers modeled this process for the students by showing them an image from a digital story they had created called "Undocumented." The photographers explained their artistic process and how they often struggled to find visual images that would impact viewers in terms of relating to how people with undocumented immigration statuses were being treated in Georgia. In an effort to evoke a sense of sadness and loss, the photographers took a photo of a pair of empty work boots. The photographers asked the students to tell their stories to each other in small groups and to explore the feelings they had and the images they saw in their minds as they pictured these stories.

To illustrate, we show samples of Edgar's photographs and his thoughts and decision-making process when selecting what to photograph. Edgar's photographs were very much aligned to his story about coming from Mexico to a new land of language and culture, but they also provided a different medium through which Edgar could explore multiple ways of representing his story in unexpected ways.

> *I took this photo of a one-way sign because that is what I felt when I heard my Mom saying we were going to leave our small town in Mexico. I remember thinking, "We are going to go to the United States. It is going to be just one way (no going way back). We could have stayed but that way was vanished. I am leaving my grandfather, my friends and*

Figure 10.3 One Way Sign

Figure 10.4 Arrival to New Home

Figure 10.5 The Yellow Bus

my community and even if I come back when I am older, it will never be the same. (Edgar's comments)
　　When I took this photo of luggage, I was thinking of when we arrived to my new home after so long. I remember feeling disappointed because when we were there before, my auntie and family lived in a different location and all my other family members were near them. I liked the new house but felt that everyone was now separate. Family for me is when everyone lives near each other and we can talk and hang out. But now in Athens, it was a small family unit. (Edgar's comments)
　　In my home town I always cycled to my school and I knew nearly everyone as they lived near my house. When I got on this yellow bus for the first time, I felt so frightened because I knew my cousin Andrew wouldn't be in the same classes as me and I didn't have any English.

Poetry Boot Camp

During the spring, we also invited Paul Ayo, a talented spoken-word poet, and the founder and director of the nonprofit organization, Art as an Agent for Change (see http://aacshutdown.org/). The mission of Paul's organization is "[t]o establish alliances with other artists, combat the plight of the oppressed, engage social apathy, promote social awareness, and build lasting human connections through the medium of art." Paul chooses to focus on the poetry because "it is an artistic medium with very few barriers to entry. I always boast that I can take a room of people from all walks of life, educational backgrounds, or geographic regions, and turn their stories into one meaningful poem" (personal interview, June 1, 2015).

　　Paul presented a poetry workshop for the CMS students on a frosty Saturday morning in March. Paul led both the students and adults in the RBYV project through a number of poetry-writing activities. Similar to our photography work, his purpose was to help the students feel connected to their homes, their families, and their communities by writing about who they were (a variation on Linda Christensen's (2009) "I Am" poems) and how they felt in their skin in their lives as dynamic young learners. Specifically, Paul hoped to draw on students' prior knowledge and to help them "understand that they have a valid story that can serve to inspire and educate others about the world" (personal interview, June 1, 2015). This requires activities that help participants become less self-conscious, and so Paul begin by leading students in a variety of improvisational games.

　　For Paul, the key to working with poetry is helping young people "understand that their stories are unique, inspirational, and meaningful." He led students through several process activities including listing memories, making word clouds, and drawing pictures. According to Paul, a central aspect of this process is that students learn to "seek their inner story and trigger meaningful personal insight." Ultimately, he has chosen these activities because he has "seen them have a profound effect on how

Table 10.1

Sometimes I Don't Feel Embarrassed Edgar Escutia Chagoya	Edgar's Comments
If I showed you how happy I am would you laugh out loud? If I showed you how sad I am would you still laugh? If I showed you how nervous I am would you laugh at me? If I showed you how excited I am would you laugh then? Or would you be excited too?	Working with Paul helped me to get to know another side of the other students in the group. Shia, for example, just wrote great poems and we got to know each other well. We are still great friends. It also helped us gain confidence about meeting other people cause it showed how to talk about feelings in another way—It made me more comfortable—reaching out to others to help them understand how I was really feeling—when people are mad, they show it in different ways so important to share what we are feeling. Writing poetry also helped me in English, helped me to give more details.

others view themselves and the world." To get them more invested in writing with rhythm, Paul also showed them how to appropriate the pacing and shape of a poem that had a given refrain and theme (as illustrated by Edgar's poem).

Reflecting on Photography and Poetry Workshops

As Edgar shared already, the photography and digital storytelling afforded users an expanded range of semiotic resources to express thoughts and feelings *and* a place to be "experts" about their real and imaginary lives (Bartholomé, 2009, p. 350). By drawing from the Internet and from artistic renderings of their homes and communities, Edgar and the other students could express and explain the cultures and languages of home to teachers and others who might not share the same background knowledge.

As Edgar comments, *"the community that shares together, ends up working much better. In my ESOL home room people share and learn how to be together like a family."*

Because photography and digital storytelling may cause subjects to rethink unexamined ideas such as belonging to a place, images also can contribute to a sense of self that simply has not been embodied physically before. Youth photographers and digital storytellers often decide to highlight human relationships that are embedded in their perceptions of place (Faulstich Orellana, 2008), or sometimes geographies stand alone as independent subjects in the students' narratives. Edgar used photos of family and of place to convey deep emotions about his Mexican hometown and his new school and community.

224 *Ruth Harman, Lindy L. Johnson, and Edgar Escutia Chagoya*

Final Curtains Up!

In May 2015, the RBYV group planned to put on another performance in Athens, perhaps this time at the local art school in the university. However, because of the tight testing schedule at CMS, we decided to present at the school to an invited group of local community members, school administrators and teachers, and other students. Each student in our group was able to invite one or two close friends as well. On the day the students presented their multimodal narratives and poems, a journalist from the local newspaper came to take photos and notes on the student stories. A photograph of Edgar with a word jumble representation of his Spanish story in the background was featured as the central image of the story in the next day's newspaper. The journalist noted in her article that "Edgar Omar Escutia Chagoya talked about his journey from Mexico to the U.S. In January, Chagoya gave his presentation in Spanish. Monday he spoke only in English" (Jackson, 2015). Edgar commented on how it felt to present his story that last time and also to see the newspaper article featuring his picture and his story.

> *When I got up in front of everyone, I felt I was now ready to explain myself in English. When I saw the photograph in the paper, I thought about how doing my best to help my family was worth it. My mother*

Figure 10.6 Athens Banner Photo
Richard Hamm, Photographer, and OnlineAthens.com & *The Athens Banner-Herald*

was very proud—she knew what I had to do to learn English during that year, the trouble it took me to get me to here. People were amazed that I could learn to speak English that fast. When seeing the photo and listening to the presentation, people could know what I can do—my parents were happy with the photographs. They said they were so glad to have a son like me (and my sister and brother who learned real fast too). (Edgar's comments)

CREATING MULTIMODAL SPACES FOR OUR STUDENTS

Our work in schools over the past decade has highlighted to us that educators and community activists need not only to have an awareness of the social inequities and injustices that their students face but also need to think about how their teaching practices can "work within and against the systems they are a part of to disrupt or challenge ideologies of social reproduction through the literacy curriculum" (Simon & Campano, 2013, p. 22). As discussed in the introduction to this book and in Chapters 1 and 5, a participatory third space environment that encourages diverse learners to interpret, remix, and embody multimodal repertoires is a democratic right of *all students* of the U.S., but it is rarely incorporated into high-stakes testing cultures of low socioeconomic school districts. Throughout our discussions over the course of the past two months, Edgar has stressed the importance of teachers having the time to listen, incorporate, and respect the multiple meaning-making processes that adolescents bring to the classroom. As he stated about Paul Ayo's poetry workshop, middle school students were afforded a range of relationships, modes, and spaces in the RBYV to engage in self-expression that led to a deeper understanding of others and self. Edgar feels that this is sorely lacking from a lot of classrooms, not because the teachers are not caring and talented but because they feel such pressure to cover an enormous amount of material in a very limited amount of time. "*We need time, we need lots of time,*" says Edgar.

Current U.S. government policies such as Race to the Top actively promote teaching-to-the-test fever among teachers (Gutiérrez et al., 2002; Ravitch, 2013). Such accountability practices give teachers very little wiggle room in terms of providing adequate space and time to all students to grow, think, and learn. Mandie Dunn, a graduate student and an experienced educator who helped out in the after-school program, stated the following about what she had learned from participating:

> Through my participation with 'Coile Serves,' an after-school organization focused on literacy projects, I've gained great understanding on how important it is to validate student voices before asking them to embody a different voice; this belief applies not just to marginalized

student voices, but to all student voices. (Dunn, personal communication, 2014)

Indeed, recent second language research has underlined the fact that for emergent bilingual learners, knowing a concept linguistically does not necessarily mean understanding the cultural contexts or appropriate use of the concept within a discourse community. Gibbons (2006) stresses the importance of supporting language learners through transmediation, with nonlinguistic modes supporting understanding of how knowledge involves a rich cultural repertoire that can further students' and teachers' grasp of social, scientific, and literacy concepts. Such an approach also supports artistic expression, critical inquiry, and academic literacy development.

As Darling-Hammond (1998, p. 91) says so compellingly in one of the quotations used by Greene, Burke, and McKenna in the introduction to this book, "For democracy to survive and flourish, those who have been silenced need to find their voices. . . . They must be able to find their dreams in the American landscape if our nation is to enact the democratic dream." At the moment we are in a crisis point in education, given the exponential increase in testing and mandates that are stifling children and teachers in Dickensian ways. Edgar's voice and the voices of his peers in similar projects worldwide provide us with deep insights about how schooling needs to be shaped, designed, and planned.

For example, Edgar, lives only 20 minutes by car from the school, but there is no form of transport in the area that he can take if he wants to meet the arts group downtown or at CMS. This compares dramatically to Edgar's life in Mexico, where public buses and close schools for bikes ensured that he had a degree of autonomy sadly lacking from his life in Athens. Edgar's plea for more autonomy in terms of public transportation and community schools leads to an essential question as to why some of our schools, like CMS, are placed in the middle of nowhere with no public transportation, shops, community libraries, and other facilities. It is not just the classroom practices that we need to reflect upon but the socioeconomic contexts of schooling (see Harman, 2007). Through community projects such as RBYV or the other culturally sustaining projects that Kelli Bivins, Alicia Coughlan, and other teachers around the country have cultivated, adolescent youth learn to question, challenge, and overcome institutional stumbling blocks in their path to becoming civic leaders. After writing this chapter, for example, Edgar decided he was going to buy a bicycle, so he would have more independence. Next we share some key elements and highlights of our process that might be of interest to multicultural educators invested in working in schools or communities in similar ways:

Multiple modes within an arts-based program: For the RBYV project, incorporating various mediums of artistic expression (storytelling, performance, photography, and poetry) provided multiple opportunities to invite students into the project and to foster and encourage the interplay among emotion, cognition, and learning. At the end of the project, several of the participating students were interviewed about their experiences participating in the various activities. Across all of the interviews, students were emotional when talking about the RBYV project. They emphasized the social and affective aspects of the experience, commenting that RBYV was a space where they could "have fun" and "talk to their friends." The students also pointed out that performing their stories in front of an audience made up of their parents, family, and community members was both challenging and exhilarating. The different arts-based programs worked to support and nurture students in various ways, depending upon the students' specific interests and passions. For some, being on stage and being the center of attention was the most important and memorable aspect of the project. For others, remediating their stories through photography was the most meaningful activity.

As Edgar repeatedly shared with us while we were writing this chapter, what was very salient for the students was the affective element of their engagement. Clearly, the role of emotions—of affect, desire, and bodily sensation—was central to the experience of RBYV students as they authored new selves and developed new and multiple literate identities (Leander & Frank, 2006). This affective aspect has been shown to have great potential not only to help students "author new selves" (Hull & Katz, 2006; Johnson, Bass, & Hicks, 2014) but also to enhance motivation and engagement in other academic areas (Vasudevan, Schultz, & Bateman, 2010). Indeed, we conceptualize the RBYV project as an approach to learning that includes a complex interplay of the affective and intellectual (Vygotsky, 1978). Engaging students in the unique mixing and remixing of semiotic modes in storytelling helped to make progress toward that unity (Hull & Nelson, 2005). As evidenced in Edgar's description of his photo selection, images and other modes such as music and performance afford an outlet for emotional qualities that would otherwise be difficult for them to put into words (Johnson & Smagorinsky, 2013).

Art and social action: The incorporation of student voices through the arts galvanized our students into seeing literacy as a material semiotic process tailored to meet the needs of authentic audiences and purposes. Students began to represent their own versions of who they were and who they wanted to be. In doing so, students developed "new and literate identities" (Hull & Katz, 2006) and also sought to transform how others saw them (Johnson, Bass, & Hicks, 2014). Edgar felt challenged by the prospect of getting up and presenting to others besides his teachers and it heightened his motivation to learn how to communicate in English. The student process also supported adult participants in learning more about and challenging the local community issues. In other words, for Ruth, Lindy, and other adult members, the students became their teachers. For example, Ruth has become active in a local immigration rights group that is challenging the inhumane practices of immigration authorities who deport hardworking fathers of families in abrupt and traumatizing ways for the family (see Floyd, 2015).

Kelli Bivins is now developing a Center for Sustainability and Humanity at the school that will support students in having rich after-school experiences to counteract the lack of public transportation and funding for the students (see Coile Cougar Cares, 2015).

Validation of languages and dialects: Our arts-based approach is informed by language and literacy research that stresses the importance of incorporating students' sociocultural and linguistic interests into the curriculum as well as providing them with carefully crafted language scaffolding (e.g., George, Raphael, & Florio-Ruane, 2003; Yoon, 2010). As Edgar shared with us, he felt validated when he got up and shared his personal story in Spanish in front of a large audience. There were no rules and norms in the group about what language or dialect to speak. Similar to Campano's (2005) second class, where students felt they were in a safe space, our students could draw from the *corriente* of languages and semiotic resources that they felt would serve them best (see Garcia & Wei, 2013).

Third spaces within school spaces: In elaborating on the concept of third space, Gutiérrez (2008) argues for a collective learning ecology mediated by a variety of resources including a privileging of students' everyday literacies and connecting everyday literacies to institutional literacies that are oriented toward critical social thought and action. The RBYV operated as a third space in which young people, teachers, and artists came together to support youth in using their artistic voices. What was very beneficial to the RBYV members was that it was very much sanctioned by the teachers and administrators at CMS. A third space can create a different configuration of time, community, and voicing even in classroom contexts if the linguistic and social repertoires of students are incorporated (see Khote, 2013). Indeed, literacy researchers have long advocated for teachers and schools to attend to the literacy practices students engage in outside of school (Alvermann, 2008; Hull & Schultz, 2001; Mahiri, 2001; Morrell, 2004) and to find ways to foster relationships between schools and communities (Kinloch, 2009).

In the end, our arts-based participatory project provided opportunities for students to improvise, experiment, and play through multiple modes in the context of multicultural and second language education. This approach aims to support students and teachers in grappling with local power relations that are dialectally connected to broader institutional and societal practices that marginalize students and teachers based on race, class, gender, and other markers of difference (Nieto & Bode, 2008). Our hope is that our telling of this particular story, our work at CMS with adult and student members, can highlight the need for educators to view learning as a collective, artistic, and social action process that positions all students as agentive members in and out of the classroom.

> *These projects are important to kids like me who need to learn English and have another way to be back at school to make friends and know*

Figure 10.7 Author at Work

> *better people who can help us. We need people to open their minds, to help us so that we can learn and grow.* (Edgar's comments)

> "*As I would say in Spanish:* Tratar las personas bien ahora para mejorar la gente de manana *(treat people well today so that we have a stronger community in the future)*."

Appendix 1
Edgar's Story

Hola! Soy Edgar. Yo tengo doce anos. Educado en México yo había terminado el 6e grado y entrado a la secundaria porque en México sexto grado es parte de la escuela nórmale y todo está organizado diferentemente. Uno dia antes de salir del 6e grado solo quedaban 3 dias para salir de al escuela, mi mama dijo [Nos vamos a ir a los Estados Unidos. 1e razón fue que toda nuestra familia estaba alla[. Todos vivian alla. La 2e razón era por la economía que era muy baja. Yo estaba muy triste y muy feliz. Estaba triste porque me iba a despedir de mis amigos de la escuela y por mi casa. Estaba feliz porque iba a ver mi familia, por ejemplo mis primos, abuelos y tios etc.

Quando salimos de nuestro pueblo, fui en autobús con sentimientos muy pesados. Por el tiempo paramos y tenemos que comer o comprar poca comida Parece una eterndiad que no puedes soportar. En mismo tiempo fue maravillosa de ver todos los pueblos y los edificios interesante y muchas cosas diferentes en viajo, aunque todavía no se los estados por donde pase en viajo.

Cuando llege a la frontera a mi mama, mi hermana, a mi hermano y a mi nos querían dejar pasar. Nos hacían muchas preguntas. Mi mama estaba muy preocupa pero al fin nos logramos y nos dejaron pasar. Quando pasamos, me sentí mejor. Cuando llege no podía creer lo que yo iba a conocer a mis primos que no habia visto en 3 anos. Realmente eran vacaciones en primero tiempo aquí. Estaba muy bien tranquillo y muy feliz, jugando con mis primos y primas. Mi primo tenia una alberca y entonces nos la pasábamos dia y noche.

Pues luego las vacaciones sabia que iba a entrar a la escuela. Primero me sentí me nervioso porque nada tenia nada unas palabras y también porque no conocía a nadie, solo a mis primos y no crei que nos iba a tocar 7 clases juntos. Quando entre, desian cosas y yo solo desia "No Talk Ingles." Luego sentí muy bien porque todos los maestros me aceptaron muy bien, aunque casi ninguno hablara español. Los que me apoyaron mucho son Ms. Bivins y Ms. Coughlan. Estoy muy agradecido con ellas y que todo salio bien y que aquí esto apoyado por buenas personas y piensa aprender y seguir con mi vida.

REFERENCES

Allexsaht-Snider, M., Buxton, C., & Harman, R. (2013). Research and praxis on challenging anti-immigration discourses in school and community contexts. *Norteamerica, Year 8,* 191–217.

Alvermann, D. E. (2008). Why bother theorizing adolescents' online literacies for classroom practice and research? *Journal of Adolescent & Adult Literacy, 52,* 8–19.

Bartholome, L. (2009). Beyond the methods fetish: Toward a humanizing pedagogy. In A. Darder, M. P. Baltodano, & R. D. Torres (Eds.), *The critical pedagogy reader* (pp. 338–355). New York, NY: Routledge.

Bauman, R., & Briggs, C. (1990). Poetics and performance as critical perspectives on language and social life. *Annual Review of Anthropology, 19,* 59–88.

Campano, G. (2005). The second class: Providing space in the margins. *Language Arts, 82*(3), 186–194.

Chappell, S., & Cahnmann-Taylor, M. (2013). No child left with crayons: The imperative of arts based education and research with language "minority" and other minoritized communities. *Review of Research in Education, 37*(1), 243–268.

Chappell, S., & Faltis, C. (Eds.). (2013). *The arts and emergent bilingual youth: Building culturally responsive, critical and creative programs in school and community contexts.* New York, NY: Routledge.

Christensen, L. M. (2009). *Teaching for joy and justice: Re-imagining the language arts classroom.* Milwaukee, WI: Rethinking Schools.

Coile Cougar Cares. (2015). *Students at W.R. Coile Middle School are committed serving Athens, our community, making it a better place for all.* Retrieved May 5, 2015, from https://sites.google.com/a/clarke.k12.ga.us/coile-serves-2012-13/

Colomer, S. E., & Harklau, L. (2009). Spanish teachers as impromptu translators and liaisons in new Latino communities. *Foreign Language Annals, 42*(4), 658–672.

Cummins, Jim. (2001). *Negotiating identities: Education for empowerment in a diverse society* (2nd ed.). Los Angeles, CA: California Association for Bilingual Education.

Curwood, J. S., & Cowell, L. L. H. (2011). iPoetry: Creating space for new literacies in the English curriculum. *Journal of Adolescent & Adult Literacy, 55*(2), 110–120.

Darling-Hammond, L. (1998). Teachers and teaching: Testing policy hypotheses from a national commission report. *Educational Researcher, 27*(1), 5–15.

Delgado, R., & Stefanic, J. (2012) *Critical Race Theory: An Introduction.* New York: New York University Press.

Faltis, C. (2013). Eradicating borders: An exploration of school artistry for embracing Mexican immigrant children and youth in education. *Journal of Language and Literacy Education* [Online], 9(2), 50–62. Retrieved from http://jolle.coe.uga.edu/

Faltis, C., & Coulter, C. (2008). *Teaching English learners and immigrant students in secondary school.* Upper Saddle River, NJ: Pearson Education, Inc.

Faulstich-Orellana, M. (2008). Space and place in an urban landscape: Learning form children's views of their social worlds. *Visual Sociology, 14*(1), 73–89.

Floyd, A. (2015). Broken families: Raids hit Athens' immigrant community hard. *Flagpole.* Retrieved June 17, 2015 from http://flagpole.com/news/

news-features/2015/06/17/broken-families-raids-hit-athens-immigrant-community-hard

Freire, P. (1970). *Pedagogy of the oppressed*. New York, NY: Continuum.

Gebhard, M., Harman, R., & Seger, W. (2007). Unpacking academic literacy for ELLs in the context of high-stakes school reform: The potential of systemic functional linguistics. *Language Arts, 85*(5), 419–430.

George, M. A., Raphael, T. E., & Florio-Ruane, S. (2003). Connecting children, culture, curriculum, & text. In G. Garcia (Ed.), *English learners: Reaching the highest level of English literacy* (pp. 308–332). Newark, DE: International Reading Association.

Gibbons, P. (2006). *Bridging discourses in the ESL classroom: Students, teachers and researchers*. New York, NY: Continuum.

Ginwright, S. (2008). Collective radical imagination: Youth participatory action research and the art of emancipator knowledge. In Julio Cammarota and Michelle Fine (Eds.), *Revolutionizing education: Youth participatory action research in motion* (pp. 13–22). New York, NY: Routledge.

Greene, M. (2001). *Variations on a blue guitar: The Lincoln Center Institute lectures on aesthetic education*. New York, NY: Teachers College Press.

Greene, S., Burke, K., & McKenna, M. (2013). Forms of voice: Exploring the empowerment of youth at the intersection of art and action. *The Urban Review, 45*, 311–334.

Gutiérrez, K. D. (2008). Developing sociocritical literacy in the Third Space. *Reading Research Quarterly, 43*(2), 148–164.

Gutiérrez, K., Asato, J., Santos, M., & Gotanda, N. (2002). Backlash pedagogy: Language and culture and the politics of reform. *Review of Education, Pedagogy and Cultural Studies, 24*(4), 335–351.Hall, D. (2014). "Emagination" and "Immigration": Multimodal representations by culturally and linguistically diverse children (unpublished doctoral dissertation). The University of Georgia, Athens.

Harklau, L. (1994). Jumping tracks: How language minority students negotiate evaluations of ability. *Anthropology and Education Quarterly, 25*(3), 347–363.

Harman, R. (2007). Critical teacher education: Discursive dance of an urban middle school teacher. Language and Education, *21*(1), 31–45.

Harman, R., & Smagorinsky, P. (2014). A critical performative process: Supporting the second language literacies and voices of emergent bilingual learners. Youth Theater Journal, *28*(2), 147–164. doi: 10.1080/08929092.2014.956956

Harman, R., & Varga-Dobai, K. (2012). Critical performative pedagogy: Emergent bilingual learners challenge local immigration issues. *International Journal of Multicultural Education, 14*(2), 1–17.

Harman, R., Varga, K., Bivins, K., & Forker, D. (2013). Critical performative literacy in an ESL middle school classroom: Latina girls speak out for undocumented workers. In S. Chapell and C. Faltis (Eds.),The Arts and English Language Learners: Building Culturally Responsive, Critical and Creative Programs in School and Community Contexts (pp. 133–142). New York: Routledge.

Harper, D. (2002). Talking about pictures: A case for photo-elicitation. *Visual Studies, 17*(1), 13–26.

Hull, G. A., & Katz, M. (2006). Crafting an agentive self: Case studies of digital storytelling. *Research in the Teaching of English, 41*(1), 43–81.

Hull, G. A., & Nelson, M. E. (2005). Locating the semiotic power of multimodality. *Written communication, 22*(2), 224–261.

Hull, G. A., & Schultz, K. (2001). Literacy learning out of school: A review of theory and research. *Review of Educational Research, 71*(4), 575–611.

Jackson, A. (2015). Athens youth share Rabbit Box stories. Retrieved on May 2015 from http://onlineathens.com/local-news/2014-05-12/athens-students-share-rabbit-box-stories

Johnson, L. L., Bass, T., & Hicks, M. (2014). Creating critical spaces for young activists. In P. Paugh, T. Kress, & R. Lake (Eds.), *Teaching towards democracy with postmodern and popular culture texts* (pp. 37–58). Boston, MA: Sense Publishers.

Johnson, L. L., & Smagorinsky, P. (2013). Writing remixed: Multimodal composing in the preservice English teacher classroom. In R. Ferdig & K. Pytash (Eds.), *Exploring multimodal composition and digital writing* (pp. 263–281). Pennsylvania: IGI Global.

Khote, N. 2013. *Engaging emergent bilinguals in the social dialogue of writing persuasively in high school*. Unpublished dissertation, University of Georgia.

Kinloch, V. (2009). Literacy, community, and youth acts of place-making. *English Education, 41*(4), 316–336.

Leander, K. M., & Frank, A. (2006). The aesthetic production and distribution of image/subjects among online youth. *E-Learning, 3*(2), 185–206.

Macedo, D. (2003). Literacy matters. *Language Arts, 8*(1), 12–13.

Mahiri, J. (2001). Pop culture pedagogy and the end(s) of school. *Journal of Adolescent & Adult Literacy, 44,* 382–385.

Martínez-Roldán, C., & Fránquiz, M. E. (2009). Latina/o youth literacies: Hidden funds of knowledge. In L. Christenbury, R. Bomer, & P. Smagorinsky (Eds.), *Handbook of Adolescent Literacy Research* (pp. 323–342). New York, NY: Guilford Press.

Medina, C., & Campano, G. (2006). Performing identities through drama and teatro practices in multilingual classrooms. *Language Arts, 84*(4), 332–341.

Mills, K. A. (2010). "Filming in progress": New spaces for multimodal designing. *Linguistics and Education, 21,* 14–28.

Moll, L. C. (2001). The diversity of schooling: A cultural-historical approach. In M. Reyes & Halcon (Eds.), *The best for our children: Critical perspectives on literacy for Latino students* (pp. 13–28). New York, NY: Teachers College Press.

Morrell, E. (2004). *Linking literacy and popular culture*. Norwood, MA: Christopher-Gordon Publishers.

Nieto, S., & Bode, P. (2008). *Affirming diversity: The sociopolitical context of multicultural education* (5th ed.). New York, NY: Allyn & Bacon.

Garcia, O., & Wei, L. (2013). *Translanguaging: Language, bilingualism and education*. London: Palgrave Macmillan.

Packard, B., Ellison, K., & Sequenzia, M. (2004). Show and tell: Photo-interviews with urban adolescent girls. *International Journal of Education & the Arts, 5*(3), 1–19.

Paris, D. (2012). Culturally sustaining pedagogy: A needed change in stance, terminology, and practice. *Educational Researcher, 41*(3), 93–97.

Pew Research. (2014). Demographic profile of Hispanics in Georgia, 2011. Retrieved May 2015, from http://www.pewresearch.org/fact-tank/2014/01/24/in-2014-latinos-will-surpass-whites-as-largest-racialethnic-group-in-california/

Rabbit Box Athens. (2015). Creating community one story at a time. Retrieved June 5, 2015, from http://rabbitbox.org/

Rabbit Box Athens Archive. (2015). *Rabbit Box Jr. stories from our youth*. Retrieved May 2014, from http://rabbitbox.org/2014/01/30/rb19-audiocast-yearyoung/

Ravitch, D. (2013). *Why I cannot stand the common core standards*. Retrieved May 27, 2014, from http://dianeravitch.net/2013/02/26/why-i-cannot-support-the-common-core-standards/

Roche, L., & Sadowsky, J. (2003). The power of stories (I): A discussion of why stories are powerful. *IJITM 2*(4), 377–388.

Simon, R., & Campano, G. (2013). Activist literacies: Teacher research as resistance to the "normal curve." *Journal of Language and Literacy Education*, 9(1), 21–39.

Skinner, E. N., & Hagood, M. C. (2008). Developing literate identities with English Language Learners through digital storytelling. *The Reading Matrix*, 8(2), 12–36.

Smagorinsky, P., & Daigle, E. A. (2012). The role of affect in students' writing for school. In E. Grigorenko, E. Mambrino, & D. Preiss (Eds.), *Handbook of writing: A mosaic of perspectives and views* (pp. 293-307). New York: Psychology Press.

Stevenson, A., & Beck, S. (2013). *¿Y si la migra se lleva a mamá cuando yo estoy en la escuela?" Familias transnacionales de estatus migratorio mixto en los Estados Unidos y la educación de sus hijos*. Paper presented at the World Educational Research Association conference, Guanajuato, México.

University System of Georgia. (2010). *New policies on undocumented students*. Retrieved September 2012, from http://www.usg.edu/news/release/regents_adopt_new_policies_on_undocumented_students/

Vasudevan, L. (2009). Critical literacy research with urban youth: Implications for teaching and teacher education. *English Education*, 41(4), 356–374.

Vasudevan, L., Schultz, K., & Bateman, J. (2010). Rethinking composing in a digital age: Authoring literate identities through multimodal storytelling. *Written Communication*, 27(4), 442–468.

Vygotsky, L. S. (1978). *Mind in society: The development of higher psychological processes*. Cambridge, MA: Harvard University Press.

Wortham, S., Murillo, E., & Hamann, T. (2002). (Eds.) *Education in the new Latino diaspora: Policy and the politics of identity*. Westport, CT: Ablex.

Yoon, B. (2010). Meeting the Cultural and Social Needs of English-Language Learners: A Middle School ESL Teacher's Practice. *Teacher Education and Practice*, 23(1), 31–43.

11 When Words Fail, Art Speaks
Learning to Listen to Youth Stories in a Community Photovoice Project

Stuart Greene, Kevin J. Burke, and Maria K. McKenna

> You gotta find out what it is [children] want to do. Because sometimes they're shy about it "Oh, I can't do that at all . . ." What do you mean you can't do that? Anyone can fly. Anyone can fly—all you have to do is try. . . . Go ahead—we're right here backing you up.
>
> Faith Ringgold

These are words that artist and author Faith Ringgold offered when she spoke to undergraduates working with local youth in a community-based learning and research course. We taught the course in cooperation with a neighborhood-based center for arts and culture and a nonprofit community partner. The sentiments Ms. Ringgold conveyed to our university students on that day buoyed our belief in the capacity of youth and the significance of fostering youth's agency as poets, researchers, change agents, and artists and echoed Greene's (2013) observations in another space:

> Children need more time in creative, supportive, and safe spaces where they know they are valued, where they can develop meaningful relationships with other children, and where they can flourish by connecting what they learn in school to their day-to-day lives. (p. 86)

In this chapter, we address the conditions for creating spaces to foster youth's sense of agency as citizens in a democracy, particularly as youth learn to take on varied community, familial, and economic roles as we describe on our work with youth in a community-based research project of almost five years. We reflect on specific examples of youth coming to know themselves in new and different ways and also examine the varied roles that educators, young adults, and community actors can play in fostering this type of youth development. We emphasize the interdependence of diverse groups of individuals; socially just, child-centered practices of teaching and learning; and civic engagement practices that seek to make a difference in the civic life of our communities (Erhlich, 2000). We argue that socially just practices (1) underscore the equitable distribution of resources; (2) ensure that everyone

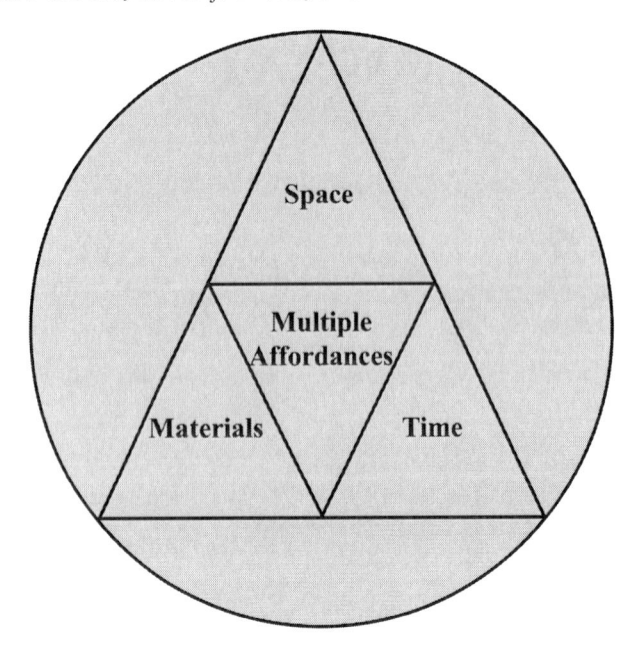

Figure 11.1 Affective, Social, Cognitive, Civic Processes

has a voice in critical decisions about the process underlying the distribution of these resources and that no one is excluded; and (3) make certain that people have access to what they need to lead full lives, personally, socially, politically, and economically (Chambers & Gopaul, 2010). Thus we advance a view of social justice that acknowledges the power inherent in education, promotes inclusion, and values an asset-based approach to education that meets the needs of all learners through an equal distribution of material, spatial, and emotional resources.

Moreover, we value the voices of children as equally vital to democratic spaces as those of adults. This is a mirror of Ginwright and Cammarota's "'socially just youth development' model of participatory citizenship" (as cited in Knight & Watson, 2014, p. 544), which allows youth to negotiate "identities as participatory citizens" as a way to "complicate questions of who may engage civically, and how they may do so, [thus] galvanizing their transformative civic potential" (p. 544). Similarly, this research supports the conclusions of Westheimer and Kahne (2004) by clarifying the varied types of participation young people can undertake as civically minded individuals. Ultimately, these socially just practices reflect a commitment to understanding literacy as a fundamental civil right where we must always provide "students with the resources necessary to become more fully human and to learn to their full potential" (Greene, 2008, p. 4). Malala Yousafzai's (2014) Nobel Peace Prize reminds us of both the potential of young people to engage civically, near and far, but also of the power of literacy, for which she is a fierce advocate.

Using youth's art, writing, and photography from our community-based research with middle and high school students, we describe in detail the *process* by which youth develop and negotiate their own sense of agency to explain the extent to which democratic engagements can foster youth voices, agency, and empowerment. We place particular emphasis on ways that socially just practices enable underrepresented youth to change inequities in the spaces they inhabit (e.g., Fox et al., 2010). More than simply describing our outcomes with the youth involved in this work or the impact these outcomes had on the adult participants, we emphasize the conditions under which transformational learning can become the norm rather than the exception. As the figure illustrates, we attend to the multiple spaces where learning occurs, the time during which kids and adults move in and out of different spaces, the materials they use to express themselves, and youth's socio-emotional development. Space, place, and the multimodalities of writing, speaking, performing, taking photographs, and creating art serve as affordances that enable youth and adults to see themselves and relationships to others in new ways.

Often missing from models of youth empowerment is an understanding of how relationships, empathy, collaboration, and generosity of time contribute to developing safe spaces that youth and adults co-construct. With this in mind, we present a robust description and analysis here of our ongoing experiences with adolescent youth engaged in an after-school Photovoice program. We adopt Paris's (2011) view of "humanistic research" within our methodological framework to stress the value of building authentic relationships with youth through power sharing, meaningful participation, and engagement. Aware that we cannot ever completely transcend differences of race, language, and culture, we learn again and again from our students that engagement depends on an ethic of care that entails meeting youth's "shouts for affirmation" with dignity and working to achieve reciprocity in an ongoing dialogic relationship. Such a view demands that we, as researchers, "claim identities and experiences" in the ways we ask youth to express themselves by asking questions, identifying shared experiences, celebrating successes, and being open about differences. Through these shared experiences, at the most basic level, children emerge as independent and fully animated community members. For children, this type of relationship is often absent in their educational and public experience and even, in some more authoritarian family spaces, home (Horgan, 2015).

We also stress the importance of taking the long and wide view of youth engagement and the emergence of self-perceived agency over time. We acknowledge the situated nature of youth empowerment and especially the value of hearing and telling stories as central to civic processes. Our work builds upon and extends models of critical youth empowerment (Jennings, Parra-Medina, Messias, & McLoughlin, 2006) that stress (1) safe spaces,

(2) power sharing between youth and adults, (3) meaningful participation and engagement, (4) critical reflection on personal and sociopolitical processes, and (5) ongoing mentoring and resources. The elaboration of the process by which young people come to feel and act empowered are important to illuminate if we are to ask adults in various fields of study to engage and adopt these democratic approaches with youth.

CONTEXT FOR THE WORK: A COMMUNITY-BASED PHOTOVOICE PROJECT

The university-community partnership program we write about here brought together middle and high school youth, university faculty, a local nonprofit agency focused on supporting healthy neighborhoods and community development, undergraduate students, and community leaders. Together, we sought to understand the history, culture, and political economy of a low-income, segregated neighborhood through mapping assets and challenges. Importantly, the Photovoice methodology we use provides youth with an opportunity to tell their own stories of how they experience the neighborhoods where they live, "to take charge of representing themselves," as Kaplan (2013) has suggested, and promotes critical dialogue among children and adults about the social distance that exists among different communities. The Photovoice methodology we use is based on Wang and Burris's (1997) Photo Novella project in which they documented the rural lives of women in China to affect policy. Thus, Photovoice is a participatory action research methodology that is inextricably tied to voice, social action, and advocacy. Such an approach gives participants, in our case, youth, who we very pointedly coin coresearchers, the opportunity to use photography to explain their lived realities and understandings of the worlds they walk in daily (Wang, 1999; Wang and Burris, 1997). We stress the use of multiple literacies with a focus on developing social capital and civic identity, particularly for the youth involved.

The project grew organically out of a community-university partnership and has continually evolved over four years. In meetings with our nonprofit partner, we formulated research questions and discussed means of evaluating the efficacy of our work to ensure that our collaborative work would be mutually beneficial. We also agreed that youth participants should act as coresearchers and that youth voices be the central focus of the work we undertook together. Ongoing communication with a variety of community stakeholders, including youth participants and public sharing of our collective work, reinforces a sense of reciprocity and mutual benefit, a key element in community-based research. The figure that follows illustrates the ways the programs we developed together within the Engaging Neighborhoods, Engaging Neighborhoods Initiative. Specifically, we developed an annual youth leadership summit to give area youth an opportunity to express how

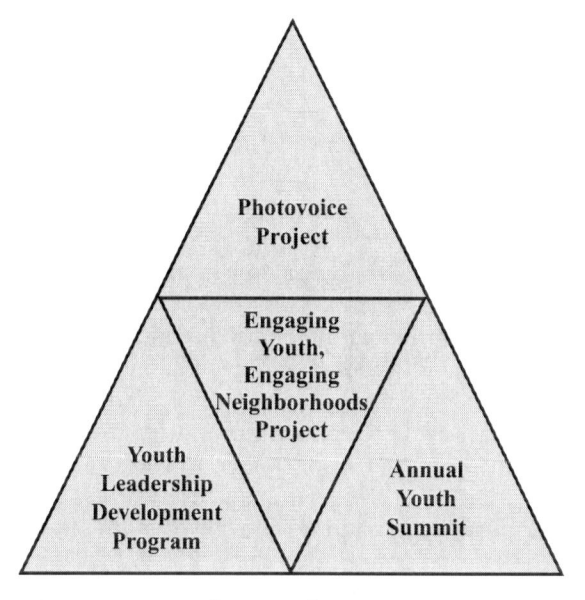

Figure 11.2 A Community-Based Partnership

[Triangle diagram with four sections: Photovoice Project (top), Engaging Youth, Engaging Neighborhoods Project (center), Youth Leadership Development Program (bottom left), Annual Youth Summit (bottom right)]

they experience life at school and in their communities; a youth leadership development program that meets monthly to discuss principles of grassroots initiatives, foster intergenerational community conversations, and enact a project to affect policy; and the Photovoice project we have developed in different parts of the community.

The Photovoice project we describe involves a cohort of youth ages 12 through 17, the fourth such cohort for the project in as many years, joined together with university students weekly for a 14-week community-based learning course that totals more than 20 hours of participation. This collaboration is part of a larger, multifaceted community engagement program coined Engaging Youth, Engaging Neighborhoods, consisting of the 14-week program, a monthly youth leadership forum, and an annual youth summit.

A NOTE ON METHOD

We placed specific emphasis on Photovoice methodology as it applies to spaces and objects within the participants' neighborhood for safety and philosophical reasons. Youth did not take photographs of people. In our use of the method, we extend out the value of visual narrative to include writing, constructing, performing, and creating art to establish multiple points of entry for young people to tell their stories. In doing so, we allow the youth involved to challenge dominant narratives about who they are, what they value, and their potential as agents of change (Burke & Greene, 2015; Greene, Burke, & McKenna, 2013, 2014).

Our 14-week program is fluid and malleable and never quite the same twice (Appendix A). It is dependent on the children involved, the researchers learning over time, the space we inhabit together, and the specific circumstances of the time period we are together. In other words, we follow the child in this work. For us, teaching and learning in this context of writing and discussion must be fluid. Sometimes we follow the kids, at other times we lead, and sometimes we work as partners as we shift conversations from familiar situations to the unfamiliar analysis of data abstracted from our coresearchers' day-to-day experiences (Goodman, 2003). Given that the young people work weekly alongside undergraduate student participants, we are attentive to the youth's needs. In this way we all become co-creators of both the process and the product. The term coresearcher stems from a methodological lens that pays the same deference to the lived realities of individuals participating in a given study as the researchers' own interpretations (Christensen & James, 2000; Mazzoni & Harcourt, 2013; Norton, 2006). We are deliberate when we identify the youth participants and our undergraduate students as coresearchers. We work to privilege children's voices in the adult-centered space of academic writing, and we value our undergraduates' perspectives as invested participants who inform our interpretations of youth's narratives and counter-narratives. Any thoughtful, child-centered youth programming must be simultaneously coherent and flexible enough to handle change of scope, pace, delivery, or content.

The children use the varied writing of Sandra Cisneros, Faith Ringgold, and George Ella Lyon to reflect on their own family stories. They use blocks and Legos to represent what they feel a flourishing community should include, construct maps of their neighborhood, and learn interview techniques to learn about the community from one another. Youth also connect with community leaders, take walks in the neighborhood, and visit local landmarks. Midway through the research process, the youth take their photographs of the community and discuss the ways they observe various community assets and challenges in their writing, map making, poetry, photographs, collages, and art. The youth also write proposals framing some subset of the challenges within the community they feel city planners and adult leaders could help solve. Our university students do the same based on their understanding of the youth's views and visions of community. In addition, our community partner participates alongside the youth and learns about the youth's perspective on community, self, and the interplay between those two spaces.

A number of researchers have documented the trend toward developing these kinds of collaborations, often cast as community-based learning and research—and they often invoke Dewey's vision of education: to prepare students to participate in a democracy (Strand, Marullo, Cutforth, Stoecker, & Donohue, 2003). We also find these efforts pertinent given the National Task Force on Civic Learning and Democratic Engagement's (2012) recently published report, *A Crucible Moment: College Learning & Democracy's Future*. The report conveys a sense of urgency in describing a steady and increasing erosion of civic participation in the U.S. at a time when a market economy has exacerbated inequalities in health, education, housing, and the workplace. Competition, individual responsibility, and the privatization of goods and services—including schools—have resulted in a diminished public sphere where policy decisions and the common good are discussed less frequently. Moreover, we find that this work contributes to a growing conversation about youth and children in the spheres of human and political geography. As Skelton (2015) recently noted, "Young people can do more than act socially or politically. Taking young people seriously has the potential to re-conceptualize political geography." With this, Skelton highlights the power that is bound in the inventiveness and potentiality of youth.

In light of this, our research process encourages youth to reflect first upon who they are and what they need as members of a community. They explore the following questions via the various activities of the program (Guajardo, 2013, p. 4):

- Who am I?
- What do I value?
- What is the foundation of my assets, challenges, and self-being?
- How do my values influence my practices as a leader?
- What is the role of leadership in making my vision for community a reality?

Underlying these questions is the assumption that personal reflection can enable kids to address their deepest conviction about what counts as a community, who will live in their community, and how residents will interact, thus reifying a solid sense of self within the larger society. With a foundation of honoring each individual child's self-definition and lived experience, we then ask the children to extend their analysis beyond themselves and into the community. In addition to the questions guided by Guajardo, we ask youth to reflect on the following:

- How do you define your neighborhood?
- What are the assets and challenges of your neighborhood and the local community?
- What is your relationship to your school community? Neighborhood? Community leaders?

As in all of our studies during the past four years (e.g., Burke, Greene & McKenna, 2014; Greene, Burke, & McKenna, 2013, 2014), we audiotape and then transcribe focus group discussions in which the children explained the thinking behind their art, writing, and photography. We also transcribe children's oral presentations to the larger groups or community leaders about children's priorities. In addition, we use the youth's photography extensively in the latter part of our time together to reflect on the visual imagery of the process and relationships alongside our recordings and transcriptions. Of particular interest to us are the youth's reflections on the following questions: (1) What do the photographs prompt the youth to think about in their lives? (2) How do the pictures or meanings relate to their everyday lives? (3) What can we learn about youth's emergent roles as community activists? (4) What can we learn about the youth's changing perceptions of their own agency? (5) What are the conditions that enable youth to become engaged in their neighborhoods? Creating space for this level of analysis with children is not only methodologically and ethically sound but also pragmatic. It allows for the authenticity of the work to emerge from the vantage point of the youth coresearchers and provides a reflective space for considering the conditions under which democratic ideals and discursive skills develop for all of the adult constituents involved.

Finally, we acknowledge our own positionality as White researchers within the context of this program. Our work with youth requires constant awareness and dialogue focused on our efforts to cross borders as participant observers. Gender, race, age, and education level are contested spaces of identity for children as much as they are with adults, perhaps even more so. By writing, performing, creating, and walking alongside youth, we work to break down some of those barriers. Along the way, we have experienced skepticism by adults and children alike. However, we adopt "humanizing approaches" rooted in "dialogic consciousness raising for both researchers and participants." Thus, we listen in ways that allow others to perceive us as "'worthy witness[es]'" to the youth's "emergent sense of engagement in the political process" (Paris & Winn, 2013, p. xvi). Still, we recognize the complexities of multiethnic, multilingual, multiage spaces that complicate our understanding of identity and what it means to share power or participate together in meaningful ways.

Likewise, our abilities to listen—and, more vitally, to hear—the stories of our students and our youth partners is, and will always be, mediated, limited, and delimited by any number of contexts but particularly, in this case, by our racialized experiences. This is especially true because we write, live, and absorb ideology within a powerful racial structure that "reinforce[s] white privilege" (Bonilla Silva, 2006, p. 9; see also Greene & Abt-Perkins, 2003). Though we seek to do humanizing research, in other words, we acknowledge as well the possibility of our own tendency toward colonization; still we hew close to the goal, from Paris and Alim (2014) of "teaching and learning" in ways with youth and especially "youth of color" that seek "not ultimately to see how closely students [might] perform White middle-class norms but to explore, honor, extend, and, at times, problematize their heritage and community practices" (p. 86). For, as Paris (2011) explains, "This ethical need for a humanizing stance emerges as both researchers and participants seek to push against inequities not only through the findings of research, but through the research process itself" (p. 9). In treating our research subjects as co-creators of new knowledge and as coresearchers within the research process, we actively seek to upend the patterns of dominance and replication of traditional research paradigms.

We base our analyses in the remainder of this chapter on observations, transcripts of interviews and group discussions, and photographic evidence. In doing so, we offer a multi-textured representation of youth and the ways youth construct spaces in which they can represent what flourishing communities can look and feel like. These multiple affordances provide a lens through which all adults, but specifically educators, can understand more fully the wisdom that youth possess in the different ways they express themselves.

By providing these examples, we not only highlight the ways in which youth challenge us to see community and engagement differently but also the very narrow definition of literacy as the capacity to read or write (or perhaps some combination of the two). This understanding of literacy, albeit easily testable, reduces literate practice to a "single story," and such a story brings with it inherent dangers of violence, hegemonic exclusion, and misunderstanding (Adichie, 2009), both real and symbolic. Adichie reminds us to attend carefully to the narratives that children are exposed to about their lives and their capacities to serve as agents of change. Thus we see value in stressing the fact that children are indeed capable of creating vibrant, truthful, and important narratives about their lives that tell us a great deal about what is possible. Consistent with Winn and Behizadeh (2011), we argue that "youth-centered scholarship focusing on cultivating critical literacy skills for urban youth can generate possibilities for disrupting and dismantling" the single story that equates illiteracy with a failure of words (p. 148). In our work, we are reminded again and again that "children are complex beings who are not simply interested in childish things; instead, they are citizens in the making who offer sophisticated observations and critiques of the inequalities and injustices around them that educators need to honor and build upon" (Mirra, 2014, p. 11).

TOWARD A MODEL OF YOUTH EMPOWERMENT, VOICE, AND CIVIC ENGAGEMENT

Throughout the project, we sought to provide safe and creative spaces for youth. In fact, space played an essential role our collective endeavor. We elected to consistently meet in a community gallery space and allowed for regular, free movement, ongoing conversation, and a general sense of openness. We allowed for the possibility that space matters to our collective goal of empowering youth to see themselves as belonging to these varied spaces. Styles's (1996) work on curriculum as "window and mirror" reminds us that when we pay close attention to our surroundings and the interactions in those surroundings, we are likely to notice how we understand those surroundings in relationship to ourselves and our own developmental process. In the following vignettes, our aim is to convey how space matters to youth's engagement of ideas, developing a sense of community, and realizing youth's agency. We are also reminded of how we see the world as a series of "windows" or "mirrors."

Window One

A small group of women gather to share their poetry. Carrie, a university student starts with a cadence similar to skipping rope on the playground (all names are pseudonyms): "Love, happy, find a way or make one . . . trees, family, cocoa butter, kisses, history, Africa, sweet potatoes, tomorrow, such and such a thing." Laughter fills the small corner of the room as she finishes her poem. Next up Gigi, who hasn't said much up until now, starts right in: "Purple, red . . . R and B, Chicago, India, Arianna, LaSalle, Elena, Jalen, honey, family, music, Takia, Bronte, Growing Kids, Ms. Terri, Ms. Brookshire . . . imagination, grandma's house, mall, dress shop, churches, parks schools, space, Notre Dame, African American." Her voice trails off as if she's wondering what they think. A barrage of questions and comments come her way: "Who are all the people you name?" "Tell me about Ms. Terri?" "I love how you started with colors." She responds with clarity and confidence. If you listen hard, you hear her vision of community full of relationships, safe adults, communal spaces, and colors—lots of bright colors.

Window Two

We gathered in the art gallery, early on in the program, sprawled out on the floor armed with art supplies to discuss Faith Ringgold's *Tar Beach*. The youth and undergraduates are reading the book aloud, and then the room fills with conversations. They discover that "tar beach" is the rooftop of a New York City apartment building and that the borders of each picture book page are rooted in the story quilting tradition of the African American community. Looking to the left, we listen to a group of young girls and university students singing quietly together as they start drawing. To the right, a smaller group of two undergraduates and a quiet, young student are having a conversation about where to start. Straight ahead in the gallery, there is an ebb and flow of youth and university students finding their afternoon snacks and bringing them back to their work spaces. At one point, one of our young coresearchers, Elise, observes, "Everyone's working here but it totally doesn't feel like school." Her group agrees and proceeds to have a conversation about why this might be the case, all the while working on their drawings of their personal "tar beach"; a seed was planted in everyone's mind about how children learn.

Window Three

The group gathers in what used to be an old gymnasium. We're reminded of the history of the building built in 1929 that we're guests in each week, a building that lay dormant for more than 25 years and was renovated a little more than a year ago. Our guide tells us that at first it was a children's dispensary started for African American families. Later it became the first community center in South Bend complete with indoor basketball and rumors of roller skating. Most recently, it has been renovated as an art studio and gallery. The youth giggle at the thought of roller skates in the gym but quickly go back to asking questions about the history of the space. We move into the art studio and get a quick lesson in various types of print making. The light flows in from the tall former gymnasium ceilings, and the students engage with the artists and the space. Toward the back of the room, PJ is a reluctant traveler in the group. His grandmother thought the program would "be good for him." PJ hangs back, writing on a stone printing block with a piece of black charcoal passed around for students to try. Once, twice, three times he writes his initials as though to remind us, and himself, that he's there. Silently he runs his hand over the block when he's done. We get a brief glimpse of his sense of possibility. Still water runs deep.

Window Four

Imagine pictures strewn everywhere; college kids and teenage kids are stepping gingerly around the piles to get to their "work." A quiet hum of a newly oiled motor fills the room. "I wrote one," Shanna says to her college partners. "Wanna hear it?" Without waiting for an answer, she begins, "Bright glistening signs. Warn you to stop for children. The unknown children." Her haiku about a photograph of street sign with the caption "Watch for Children" strikes everyone as haunting and beautiful at once. Her granny runs a child care business. She helps out all the time. She notices everything about kids.

In each vignette we see the emergence of a young person sharing often personal thoughts or actions with those around him or her. We hear possibility in the youth's poetry and the eagerness to learn more, do more, and think deeper. We notice the subtle movements and actions that we might have missed if not for close observation and careful attention. We feel the weight that laughter and music lift from the monotony of typical school days, and we sense the feeling of kinships and belonging. As the university students work alongside the youth, a relational space of learning and listening emerges.

Over the course of a number of weeks in a variety of contexts, we listened to the youth debate whether or not they know something. Some even told us that they are *not* leaders who can affect change. They doubt themselves. Yet only days apart we observed the youth using blocks to build a model of a flourishing community and teach their peers about hope and the value of supporting those in need by having homeless centers, food pantries, and spaces for those who get involved with drugs to rehabilitate. We observed kids' reticence in some artistic or writing contexts, but then in other different spaces, we watched as they took on the role of organizing their peers to make decisions about what problems they can begin to address in their neighborhoods (e.g., demolishing abandoned houses and constructing a park, reclaiming a legacy of Latino education, or fixing sidewalks). We learn that not every child will be literate in the same way, in the same space, in the same time, but with consistent encouragement, multiple opportunities to make meaning, and ample time, all youth have important ideas about themselves and their lived realities to share. In fostering democratic spaces, we provide the conditions that enable youth to form the foundation of civic identity.

Just last year, at an academic conference presentation where a small group of our youth participants accompanied us to present on our work together, the youth questioned their ability to present their ideas to other adults only to have the adults in the room ask them for advice on how to teach and engage young people at the end of their presentation. If youth are to become more engaged, then they need to trust one another and know that others care about what they think and feel. They also must have adults who craft spaces for practicing democracy and civic-minded behaviors, especially if we are seeking to do more than engender an oversimplified, "charitable" view of citizenships as Westheimer and Kahne (2004) describe. What we hope to suggest here is a robust argument for civic-minded, child-centered action in classrooms in and out of schools rooted in a sense of what Biesta (2014) would call an " 'act' of educational creation" (p. 139). We believe that the process itself holds potential for reconceptualizing how civic identity develops in youth and the potential for educational spaces to assist in this process. The program we describe is not rooted in community service or one-off field trips, nor is the value measured in typical academic ways. Rather, we present a path that is predicated on a theory of change that is both relational and introspective. In the process, youth gather evidence and conduct research about problems that matter to them.

Window Five

A conversation occurs between Summer and her undergraduate partners as they walk the neighborhood, taking pictures as they wander the streets following a major snow, with the sidewalks largely impassable. We note that the undergraduates are clear with Summer that this is a space where they are listening and she is expert:

> UGS: You're in charge here. We're just going to [listen].
> SUMMER: I don't like . . . I walk a lot because my dad is visually impaired and he can't drive and so we talk about, we have problems with the sidewalks. He can't see the cracks. What we like is, sometimes people highlight the cracks in yellow spray paint. But sometimes, like the city over by the Martin's [a local grocery chain], they put in really nice [aural] walk signals. They fixed up the sidewalks and stuff, but they rounded the corners so people [turning the corner] can just speed and they don't . . . it's dangerous. So it's really hard waiting at the signal and you can't get too close to the edge because cars come really close to the edge. And, ah, the other day we were walking to Martin's. Bridges are the city's property and the city didn't shovel them so it was like a foot of snow and we had to walk through on the sidewalk.

As Summer narrates her concerns about the condition of the sidewalk and even the city's attempt to mitigate danger—poorly executed—they listen silently, capturing it all on audiotape. This exchange informs both the letter writing campaign proposed by our youth participants about unsafe sidewalks and rundown properties independent of the college students and also the final project of one group of undergraduate coresearchers as well. The undergraduate project has become a Madonarri chalk festival to raise money for fixing, and to draw awareness to, the crumbling sidewalks in the neighborhoods in the city. What we're struck by, however, is the wisdom of a child whose lived experience has come to inform her budding activism. Her research partners have become, as Paris (2011) notes, "friend[s] who understand fully" (p. 7). This understanding comes through children trusting that adults are fully present, and it develops in safe spaces where kids are given room to practice and rehearse their ideas about what they think and feel about themselves, their families, their neighborhoods, and the broader community.

This rehearsal often sheds light on youth's insecurities about their capacity for change and even their belief that their ideas are valid at all, but it also allows them to develop supportive relationships where the power of the collective is asserted. Additionally, within this space, we present youth with opportunities that challenge their relative familiarity of the voicelessness of childhood.

Window Six

Two weeks after Summer's conversation with her undergraduate partners, Maria facilitates a discussion about the photographs the youth have taken. The youth cut up the photographs that they took of the neighborhood and placed them on two posters. One conveys what youth see as positive traits of the city, and the other reflects the issues the youth want to address to better the city. The youth coresearchers huddle around the posters trying to remember what they put on the large boards the week before. Our university students sit quietly, listening silently behind the youth. The kids teach one another and the student and faculty observers a very real lesson in perceptions about leadership:

> MARIA: Your job is to explain what these posters mean to the [undergraduates seated] behind you.
> SHANNA: We decided that we didn't necessarily like old buildings. You could knock them down or refurbish or rebuild them. Then on this poster, with a lot of pictures, we were talking about what brings your eye to a picture first and mostly people said the sunset. It's because it's brighter than everything else. And then there are things like churches and food and water (a shot of a tree reflected in a puddle) that's pretty.
> GIGI: I said I like the city cemetery because it shows that common people have, let me put it a different way. ., . all the people who are in the cemetery, they have turned the city into a nice or a broken down city. There's a history.
> MARIA: So tell me two things to improve the community.
> SHANNA: Everything we need requires money and we don't got any money. Fix the messed up houses and streets. The potholes are bad.
> GIGI: Homeless people. Make houses for them. I'd tell him take care of the homeless . . . make houses for them. I mean, not just homeless people, but like, people who need help. Like, someone who has diabetes or cancer, someone who is on the street or who doesn't have food. Do a fundraiser, earn money and help them.
> PJ: Fix up the houses. Fix up the streets.
> GIGI: But we're kids we don't know what we're talking about.
> SHANNA: But we do know what we're talking about. The houses need to be fixed and the streets need to be fixed, so . . .
> MARIA: GiGi, why do you think you don't know what you're talking about because you're "just kids"?
> GIGI: Our voice does matter, but they have to take into account what we want, but sometimes people are too stuck up to listen to little kids.
> MARIA: Do you think kids can be advocates for other kids?
> SHANNA: You have to be a role model. So you do the right thing and others follow you.
> GIGI: I'm a big sister, so I have to set the right example for her.
> MARIA: PJ, who are you a role model for?
> PJ: Nobody.

When Words Fail, Art Speaks 249

> SHANNA: I think he is a role model because when I was little in our Church they would announce his name cause he's smart, like "PJ got all 'A's,'" yeah so I like, always try to get all 'A's.'

This is just a snippet of a much longer conversation where the youth narrow their concerns about what might be changed within the community for the undergraduates and very clearly for themselves. It should also be situated in the larger contexts of ongoing weekly conversations about community and what children need to flourish. What we note is the power of relationships among the youth. Given the space and time to express their ideas, they are very clear about what needs to be done to improve the city, and they progressively talk themselves through the notion that they are not only powerful, but they are role models. Notably, they are engaged with one another and take the conversation in a variety of directions with little prompting from Maria. The youth carried on this particular conversation for almost an hour, challenging one another and using the data collected in the form of photographs to support their thinking. Interestingly, as with most of our conversations with the young people involved in this work, schools are noticeably absent for them as specific or detailed community fixtures. The idea of schools is important but only really in an idealized sense. Whether this is because they do not see schools as spaces where change is possible or they simply wish to focus on other aspects of community is unclear.

Also worth noting is the way in which conversations about community shift to relationships and leadership so fluidly. When PJ fails to see himself in a leadership role, Shanna illustrates the seemingly imperceptible ways he has influenced her. This is significant. In our layered, multiple literacy-laden process, we consistently consider and explain the important ways relationships and associations matter to the democratic process. The kids' sense is striking. They suggest that both community and government leaders have a moral obligation to provide money and homes for the less fortunate. This empathy emerges, we think, through relationships and trust over time. These youth were, by this point, three-quarters of the way through the program, used to being positioned as experts, and had been asked in a number of ways to connect their art with larger social issues. In this space, they begin to speak the language of cooperative and supportive empowerment necessary for taking up future leadership roles in the neighborhood and city.

Window Seven

During another walking tour, a small group of undergraduates is led by Lindsay, a middle schooler who has distinguished herself from her peers by her sheer boisterousness. They enter the historic city cemetery, which houses monuments dating back to the middle of the 19th century, including former Vice President of the United States Schuyler Colfax. This cemetery is also one of the earliest integrated spaces in the community. Black and White families are buried side by side in sections of the cemetery that house the remains of Union dead from the Civil War. Struck by the tumbledown nature of some of the headstones, Lindsay muses about her great grandmother:

> I wonder where my great-granny is. My mom's side. Her, gosh, her name was Adie Hawkings and her parents were slaves. She lived to be like 90 or 91. She, in her younger years, was probably a slave as well. I always wondered what her name stood for. I knew her my entire life, ever since I was a baby so that's why her death affected me.

The undergraduates remain silent, perhaps unable to come up with the words to mitigate Lindsay's seemingly still-raw grief but perhaps also considering the literal historical closeness of the institution of slavery for this young woman. They continue walking, and Lindsay comments on a grave that has fallen over, wishing someone would fix it. As they leave the cemetery and head back to the community center, Lindsay connects the experience to her memory of reading about the Holocaust in school, asserting that everyone should have a proper burial. In the silence that follows, the pain of not knowing where Great-Granny is hangs heavily.

We relate this tale simply to reassert forcefully the value of walking with kids in the cities they inhabit. This walking is essential to our understanding of what types of spaces and activities are needed for children to develop authentic visions of their civic selves. We understand our neighborhood walks with children as a collaborative process of mental mapmaking about their community. Most importantly, these walks through the neighborhood situate history as living and connected to the present. This cemetery is not a space that Lindsay "knew" prior to our time together. Having the freedom to wander, and the bond of trust with her undergraduate partners, allows her to make connections to a painful family past (one literally enslaved) with a beloved relative while slowly building toward a sense that the civic space of the cemetery ought to be restored out of respect for the dead. Additionally, this experience allows Lindsay to continue the conversation at later points in the program, providing opportunities to compare other young people's experiences with those same spaces to her own.

This link to the past is almost hauntingly resonant as the cemetery falls into disarray, too far from the city center and corridors that are being developed in an effort to bring about new investment. This policy, on the city's part, of "planned shrinkage" toward the urban core focuses wholly on "policies . . . [with] a precedent for economic development as a 'public purpose'" (Rosenman, Walker, & Wyly, 2014, p. 50) that center mostly on land appropriation and tax increment financing (TIF). Recently, the city announced that a design firm has been hired to create a master plan for the cemetery focused on rehabilitation but also marketing. Missing in the plan (http://bit.ly/1ArKnFM) is any sense that citizens, and particularly children, might be engaged in thinking about what might best be done with, to, and in the space.

Nonetheless, Lindsay finds pedagogical purpose here; this space matters and informs her mental map of her community. In fact, it is not unrealistic to say that the walk and her thinking transformed in some small (or large) way her understanding of her personal place in history and her connection the past of her community. That she has not made connections to in-school texts is not surprising; what is surprising is that this opportunity to wander with kids finds so little room in the imaginary of a curriculum in schools that doesn't "give a shit about what you feel or what you think" (Coleman, 2011).

Window Eight

Fast-forward one year. A new Photovoice cohort is about to begin. Our research assistant and former university student from last year's project walks in and asks, "Hey, I just got a text from PJ. He wants to know if he can do the "class" again? He says his grandma isn't even making him this time and wants to come back. What should I tell him?"

Tell him, "Welcome back, PJ. Welcome back."

YOUTH'S VISION FOR COMMUNITY

In this chapter, we argue that educators can cultivate skills in youth so that they can be future leaders and innovators. We can do so by balancing the teaching of skills and craft with rigor (Watson, 2014); encouraging youth to examine social issues; creating spaces in which youth can ask difficult questions and rehearse their roles as problem solvers, innovators, and leaders; and ensuring that what is going on in youth's day-to-day realities plays a key role in what we do inside the classroom—whether it's an art studio, the neighborhood's sidewalk, or the more formal setting of the civil rights institute. Moreover, we acknowledge the relational nature of the dialogic and the time that it takes to build supportive, collaborative foundation for this deeply personal and important work. As educators for social justice and democratic citizenship, we also seek to honor and extend the cultural competence and diversity of young people. We maintain the value of marginalized youth's varied funds of knowledge as resources for increasing student engagement and learning (Paris, 2011; Yosso, 2005).

Stressing the idea that literacies are a civil right, we cannot help but underscore the kind of teaching that prepares youth to be critical thinkers and participants in our fragile democracy. We highlight the ways in which varied spaces, modalities, and interactions create the kind of community that enables youth to change the inequitable conditions plaguing low-income communities. Building community undergirds freedom. This understanding of literacies as a civil right leads us to assert that spaces for engaging youth's agency are not only good but essential to youth's well-being and the health of communities writ large. As Allen (2014) points out, "we get our freedom from participating as citizens in this shared endeavor." Unfortunately, education reform and economic development have ignored the very skills and perspectives necessary for building the diverse world in which we want to live. In the end, we maintain with Winn and Behizadeh (2011) that youth need opportunities in and out of school to understand that their voices matter. In this work we only begin to peel back the layered complexity of how we must engage youth for such practices to become the norm and not the exception. As these researchers argue, "to be critically literate . . . must be the right of all children and youth" (p. 167).

Given the erosion of public spaces and neighborhood schools in the current climate of education reform, we contend that it is more important than ever to understand the contexts and relationships that enable youth to carve out and engage with spaces where they can flourish, discover their voices, and reflect critically on their own literate and democratic practices. Youth's stories prompt us to reimagine after-school programs as places that can serve as bridges between the struggles students experience in the neighborhoods they inhabit and the vision for community they may offer with their stories. Youth's stories also prompt us to maintain an activist stance about what schools are foregoing in their myopic focus on achievement scores and narrowed definitions of what it means to be well educated. As Goodman (2003) points out, reimagining the school day for urban kids "can create opportunities to connect and bring relevance to their varied experiences of school, mass media culture, and community life" (p. 100). And so, grateful for the out-of-school spaces that we work with, we also recognize the limits of "unlearning" and "unschooling" practices outside of the traditional school and classroom context. Our hope is that within the transformative experiences of these programs, a powerful narrative of what children need to flourish as change agents emerges powerfully enough for formal educational spaces to take notice and respond.

We argue that programs like the one we discuss here provide a logical starting place for asserting the value of children's counter-narratives about their lives and reinvesting time and energy in opportunities for relationship building with children in and out of school. Relationships are a necessary precondition, we learned, for creating space for these counter-narratives to be told and, more importantly, heard safely, for fostering connections to community, and for cultivating an ethic of civic engagement. Still, in many moments of our work, the youth remind us of their overall of the skepticism, not just about their own agency, although there is that, but the willingness of the adult world to engage them fully and seriously. The youth regularly make comments about how they "aren't sure that their ideas will matter" and remind us that in their eyes we are "different" from other adult actors in their lives.

Thus, we also think it is vital to understand how an anchored, community-based organization provided the kind of structure necessary for kids to flourish and how community leaders can be informed by youth voices. The argument for community and university partnerships requires that we recognize how educators, community leaders, and activists can work together to ensure youth develop strong civic identities; understand the nuanced ways one must engage in various political, economic, and social spheres; and envision themselves as having a continued voice in community change processes. To marginalize the kinds of experiences we describe risks further "isolating youth from the communities" where they live and limits educators' abilities to understand children's emotional, social, and intellectual needs (Goodman, 2003, p. 101). Understanding youth's perspectives on what it means to flourish is especially important at a time when neighborhood schools are disappearing and neoliberal policies have eroded public spaces (Lipman, 2011) where youth have opportunities to build relationships and a sustaining sense of community. With fewer and fewer schools as anchors in neighborhoods, it is more essential than ever to understand how to create and maintain vibrant communities. One of our undergraduates (Fusco, 2014) reminds us that "literacy . . . which exist[s] in a multitude of forms . . . is the ability to understand and express one's self. It's the process through which we interact with our surroundings—with the world" (p. 3). Her words speak to the ways multiple literacies and discursive spaces can foster this sense of identity and agency.

The work here addresses, at least implicitly, the role that universities can play in a distributive model of social justice for the youth, college students, and community actors. In particular we saw students from across the U.S. enrolled in our course come to understand the historical and geographical context of the city that surrounds their university (very much a purposefully separate space according to many community members). We also saw them become passionate advocates for improving a city that was not their home. They came to see the boundary between their college and the spaces of their youth partners as arbitrary, unnecessary, and often harmful. In this way, they too were coming to know themselves as democratic agents, especially in relationship to the youth they felt responsible to, and for, through the heartfelt relationships they developed with the children. They did this by taking the time to be empathic, respectful listeners to the concerns of the youth.

We are inspired by work done in the same vein from Kaplan (2013), and we see this manner of community-engaged course work as at least one response to ongoing concerns about educational tourism (e.g., Biddle, 2014). Universities have access to assets that might benefit youth in the communities that jostle (often uncomfortably) against them; often the best and most plentiful of those assets is the student body, eager for connection and challenge, as we saw play out in our partnership. This is the vision of Newman (1982) of a university as "a place of teaching universal knowledge" for the common good, where the universe that immediately surrounds the college is not held at arm's length in favor of something more exotic or esoteric.

Finally, we argue that it is not enough to provide opportunities for analysis and critique of the discursive tensions between what is and what could be (Weinstein & West, 2012). Low (2011) puts it well when she observes that teachers and after-school programs can forge connections between home and school to foster children's emerging sense of leadership, creativity, initiation, and civic responsibility as a form of social action. It is important that these things are "recognized and supported in both places" (Low, 2011, p. 151). Youth engagement also has the potential to forge connections in those in-between spaces that are not home or school and where we rarely, if at all, attend to youth practices and voices as communities. The multiple literacies model serves as a space for discursive action and engagement through which we both examine the tensions and structures that stand in the way of a more equitable distribution of material resources, power, and voice that would enable youth to flourish but also take action to remedy these tensions and structures.

By helping to give voice to the tensions that exist between what is and what could be, we would be remiss if we also did not take responsibility for helping kids navigate the political, economic, and institutional barriers that they confront each and every day, especially those barriers related to the work that they choose to undertake within the program (see also Weinstein & West, 2012). In fact, we see these acts of assistance as buoying youth agency and as a key responsibility of youth advocates. Youth can't navigate that which they don't know or have access to. The same can be said for our undergraduate students who, when presented with an opportunity to engage the local community, did so with humility and eagerness. Put more strongly, youth and young adults cannot be asked to participate in spaces of civic engagement without this scaffolding. To fail to provide youth with these tools would be setting them up for failure and simply reify those spaces when adults pay lip service to children and young adult voices but nothing more. We must work to act simultaneously as conduits for youth's ideas while also reframing adult views of children and the value (or lack thereof) of children's voices with other adult players in the community.

In closing, we agree with Levinson's (2012) admonition to social justice educators. Civic identity develops over time through deep inquiry and engagement of real issues. Education can serve as a site of possibility and cultivate in children and young adults an ethic of action, democracy, dialogue, and positive interdependency. In one of our undergraduate's words (Mullins, 2014), "Every student deserves to have a space where they always hear Ringgold's wise words: 'Go ahead—we're right here backing you up'" (p. 10).

Appendix A
Engaging Youth, Engaging Neighborhoods Photovoice Program

Session	
#1	Introduction of project "To say the name is to begin the Story": Name games and artistic representations of names Youth and university students interview one another
#2	Children create/map their neighborhoods with blocks Two dimensional neighborhood/community maps
#3	Restorative Justice "Circle Process" Reading from Sandra Cisneros' *House on Mango Street*
#4	Listen and discuss "Where I am from" by George Ella Lyon Compose "I am from" poems Collages of "I am from" poems
#5	Build flourishing communities with blocks Reading, of Faith Ringgold's *Tar Beach* Dramatization and/or art of Faith Ringgold's *Tar Beach* Distribution of take home cameras
#6	Civil Rights Heritage Center visit w/community leaders Performances of "I am from" poems Photography 101
#7	Neighborhood walk Photography of Neighborhood
#8	Watch clip of *Echoes of Brown* Local community leader exploration/visits
#9	Discussion of photos Create abstract collage, haiku poetry of individual photographs Write narrative descriptions of photos
#10	Group photo collages (Digital or handmade)
#11	Collage and photo narrative discussion Asset mapping/coding
#12	Post-it work to understand photos Formulate proposal for change Write proposals

Session	
#13	University students share biographical digital narratives of youth. Children's Reflections
#14	Public Gallery Opening Youth Photo Exhibit and Poetry Reading
#15	Public presentation of change proposals with youth and/or university students

REFERENCES

Adichie, C. (2009). *The danger of a single story.* Retrieved from http://www.ted.com/talks/chimamanda_adichie_the_danger_of_a_single_story

Allen, D. (2014). *Our declaration: A reading of the Declaration of Independence in defense of equality.* New York, NY: Liveright Publishing Corporation.

Biddle, P. (2014). The problem with little white girls, boys and voluntourism. *The Huffington Post.* Retrieved August 16, 2014, from http://www.huffingtonpost.com/pippa-biddle/little-white-girls-voluntourism_b_4834574.html

Biesta, G. (2014). *The beautiful risk of education.* Boulder, CO: Paradigm.

Bonilla-Silva, E. (2006). *Racism without racists: Color-blind racism and the persistence of racial inequality in the United States.* New York, NY: Rowman & Littlefield.

Burke, K., & Greene, S. (2015). Participant action research, youth voices and civic engagement. *Language Arts, 92*(6), 387–400.

Burke, K. J., Greene, S., & McKenna, M. K. (2014). A critical geographic approach to youth civic engagement: Reframing educational opportunity zones and the use of public spaces. *Urban Education, 51*(2016), 143–169. doi: 10.1177/0042085914543670

Chambers, T., & Gopaul, B. (2010). Toward a social justice-centered engaged scholarship: A public and private good. In H. Fitzgerald, C. Burack, & S. Seifer (Eds.), *Handbook of engaged scholarship: Contemporary landscapes, future directions* (pp. 55–70). East Lansing, MI: Michigan State University Press.

Christensen, P., & James, A. (Eds.). (2000). *Research with children: Perspectives and practices.* London, UK: Falmer Press.

Cisneros, S. (1989). *The house on Mango street.* New York, NY: Vintage Books.

Coleman, D. (April 2011). *Bringing the common core to life.* Paper presented to the New York State Department of Education in Albany, New York. Retrieved August 16, 2014. http://usny.nysed.gov/rttt/docs/bringingthecommoncoretolife/part6transcript.pdf

Erhlich, T. (2000). *Civic responsibility and higher education.* Lanham, MD: Rowman & Littlefield Publishers.

Fox, M., Mediratta, K., Ruglis, J., Stoudt, B., Shah, S., & Fine, M. (2010). Critical youth engagement: Participatory action research and organizing. In L. Sherrod, J. Torney-Puta, & C. Flanagan (Eds.) *Handbook of research and policy on civic engagement with youth* (pp. 621–650). Hoboken, NJ: Wiley Press.

Freire, P. (1983). *Pedagogy of the oppressed.* New York, NY: Continuum.

Fusco, K. (2014). Letter from the editor. *The Juggler: Literature, Art, Design at Notre Dame, 79*, 3.

Goodman, S. (2003). *Teaching youth media: A critical guide to literacy, video production, & social change.* New York, NY: Teachers College Press.

Greene, S. (2008). Introduction: Teaching for social justice. In S. Greene (Ed.), *Literacy as a civil right: Reclaiming social justice in literacy teaching and learning* (pp. 1–25). New York, NY: Peter Lang.

Greene, S., & Abt-Perkins, D. (2003). How can literacy research contribute to racial understanding? In S. Greene & D. Abt-Perkins (Eds.), *Making race visible: Literacy research for cultural understanding* (pp. 1–31). New York, NY: Teachers College Press.

Greene, S., Burke, K., & McKenna, M. (2013). Forms of voice: Exploring the empowerment of youth at the intersection of art and action. *The Urban Review, 45*, 311–334.

Greene, S., Burke, K., & McKenna, M. (2014). Re-framing spatial inequality: Youth, photography and a changing urban landscape. In H. R. Hall, C. Cole-Robinson & A. Kohli (Eds.), *Shifting demographics: A cross-disciplinary look at race and class in 21st century America* (pp. 107–127). New York, NY: Peter Lang

Guajardo, F. (2013). *Digital storytelling and the Llano Grande Center.* Paper presented at annual meeting of the American Educational Research Association, San Francisco, CA.

Horgan, D. (2015.) *The bordered contexts of children and young people's participation and engagement in everyday life.* Paper presented at the International Conference on the Geographies of Children, Youth and Families, San Diego, CA.

Jennings, L., Parra-Medina, D., Messias, D., & McLoughlin, K. (2006). Toward a critical social theory of youth empowerment. *Journal of Community Practice, 14*, 31–55.

Kaplan, E. B. (2013). *We live in the shadow: Inner-city kids tell their stories through photographs.* Philadelphia: Temple University Press.

Knight, M. G., & Watson, V. W. M. (2014). Toward participatory communal citizenship: Rendering visible the civic teaching, learning, and actions of African immigrant youth and young adults. *American Educational Research Journal, 51*(3), 539–566.

Levinson, M. (2012). *No citizen left behind.* Caimbridge, MA: Harvard University Press.

Lipman, P. (2011). *The new political economy of urban education: Neoliberalism, race, and the right to the city.* New York, NY: Routledge.

Low, B. (2011). *Slam school: Learning through conflict in the hip-hop and spoken word classroom.* Palo Alto: Stanford University Press.

Mazzoni, V., & Harcourt, D. (2013). An international experience of research with children: Moving forward on the idea of children's participation. *Qualitative Research.* doi: 10.1177/1468794112468470

Miller, P. (2011). Mapping educational opportunity zones: A geospatial analysis of neighborhood block groups. *Urban Review, 44*(2), 189–218.

Mirra, N. (2014). Interest-driven learning: Student identities and passions as gateways to connected learning. In A. Garcia (Ed.), *Teaching in the connected learning classroom* (pp. 10–11). Digital Media and Learning Research Hub and the National Writing Project.

Mullins, K. (2014). *Rethinking spaces for confident voices and creative expressions* (Unpublished manuscript). Notre Dame, IN: University of Notre Dame.

National Task Force on Civic Learning and Democratic Engagement. (2012). *A crucible moment: College learning and democracy's future*. Washington, DC: Association of American Colleges and Universities.

Newman, J. H. (1982). *The idea of a university*. Notre Dame, IN: University of Notre Dame Press.

Norton, N. (2006). Talking spirituality with family members: Black and Latina/o children co-researcher methodologies. *The Urban Review, 38*(4), 313–333.

Paris, D. (2011). *Language across difference: Ethnicity, communication, and youth identities in changing urban schools*. New York, NY: Cambridge University Press.

Paris, D., & Alim, H. S. (2014). What are we seeking to sustain through culturally sustaining pedagogy? A loving critique forward. *Harvard Educational Review, 84*(1), 85–100.

Paris, D., & Winn, M. T. (Eds.). (2013). *Humanizing research: Decolonizing qualitative inquiry with youth and communities*. Thousand Oaks, CA: SAGE Publications.

Rosenman, E., Walker, S., & Wyly, E. (2014). The shrinkage machine: Race, class and the renewal of urban capital. In H. R. Hall, C. C. Robinson, & A. Kohli (Eds.), *Uprooting urban America: Multidisciplinary perspectives on race, class & gentrification* (pp. 41–76). New York: Peter Lang.

Skelton, T. (2015). *The importance of 'geography' in children and young people's geographies*. Lecture presented at the International Conference on the Geographies of Children, Youth and Families, San Diego, CA.

Smagorinsky, P. (2014). *Response to the new NCTQ teacher prep review*. Retrieved August 16, 2014, from http://radicalscholarship.wordpress.com/2014/06/17/peter-smagorinsky-response-to-the-new-nctq-teacher-prep-review/

Strand, K., Marullo, S., Cutforth, N., Stoecker, R., & Donohue, P. (2003). *Community-based research and higher education*. San Francisco, CA: Jossey-Bass.

Style, E. (1996). Curriculum as window & mirror. *Social Science Record, 33*(2), 35–42.

Wang, C. (1999). Photovoice: A participatory action research strategy applied to women's health. *Journal of Women's Health, 8*(2), 185–192.

Wang, C., & Burris, M. (1997). Photovoice: Concept, methodology, and use for participatory needs assessment. *Health Education, and Behavior, 24*(3), 69–87.

Watson, R. (2014). *The role of art in social justice: Using the arts to celebrate, critique, and change our world*. International Symposium of Cultural Diplomacy at the United Nations Headquarters in New York City. Retrieved from http://reneewatsonauthor.tumblr.com/post/90056578488/renee-speaks-at-the-un-i-was-invited-to-give-this

Weinstein, S., & West, A. (2012). Call and responsibility: Critical questions for youth spoken word poetry. *Harvard Educational Review, 82*(2), 282–302.

Westheimer, J., & Kahne, J. (2004). What kind of citizen? The politics of educating for democracy. *American Educational Research Journal, 41*(2), 237–269.

Winn, M. (2013). Toward a restorative English Education. *Research in the Teaching of English, 48*(1), 126–135.

Winn, M., & Behizadeh, N. (2011). The right to be literate: Literacy, education, and the school-to-prison pipeline. *Review of Research in Education, 35*(1), 147–173.

Yosso, T. (2005). Whose culture has capital ? A critical race theory discussion of community cultural wealth. *Race, Ethnicity, and Education, 8*(1), 69–91.

Contributors

Rebecca L. Beucher, PhD, is assistant research Professor with the Center for Gender Equity in Science and Technology (CGEST) at Arizona State University, U.S. Her research and theoretical interests include urban education, New Literacy studies, multimodal and nontraditional literacies, and feminist and queer theories.

Kevin Burke, PhD, is assistant professor of literacy education at the University of Georgia, U.S. His recent work in literacy has focused on the ways in which multiple affordances of art can be leveraged to provide fruitful spaces for developing youth voice in civic political processes, particularly through university and community partnerships.

Mark Cantú is a doctoral candidate in school improvement at Texas State University, U.S., where he is exploring the spaces between theory, action, and formal and informal learning practices as a way to inform continuous school improvement. He taught middle school English language arts and ESL for several years at his alma mater, Edcouch–Elsa ISD. While teaching, he obtained a master's degree in educational administration from the University of Texas Pan-American.

Edgar Escutia Chagoya comes from Moroleon, Guanajuato, and lives in Athens, Georgia, U.S. He is a middle school student and is a very independent person who likes to do sports, work for tangible goals, and be with his family. His greatest fear is losing his family because he loves them so much. For his future he is excited about going to college and studying law, agriculture, or engineering.

Melissa A. Gallagher is a doctoral candidate in teaching and teacher education at George Mason University, U.S. She is a former elementary teacher and National Board Certified Teacher and teaches courses to preservice elementary teachers. Her research interests include preservice teacher education, literacy education, mathematics education, student engagement, and English learners (ELs).

Keisha L. Green, PhD, is assistant professor of secondary English education at the University of Massachusetts Amherst, U.S., and her publications appear in *Race, Ethnicity, and Education*, *Equity & Excellence in Education*, *Reading African American Experiences in the Obama Era: Theory, Advocacy, Activism*, and *Humanizing Research: Decolonizing Qualitative Inquiry With Youth and Communities*.

Stuart Greene, PhD, is associate professor of English with a joint appointment in the department of Africana Studies at the University of Notre Dame, U.S. His research has examined the intersections of race, poverty, and achievement in public schools, and his current work focuses on literacy, youth empowerment, and civic engagement.

Miguel A. Guajardo, Ph.D., is associate professor in the Education and Community Leadership Program and a member of the doctoral faculty in School Improvement at Texas State University-San Marcos, USA. His research interests include issues of community building, community youth development, leadership development, race and ethnicity, university and community partnerships, and Latino youth and families.

Francisco J. Guajardo, PhD, is professor and C. Bascom Slemp endowed chair in Education at the University of Texas Pan American, U.S. He is a founding member of the Llano Grande Center for Research and Development, an education nonprofit organization he founded in the mid-1990s when he was a classroom teacher at Edcouch-Elsa High School.

Marcelle M. Haddix, PhD, is a dean's associate professor and chair of the Reading and Language Arts Department in the Syracuse University School of Education, U.S. Her scholarly interests center on the experiences of students of color in literacy and English teaching and teacher education. Her awards and recognitions include the American Educational Research Association Division K Early Career Award, the National Council for Teachers of English Promising Researcher Award, and the Syracuse University Meredith Teaching Award, one of SU's most prestigious teaching honors.

Horace R. Hall, PhD, is associate professor at DePaul University in the Department of Educational Policy Studies and Research and the Center for Diaspora Studies, U.S. Dr. Hall's academic courses, as well as his body of scholarship, focus on economic sociology, ideological discourse, and youth mentoring and activism. His most recent book, *Uprooting Urban America: Multidisciplinary Perspectives on Race, Class and Gentrification* (Hall, Robinson, & Kohli, 2015) examines rifts in America's socioeconomic fabric, the ill effects these divisions are having on underprivileged groups, and policy strategies for maintaining fair housing, education, health care, and employment practices.

Ruth Harman, PhD, is associate professor in the TESOL and World Language Education Program at the University of Georgia, U.S. Her research, teaching, and service focus on exploring how best to support the literacy and language development of emergent bilingual learners in K–12 classrooms, especially in the current climate of high-stakes school reform and anti-immigration discourses.

Lindy L. Johnson, PhD, is assistant professor of English education at the College of William and Mary, U.S. Her research interests include new and digital literacies, teacher education, and critical discourse analysis; she served as principal editor of the *Journal of Language & Literacy Education* from 2012 to 2013, and she was selected as a Digital Media and Learning Summer Research Fellow in 2013.

Valerie Kinloch, PhD, is professor of literacy studies, chief diversity officer, and director of the office of diversity and inclusion in the College of Education and Human Ecology at Ohio State University. Her research examines the language, literacies, and community engagements of adolescents and adults inside and outside schools. One of her books, *Harlem on Our Minds: Place, Race, and the Literacies of Urban Youth*, received the 2012 Outstanding Book of the Year Award from the American Educational Research Association (AERA), and in 2015 she received the Rewey Belle Inglis Award for Outstanding Women in English Education from the National Council of Teachers of English (NCTE).

Liz Long is an alternative education teacher and Language Arts Department chair at New Dominion Alternative Center in Manassas, Virginia, U.S. Her responsibilities include teaching sixth and eighth grade, preparing interactive station-based lesson plans, evaluating student progress, managing the classroom, and acting as a mentor for her students. She leads the language arts service learning project where students write horror or science-fiction stories. She is currently enrolled in George Mason University's master's program for teaching reading and writing.

Alvina Mardhani-Bayne is a doctoral candidate in literacy education at Syracuse University, U.S. Her research explores strategies for supporting educators who provide literacy instruction in nonclassroom settings. Her aim is to enable literacy programming in libraries and other out-of-school spaces to best respond to the needs of those educators and the communities they serve.

Maria K. McKenna, PhD, is assistant professor of the practice at the University of Notre Dame, U.S., in the Department of Africana Studies and the interdisciplinary minor, Education, Schooling, and Society. A qualitative researcher, McKenna's work focuses on marginalized voices in education, especially children and families of color, and attentiveness to care

262 *Contributors*

within learning environments. Her work has been published in a number of edited collections as well as in *Urban Education, Urban Review*, and *School Community Journal*. She also has a TEDx talk on caring and human integrity.

Anthony M. Pellegrino, PhD, is an assistant professor of secondary education at George Mason University, U.S. His research interests include preservice teacher education, history education, youth civic engagement, and multimodal instructional practices in social studies. He has published research and practitioner articles in journals such as *Action in Teacher Education*, the *Teacher Educator*, the *Journal of Social Studies Research*, the *History Teacher*, and *Social Studies Research and Practice*. His book, *Let the Music Play: Harnessing the Power of Music for History and Social Studies Classrooms*, was published in 2012.

Timothy San Pedro, PhD, is an assistant professor of multicultural and equity studies in education at the Ohio State University, U.S. His scholarship focuses on the intricate link among motivation, engagement, and identity construction to curricula and pedagogical practices that refocus content and conversations upon indigenous histories, perspectives, and literacies. Recent publications appear in the *Journal of American Indian Education* and *Multicultural Perspectives on Race, Ethnicity, and Identity*, and two articles are in press with the *Equity & Excellence in Education* and *Research in the Teaching of English* that discuss the agentive uses of American Indian student silence.

Beverly J. Trezek, PhD, is associate professor of special education and the codirector of the Reading Specialist Program at DePaul University in Chicago, Illinois, U.S. Her research focuses on reading instruction for beginning and struggling readers with a particular emphasis on investigating the role that phonemic awareness and phonics play in the development of literacy skills for students who are deaf or hard of hearing. Dr. Trezek serves as a literacy intervention consultant for several schools throughout the U.S. and is the lead author of the book *Reading and Deafness: Theory, Research and Practice* (Trezek, Wang, & Paul, 2010). Her second book, *Early Literacy Development in Deaf Children* (Mayer & Trezek, 2015), was published recently by Oxford University Press.

Lawrence T. Winn is a doctoral student in the School of Human Ecology in the Civil Society and Community Research Program at the University of Wisconsin, Madison, U.S. His research explores the role of social capital in the educational, leadership, and career trajectories of youth of color. Since 1999, Winn has worked and managed community-based nonprofits. As a consultant for the Race to Equity Project, he coauthored *Race to Equity: A Baseline Report on the State of Racial Disparities in Dane*

County. Winn also coauthored *Expectations and Realities: Education, the Discipline Gap, and the Experiences of Black Families Migrating to Small Cities* (with Maisha T. Winn).

Maisha T. Winn, PhD, is the Susan J. Cellmer endowed chair in English education and professor of language and literacy in the Department of Curriculum and Instruction at the University of Wisconsin, Madison, U.S. Her program of research examines the ways in which teachers and/or adult allies for youth in schools and in out-of-school contexts practice "justice" in the teaching of literacy. Dr. Winn received the William T. Grant Foundation Distinguished Fellowship (2014) and the American Educational Research Association Early Career Award (2012). She is the author of several books including *Girl Time: Literacy, Justice, and the School-to-Prison Pipeline*, and she is coeditor of *Humanizing Research: Decolonizing Qualitative Research* (with Django Paris).

Kristien Zenkov, PhD, is professor of education at George Mason University, U.S. He is the author and editor of more than 100 articles and book chapters and six books focusing on teacher education, literacy pedagogy and curricula, social justice education, school-university partnerships, and professional development schools. Dr. Zenkov codirects "Through Students' Eyes," a YPAR and Photovoice project based in northern Virginia, Cleveland, Haiti, and Iraq, through which youth document with photographs and writings what they believe about citizenship, justice, school, and literacy.

Index

Page numbers in *italics* refer to figures and tables.

A
academic discourse 84
activism 193
African American teachers 117–19, 126–7
African American youth: Afrocentric worldview 203–5; agency 164; arts-based projects 212; barriers to success of 112, 163–4; citizenship and 190, 202–4, 206; consciousness-raising 194, 204; critical service learning 207; cultural identity 205–6; culturally biased interventions 149, 163–4; historical literacy 194, 196, 205; inequities and 122, 126–7, 155, 206; institutionalized silencing 155; media literacy skills 197, 206; mentoring programs 149, 163–4; oppressive framing of 133; policing and 117–19, 126; protesting 201–2; reading skills 151, 155–7; schooling and 117, 126–8, 132; storytelling 215; YPAR projects 112–28, 207; *see also* students of color; urban youth; youth
after-school programs 219, 225, 228
agency: creating spaces for 235; critical awareness and 8; digital storytelling and 52–3; mentoring programs and 164; nondominant discourse 54; process of developing 237
air-shifting 195–7
Alliance (student group) 112–19, 125, 128
anti-immigration discourse 210–11

Arie, India 195–6
Art as an Agent for Change 222
arts-based projects 212–28
asset mapping 170–1, 181
authentic writing 131–3, 136–7, 143, 145
autobiography 50–63
Ayo, Paul 222–3, 225

B
Bartolomae, L. 97
Beyond the Black Berry Patch project 96
"Beyond the Methods Fetish" (Bartolomae) 97
bidialectal youth 212
bilingual students: arts-based projects 211–19, 224–5, 227–8; counter-narratives and 211; marginalization of 210–12, 218; transmediation and 226
Bivins, Kelli 214–16, 226, 228
Black radical traditions 191, 200, 205
Black Radical Tradition Toolkit 206
Black youth *see* African American youth
Brown youth 197
Buchannan, Kira 54, 63
Burris, M. 238
Butler, Judith 50

C
Campano, G. 97
Cantú, Mark 169
Cárdenas, B. 169
Cardenas, J. A. 169
career/college readiness activities 151–2, 162–3

266 *Index*

Carnegie Foundation 92
Cee-Lo 196
Center for Rural Strategies 178–9
Chagoya, Edgar Escutia 210, 216–18, 220, 223–30
Chall, J. S. 159, 163
change 120–5, 127
Change Agents (student group) 112, 116, 120–5, 127
Chicano scholarship 180, 182
Children's Defense Fund (CDF) 122–3
circle practice 174–84
Cisneros, Sandra 240
citizenship: African American youth 190, 202–4, 206; questionnaire on 43–4; service learning and 94; youth perspectives on 32–3, 35, 37
civic activism 51, 53, 193
civic empowerment gap 31
civic engagement: African American youth and 190, 197–207; critical awareness and 8; literacy and 29–30; youth and 9–10, 42, 236–7, 241, 251–2, 254
civic literacy 30
civics education 30–1, 41–2, 190, 202, 246
Civil Rights Movement 194, 206
civil society 30
Cochran-Smith, M. 97
Coile Middle School (CMS) 212, 214, 224–8
Coile Serves 214, 225
collaboration 128, 164
collages *142–3*
collective arts processes 211–12, 218–25, 228–9
college preparation programs 169–71
Collins, Suzanne 156–7
Common Core Learning Standards 145
communities: advocacy for 178–9; asset mapping 170–1, 181; defining 114–16; oppressed 113; police and 117–19; publicly engaged scholarship and 92–3; school and 70, 81, 88–90, 95–7, 104, 131–2; service learning and 94; unity within 135–6; university partnerships 91–2, 238–54; urban 88, 96; youth leaders in 171–2, 191
community-based organization (CBO) 191

community-based participatory research (CBPR) 92, 170–2, 175–7, 237–40, 242; *see also* publicly engaged scholarship
community engagement: community garden example 97–101; course in 89, 96; defining 91–2, 135–6; Design Team example 102–4; group membership and 197–8; problem solving 199–202; students and 89–93, 95–105, 170–2, 177–84; youth media and 192–3, 197–202, 207; youth perspectives on 239–53; youth writers and 138
Community Learning Exchange 174–5
community radio 195–7
community spaces 131–2, 139, 145
conscientization/consciousness-raising 82, 173, 193–4, 204
consciousness vision and strategy (CVS) analysis 194
Corrective Reading-Decoding 151, 156, 163
Coughlan, Alice 215–16, 226
creative writing workshops *see* writing workshops
critical discourse analysis (CDA) 52
critical listening 84
critical literacy practices 52, 196–7
critical pedagogy 149–50, 152–4, 163–4
critical place pedagogy 72
critical self-awareness 173, 181
critical service learning: African American youth and 207; community garden example 97–101; course in 89, 96; defined 91; Design Team example 102–4; relational nature of 93–4; social justice and 94–5; students and 89–91, 97–105
A Crucible Moment (National Task Force on Civic Learning and Democratic Engagement) 241
cultural citizenship 31
culturally responsive design 206
culturally sustaining pedagogy 211–12

D

democracy 10; *see also* citizenship
Design Team 101–3

Index 267

Digital Media Project (DMP) 51
digital storytelling: autobiographical 50–63; civic activism and 53; counter-narratives and 53, 56–63; multimodal 51, 53, 55, 59; music in 64; photography and 220–3
"Discipline or Punish?" (Yang) 128
discipline policies 112, 115–17, 120
discourse 53–4, 56, 58, 64, 84
dominant discourse 53–4
Du Bois, W. E. B. 125
Du Bois High School 115, 119, 127–8
Dunn, Mandie 225–6

E
Edcouch-Elsa High School 169–70, 177, 179–80
education: assessment-based 8; political 193–4; popular 193–4; social justice and 235–6; *see also* high schools; schools
emergent bilingual learners 210–11, 213, 226
Engaging Youth, Engaging Neighborhoods Initiative 238, 255
English language learners (ELL) 28
English-only mandates 210–11
Epperson, Matthew 215, 218
equity, youth perspectives on 32–3, 35
equity-oriented scholars 112
Eyes on the Prize 194, 206

F
Franklin, V. P. 196
Freedom Riders 201
Freire, P. 150, 153–4, 172–3
Fye, Michelle 96

G
Good Seed Community Garden 97–103
Greater Linden Development Corporation (GLDC) 88
Grimes, Erica 96
Guajardo, Miguel A. 169
guidelines 199–200

H
Harman, Ruth 212, 214, 227
Hernandez, Jesse 217
Hicho, donna 88–92, 97, 104
high schools: college preparation programs 169–71; community engagement and 97, 101–5; critical service learning and 91, 93–7; discipline policies 112, 115–17; indigenous knowledge in 68, 70; mentoring programs 148–63; school culture 119, 125–8; writing workshops 131
hip-hop culture 64
history instruction: Eurocentric 82–3; Native American 77–81; as perspective 73–83; re-centering 77–81
hooks, bell 104
humanizing research 242–3
The Hunger Games (Collins) 156–7

I
"I am" poems 51, 142, 222
image-based tools 27, 29, 31–3
Immigrant Students and Literacy (Campano) 96
immigration policies 210–11, 227
indigenous research methods 71–3
inequity 37, 117, 122, 126–7, 154–5
Inside/Outside (Cochran-Smith and Lytle) 97
institutionalized silencing 155
instruction: asset-based 206; challenges of 39–40; child-centered 246; culturally responsive 63–4, 206; diverse perspectives in 63, 73–6; genre-based 214; multimodal 25–7, 29, 225–7, 231; social justice and 235; transformative praxis 73, 80–2

J
Johnson, Lindy L. 212, 227
Johnson, Rhonda 104
justice, youth perspectives on 32–3, 35, 37

L
Latino/a youth: arts-based projects 212–13; health issues 96; marginalization of 210–11; schooling and 128; storytelling 215; *see also* urban youth
Latinos y CSIA project 95
learning: affective processes 236–7; civic processes 236–7; social cognitive processes 236–7
liberation discourse 58, 191, 193, 205
listening 84

268 Index

literacy: authentic writing 131–3, 137–8; civics and 29–30; code-related skills 159; critical 52, 196–7, 243; cultural 8–9; defining 28–9, 134; emergent bilingual learners 210–11, 213, 226; as a fundamental right 236–7, 251; historical 196, 205; media literacy skills 194, 197; mentoring programs 150, 155–64; multimodal 29, 238, 240, 242, 246, 253–4; performance and 213; range of 134–5; social justice and 145; as a social practice 9, 227; sociocultural perspectives 212–13; storying as 84–5; storytelling and 218; student engagement and 97–104; third space 228; word collages 138; writing workshops 131–46
literacy for liberation philosophy 191
literacy tutors 152, 157–63
Llano Grande Center for Research and Development 169–83
Lugones, María 63–4
Lyon, George Ella 240
Lytle, S. L. 97

M
media literacy skills 194, 197, 206
mentoring programs: agency and 164; career/college readiness activities 151–2, 162–3; compensation for 158; critical pedagogy 150, 152–4, 163–4; deficit-focused 149; goals of 150, 164; literacy and 150, 155–7; mentee responses to 153–8; mentor energy 157–8, 163; participation in 153, 162–3; range of 149; reciprocal 164; trust in 154–6; tutor responses to 158–61; *see also* school-based mentoring (SBM) programs
Merry, Johnny 96
Mexican American youth: asset mapping 170–1, 181; college preparation programs 169–71, 180–1; *pláticas* (talks) and 174–8, 180–4; schooling and 169; self-awareness 181
Mfume, Ayinde 195

middle schools 210–14
"The Moth" 214
multicultural education 226–7
multiple literacies 238, 240, 242, 253–4
music 64

N
National Assessment of Educational Progress 151
National Center for Education Statistics (NCES) 151
National Task Force on Civic Learning and Democratic Engagement 241
Native Americans: history instruction and 76–81; stereotypes of 68–9
neighborhood walks 246–51
New England Resource Center for Higher Education 92, 103
new literacy studies (NLS) 52–3
Nieves-Ferguson, Brenda 96
nondominant discourse 54

O
oppressive discourse 56
oral history 170–5

P
participatory action research *see* YPAR methods
pedagogy of disruption 195
performance: critical use of 211–12; literacy and 213; storytelling and 216–18, 224
perspective activity 73–80, 83
photo elicitation projects 25–6, 37–8
photography 31–2, 219–23, 242
Photo Novella 238
Photovoice methods 25, 31, 36, 41, 237, 251, 255
pláticas (talks) 171–84
poetry: "I am" poems 51, 142, 222; slam poetry 29; storytelling and 222–3; youth empowerment and 244
police: African American youth and 117–19, 126; community relations and 117–19
political education 193–4
popular education 193–4
post-structural feminist theory 54
praxis 81–4, 154, 172
preservice teachers: anecdotal records 36–9, 45; education of 27–8,

41–2; Photovoice methods 25–6, 31–2, 36; student relationships 39–40; tutoring 158–63; YPAR methods 27, 31–6, 39, 42
protesting 201–2
publicly engaged scholarship: approaches to 88–93; defined 92; youth and 93, 105
public transportation 226

R

Rabbit Box Youth Voices (RBYV) project 210, 213–19, 222–8
Race to Equity Report 125
Race to the Top 225
racism 10, 122, 127, 189
radio collectives 191–2, 195–6, 205–7
reading: mentoring programs and 150–1, 155–7; strategies for 151, 159; student achievement in 151, 155, 159–60, 163
Reading Mentors project 96
Reading Your World (RYW) 149–50
Reading Your World-Literacy 152–64
reflection 82, 193, 200, 241–2
research: multimodal 27; process of 113–15; student engagement and 117–18; students and 119, 125–6; *see also* YPAR methods
Richardson, L. 97
Ringgold, Faith 235, 240, 244

S

school-based mentoring (SBM) programs 148–64
school culture 119–27
school reform 175–7
schools: African American youth and 127–8, 132; bilingual students 210–11; change in 120–5, 127; civics education 202; classroom discourse 53; community and 70, 81, 88–90, 95–7, 104; empowerment in 204–5; high-stakes testing 210–11, 225; home-school connections 254; inequities in 117, 155; limitations of 131–2; mentoring programs 148–9, 152; Mexican American youth and 169; multicultural education 226–7; praxis in 81–3; safe spaces in 81–4; socioeconomic contexts of 226; student achievement in 157–8; teacher-driven 128; visual representation in 68–70; youth views on 34, 117, 125–7; *see also* teachers
school-to-prison pipeline 3, 6, 14, 18, 112, 117, 207
second language acquisition 212–13
service learning: citizenship and 94; critical 89–95; social justice-oriented 94–5
slam poetry 29
social justice: arts-based projects and 227; authentic writing and 145; protesting and 201–2; in teaching and learning 235–6; university-community partnerships 253–4; YPAR methods and 111
social justice-oriented service learning 94–5, 98–105
socially just youth development 236–7
South Works 190
Spanish Institute 171, 177–8
The Stand newspaper 139–40
The State of Black Children and Families (CDF) 122
storying: defined 73; listening 84; as literacy 84–5; sharing 73; visual 77–81; youth narratives in 85
StoryJumper.com 143, 145
storytelling: college preparation programs and 170–2; community projects in 214–18; critical self-awareness 173; digital 50–2, 220–3; indigenous research methods 71–3; oral history 171–5; performance and 216–18, 224; subversive 52; youth and 215–18, 222
student engagement: affective element of 227; critical 27; multimedia and 29, 194; participatory action research 116–25; writing and 37–8
students: arts-based projects 219–28; career/college readiness activities 151–2, 162–3; civic knowledge and 30–1; college preparation programs 169–71; community engagement 89–105; critical service learning 91–105; institutionalized silencing 155;

270 Index

internal struggles and 36–7; personal narratives 219–20; photo elicitation projects 25–6, 37–8; photography and 219–23; poetry and 222–3; reading skills 151, 155–7, 163; research and 117–19, 125–6; self-determination 82–3; storytelling 215–18, 222; *see also* youth
students of color: as writers 131–5; *see also* African American youth; Latino/a youth

T
Tar Beach (Ringgold) 244
"Teacher Research Movement" (Cochran-Smith and Lytle) 97
teachers: African American 117–19, 126–7; constraints on 145; effective instruction 157; homogeneous 134; as mentors 41–2; in-service education 89–90, 96; White 126–7, 134
Texas State University-San Marcos 175–6
third space 228
transformative praxis 73, 80–4
trust 111–14, 154–6
tutoring 148, 152, 157–63

U
unity 135–6
university-community partnerships 91–2, 238–54
urban communities: achievement gap in 133; positive views of 104; publicly engaged scholarship in 88–9; youth in 104, 133
urban pedagogies 128
urban youth: oppressive framing of 133, 142; schooling and 133–4, 136; as writers 131–46; *see also* African American youth; Latino/a youth
U.S. Social Forum 201

V
visible narratives 72–3
visual narratives 238–42
visual representations: re-centering 73, 77–81; in schools 68–70, 73; social identity formation and 219

visual sociology 25
visual storying 77–81
Vygotsky, L. 212–13

W
Wang, C. 238
Washington, Booker T. 125
Watson, Lilla 135
White teachers 126–7, 134
worthy witnessing 114–15
writing: authentic 131–3, 136–7, 143, 145; process of 146; school genres of 134; self-guided 135
"Writing" (Richardson) 97
Writing Our Lives program 131–3, 135–40, 143, 145–6
writing skills 37–8
writing workshops: image-based tools 143, 145; models of 134, 140–1; ownership of 140; urban youth and 131–4, 136–46

Y
Yang, Wayne 128
Yousafzai, Malala 236
youth: adult allies 111–14, 193; agency 52–4, 235, 237; air-shifting 195–7; aspirations 39; barriers to success of 254; as change agents 196–7; civic activism 51; civic identity 254; community engagement 104, 171–2, 199–202, 243–53; conscientization 82–3, 173, 193–4; digital storytelling 50–4; empowerment of 237–8, 244–54; as experts 31–3; group membership 197–8; identity 53; leadership 191, 198, 238–9, 249; literacies 97–104; media and 191–3; narratives 85, 252; perspectives on citizenship 32–3, 35, 37; perspectives on justice/equity 32–3, 35, 37; publicly engaged scholarship and 93, 105; reflection 193, 241–2; as researchers 25–7, 31–2; safe spaces for 237, 243–54; self-awareness 181; social justice and 236–7; trust-building 113–14; views on school 34, 117, 125–7; visual narratives

238–43; *see also* African American youth; students
youth initiatives 171, 177–8
youth mentoring *see* mentoring programs
youth participatory action research (YPAR) *see* YPAR methods
Youth Radio 191
youth voice 136–7, 195–205, 207, 226, 252
Youth Voices (radio show) 189–207
youth writers 131–46

YPAR methods: adult allies 112–14; bilingual students 211; collaboration and 128; community engagement and 111, 119; designing 128; multimodal techniques in 27; multiple literacies and 238, 240, 242; ownership of 122; preservice teachers and 39, 42; student engagement and 25, 31–2, 116–25; trust-building 113–14; trustworthiness of 33; value of 111